Communication, Society and Politics

Editors

W. Lance Bennett, *University of Washington*

Robert M. Entman, *The George Washington University*

Politics and relations among individuals in societies across the world are being transformed by new technologies for targeting individuals and sophisticated methods for shaping personalized messages. The new technologies challenge boundaries of many kinds – between news, information, entertainment, and advertising; between media, with the arrival of the World Wide Web; and even between nations. Communication, Society and Politics probes the political and social impacts of these new communication systems in national, comparative, and global perspective.

OTHER BOOKS IN THE SERIES

(continued after the index)

Consumer Democracy
The Marketing of Politics

This book argues that marketing is inherent in competitive democracy, exploring how we can make political marketing more democratic. Margaret Scammell argues that consumer democracy should not be assumed to be inherently antithetical to "proper" political discourse and debate about the common good. Instead, Scammell argues that we should seek to understand it – to create marketing-literate criticism that can distinguish between democratically good and bad campaigns and between shallow, cynical packaging and campaigns that at least aspire to be responsive, engender citizen participation, and enable accountability. Furthermore, we can take important lessons from commercial marketing: enjoyment matters; what citizens think and feel matters; and, just as in commercial markets, structure is key – the type of political marketing will be affected by the conditions of competition.

Margaret Scammell is currently visiting senior lecturer in Media and Communication at the London School of Economics (LSE). Prior to her time at LSE, she worked as a lecturer at the University of Liverpool and as a Research Fellow at the Joan Shorenstein Center on the Press, Politics and Public Policy at the John F. Kennedy School of Government, Harvard University. She worked as a local, sports, and politics journalist for a number of news organizations before receiving her PhD at LSE. Her book *Designer Politics* (1995) became a standard reference for use in marketing and public relations in the United Kingdom. She has published widely on many aspects of political communication, including political campaigning, Americanization of campaigning worldwide, government and news management, consumer activism, and the appropriate role of media in democracies. She is the co-author of *On Message: Communicating the Campaign* (1999) and co-editor of *The Media, Journalism and Democracy* (2000) and *The Sage Handbook of Political Communication* (2012).

Consumer Democracy

The Marketing of Politics

MARGARET SCAMMELL
London School of Economics

CAMBRIDGE
UNIVERSITY PRESS

CAMBRIDGE
UNIVERSITY PRESS

32 Avenue of the Americas, New York, NY 10013-2473, USA

Cambridge University Press is part of the University of Cambridge.

It furthers the University's mission by disseminating knowledge in the pursuit of
education, learning, and research at the highest international levels of excellence.

www.cambridge.org
Information on this title: www.cambridge.org/9780521545242

© Margaret Scammell 2014

First published 2014

Printed in the United States of America

A catalog record for this publication is available from the British Library.

Library of Congress Cataloging in Publication data
Scammell, Margaret.
Consumer democracy : the marketing of politics / Margaret Scammell.
    pages cm. – (Communication, society and politics)
Includes bibliographical references and index.
ISBN 978-0-521-83668-5 (hardback)
1. Advertising, Political.   2. Marketing – Political aspects.   3. Public
relations and politics.   4. Communication in politics.   5. Campaign
management.   6. Political campaigns.   1. Title.
JF2112.A4S295   2013
324.7′3–dc23   2013027298

ISBN 978-0-521-83668-5 Hardback
ISBN 978-0-521-54524-2 Paperback

In memory of Pauline, Helen, and Patricia

Contents

Tables, Figures, and Images

TABLES

FIGURES

IMAGES

Acknowledgments

This book took quite a time to get together, and there are many people to thank for helping me through the long haul. Thanks to all those students who took my Political Communication classes at the London School of Economics. Your enthusiasm was inspirational and your criticism invaluable. Much gratitude to W. Lance Bennett, Lew Bateman, and the editorial staff at Cambridge University Press, for their support, professionalism, and Job-like forbearance.

Big thanks to all those colleagues who helped in various ways, from reading chapters to moral support: Sonia Livingstone at the LSE, Jon Simon (Indiana University), Martin Harrop (formerly of Newcastle University), Katherine Jocz (Harvard Business School), and Julia Hallam (Liverpool University). Special appreciation for Robin Mansell (LSE) and Ana Langer (Glasgow University). You are wonderful friends as well as great colleagues, and so many thanks for commenting on all those multiple drafts without ever betraying an ounce of irritation.

The book draws heavily from help and access given to me over the years by practitioners, in both journalism and politics. While there are too many to name, I would be horribly remiss not to mention Chris Moncrieff, into his eighties and sharp as ever at the Press Association, and the late Philip Gould, whose insight and energy are irreplaceable. Graeme Trayner's help was invaluable, and thanks to him also for reading a draft chapter. A special mention too to Mark McKinnon for generously supplying advertising material. A good number of people and organizations have given me permission to reproduce material or cite from unpublished papers. I thank them all. The following were either single or lead authors: David Farrell (University College, Dublin), Fritz Plasser (University of Innsbruck), James Donius (Marketplace Measurement Worldwide and Fordham Graduate School of Business), Todd Belt (University of Hawaii), and Richard Barberio (SUNY College at Oneonta). Thanks to Charles Trevail and colleagues at Promise Corporation who gave permission to cite extensively from their work on rebranding Prime Minister Tony Blair. Thanks also to branding consultancies Landor PSB Associates and Chernoff Newman for permission to reproduce images created by them.

My family has its own particular style of encouragement. "Are you *still* writing that," they'd giggle while carving the Sunday roast. I feel their pride and love them for it. Thanks too to my closest friends, just for being my friends, knowing when to hang back and when to offer a hand. Most of all thanks to my partner Lesley. There is simply no way I'd have managed this without her, and I promise faithfully that the next book will shake out smooth as silk. Maybe I should have put an "if" somewhere in that sentence.

Ultimately, despite the help of so many, there are doubtless errors and omissions in this book. They are solely and wholly my responsibility.

Preface: The U.S. Presidential Election of 2012

What did we learn from the 2012 U.S. presidential election? Its fascination lies partly in the difficulty of characterizing it easily. It presents us with an array of seemingly contradictory verdicts, many of which have at least surface plausibility.

On the one hand, it was the nothing-much-happened election; it was the most costly race in history that ended up delivering the status quo in the White House and relatively minimal change on Capitol Hill. On the other, it marked a watershed result that may cast the Republicans into the wilderness, ideologically alienated from women, nonwhites, youth, and the "new Americans" from Latin America and Asia. On the one hand, it was a race of tight margins; just a few hundred thousand votes in four key states separated former governor Mitt Romney from the White House. The real decider was not the Republican "value set" but their organizational failures in the ground wars; they were outfought and outthought on the data-driven turnout operations in the places where it mattered (Stutts, 2012). On the other hand, it was an "ass-whuppin'," in the words of Democratic consultants Carville and Greenberg (2012a), in which the Republicans were crushed in the Electoral College, fell short in almost all the main battleground states, and fared badly with virtually all demographic segments of society apart from white men and those over forty-five.

It is plausible to view 2012 as a dispiriting anticlimax after the grassroots enthusiasm of 2008's election of a lifetime. It could easily be seen as a regressive rerun of big money, negative, advertising-dominated politics as usual. Equally, it could be seen as a seminal election; it might carve the American political landscape as decisively as Franklin Delano Roosevelt's New Deal of the 1940s. Obama, just as FDR, defied the normal economic logic of elections. He became the first incumbent since FDR to be reelected with an unemployment rate of around 8 percent. Just as FDR's victories entrenched Social Security as the untouchable "third rail" of American politics, so Obama's Affordable Care Act may come to be regarded historically as a great achievement, argues American historian Gary Gerstle (2012). Just like FDR, Obama is associated with the future, while the Republicans have become overreliant, not just on the relatively declining demographic of white men, "but on an institution – heterosexual marriage – that encompasses a smaller group of Americans than it has at any time in the past two hundred years."

Typically the aftermath of general elections generates competing narratives of success and failure as practitioners, pollsters, pundits, and academics dissect the data. In the post-2012 analyses a cluster of possibly decisive factors has emerged. Some of these are long-term factors, such as the changing demographics of the United States. "This isn't your father's America," as veteran political consultant Dick Morris told the election night _NewsHour_ PBS program. Some are short-term factors, such as the influence of particular issues: the economy, social welfare, women's reproductive rights, and so on. Some factors are linked to ideology and especially its resurgence on the Republican right; Carville and Greenberg (2012b) characterized the election as a "class war" for middle-income America; not "it's the economy, stupid," the slogan that propelled Bill Clinton's 1992 success, but "it's the middle class, stupid." Other factors relate to campaign effectiveness of specific elements, the qualities of the candidates, the efficacy of targeted ground and air wars, and the sophistication and efficiency of software.

Fascinating and fundamental as these issues may be, it is not my purpose here to try to resolve them. In any event, consensus around the most compelling explanations will take time, as history unfolds and as analysts drill beneath the numbers, offering perspective and order to all these various elements. Rather, the point is to indicate how these debates connect to the key themes of this book: trends of political salesmanship and the significance of marketing frameworks to understanding these; the importance of structures of competition in determining styles of political marketing; the relationship between ideology and the work of the political marketers; and the quest to understand exactly what is a "good" campaign, both in terms of effectiveness and more broadly with respect to systemwide democratic dimensions. The following chapters work through these issues, but for now the general point can be made by picking up just two of these themes: the significance of marketing analysis and the problem of "good" campaigns.

MARKETING ANALYSIS AND THE 2012 ELECTION

A marketing analysis takes the conditions of competition as a guiding principle. It is in essence an economic perspective that sees politicians and parties as goal-directed actors in direct contest with rivals for particular rewards, for example, control of issue agendas, share of the vote, or ultimately electoral victory. Modes and styles of campaigning are directly shaped by the structure of competition: oligarchy or multiparty, first-past-the-post winner-take-all contests, or proportional representation where vote share across the electorate may matter more than individual constituency majorities. This emphasis on competitive structure renders marketing analysis as an alternative perspective on campaigning change compared to the usual political communication accounts that highlight mediation, media power, and communications innovation (see Chapter 1).

While these perspectives (competitive structure and mediation) are by no means mutually exclusive, they can lead to strikingly differentiated conclusions. Thus, from a media-centric viewpoint, the 2012 election may seem a curiously backward step compared to 2008. Obama's first victory heralded the power of the Internet; it offered a dramatic demonstration of how technology can alter the campaigning landscape. It held out the possibility of democratized campaigning, with Internet-enabled initiative and participation on a grand scale. However, if 2008 proclaimed social media and the collective influence of small donors, 2012 reminded us of older structures of power. This was exemplified by the continuing significance of big money, epitomized by the war of the "Super PACs." In the wake of the Supreme Court's *Citizens United* ruling, political action committees had no limits on the funds they were able to raise from corporate and individual donors, and this led to "historic spending levels spurred by outside groups dominated by a small number of individuals and organizations making exceptional contributions," according to Sheila Krumholz, executive director of the Center for Responsive Politics (Center for Responsive Politics, 2012).

If 2008 was all about the Internet, 2012 revived good old-fashioned "big money" TV advertising wars, with some estimates at nearly $1 billion spent on advertising in the ten battleground states of Ohio, Florida, Virginia, Colorado, Iowa, North Carolina, Nevada, Wisconsin, New Hampshire, and Pennsylvania. *Campaigns & Elections* reported that about $197 million was spent on political advertising, much of it negative, in Ohio alone (Trish, 2012). In short, 2012 apparently returned us to pre-Internet themes: big money, powerful interests, negative television advertising, and grassroots organization.

However, from the marketing perspective, media use in this campaign was not surprising. Rather, it exemplified fierce oligopoly competition for relatively small but decisive segments of the market. In 2012 the standout political marketing lesson was pinpoint micro-targeting enabled by "Big Data." The "Obama team assembled a team of top-notch technical talent and developed one of the most sophisticated data-driven marketing campaigns the world has ever seen," according to an admiring analysis in *Forbes* magazine (Severinghaus, 2012). Vast data banks combining electoral rolls and household- and individual-level consumer and social media information facilitated personalized targeting for messaging and fund-raising. Data analysis underpinned all aspects of communication, whether through video advertising to specific program audiences, social media messaging, or personal contacting via the telephone or on the doorstep. Among campaigners, both in the United States and elsewhere, the Obama camp's data advantage has come to be regarded as one of the decisive factors influencing the result. "Big Data," allied to intelligent analysis and military-precision organization, is the key lesson of 2012.

From the perspective of marketing analysis, this was predictable; the trend toward data-informed micro-targeting has been evident in both politics and commerce for some time. Data mining, including cookie-enabled tracking of online consumer behavior, has led to the applied "science" of "predictive analytics" in the retail sector, to facilitate marketing to ever more precisely identified potential customers. Especially in times of relative austerity, business is forced to work harder for a smaller slice of the pie. Predictive analysis enables companies not to wait until customers come through the door, but to approach selected targets much earlier in the purchase decision-making process. Bob Moritz, chairman of PricewaterhouseCoopers, described the data effect as transformational, using the example of a large mortgage insurer (Hellweg, 2013). Typically customers would seek out insurance agents only after they had already selected a house, he said: "We worked with the insurer to supply the agents with more data so they could contact clients further upstream, say three months before the purchase. Then they could provide information on the insurance, obviously, but also on the demographics of the area, comparable homes with insurance info, data on schools – that kind of thing. The data turned what had been a transaction into a service and an experience."

A similar process is evident in the 2012 presidential election. Two fierce rivals competing in a relatively diminishing market exploited data to target potential supporters. Both the Obama and Romney campaigns "broke new ground" in data exploitation (Trish, 2012), sifting through personal information on spending patterns, cultural tastes, church attendance, and so on to approach and motivate possible donors, activists, and voters. The main difference between them is that Obama waged the more effective Big Data war. His dream team of software engineers, with experience in Facebook, Twitter, and Google, is credited with amassing more volunteers and small donors than they had in 2008 and with running an awesomely efficient turnout operation on Election Day. In contrast, Romney's digital data platform, Orca, famously crashed on polling day (Madrigal, 2012).

THE "GOOD" CAMPAIGN

It is clear already that it is nearly impossible to talk about the 2012 election and not engage with that key question: what is a good campaign? The election exposed once again some raw democratic nerves. The highly polarized and aggressive character of American political discourse has been a matter of public concern for some years now, and the 2012 campaigns were remarkable for the amount of attack ads in the national races. It is well known that citizens dislike the mudslinging, and Pew's exit polls (2012) tell us that voters hated the ugly negativity, resented a lack of debate about substantive issues, and graded the candidates' campaigns lower than their counterparts in 2008. The potentially corrupting influence of big money, a perennial theme of American politics, emerged with intensified force following the *Citizens United* ruling. It was not just the basic issue of fairness and inequality of resources, but also that vast sums of money from corporations and wealthy donors could avoid disclosure, being funneled through a succession of political action committees, such that it is nearly impossible to trace the original source. A further, and relatively new, trouble spot is exposed by Big Data. Its prominence now in commerce and politics inevitably raises issues of the invasion of privacy of unwitting citizens. Moreover, in politics there are fundamental issues at stake. What are elections for, asked a postelection feature in the trade journal *Campaigns & Elections*, if what should be competing visions about the way to run the country – debates about the common good – are reduced to contests of social engineering of a ruthlessly selected group of target voters (Trish, 2012)?

Just what constitutes a good campaign is a driving question of this book, and we can see even from this limited discussion that there are two key strands in play. The first concerns the democratic dimensions: how closely did this campaign match up to requirements for free and fair elections, in which informed citizens express preferences and judgments about competing candidates' track records, issue stances, and general visions for a common future? Elections provide key tests of the well-being of democracy, the quality of the information environment, and the extent of public knowledge and citizen engagement, political responsiveness to public concerns, and accountability for political actions. The second strand has to do with effectiveness; it is most typically, but by no means exclusively, the practitioner perspective. What worked? What turned this election? What factors could have been influenced by strategy and tactics, and what were outside campaigners' control? Did the campaign matter at all in influencing the outcome?

There is a common tendency to view these two, the practitioner and democratic dimensions perspectives, as being in conflict with each other. The pragmatic, if you like, is posed as the enemy of the ideal. The cold reality of an imperfect world will tempt practitioners (the political marketers) to do the graceless necessary: to go negative, to hide and bias information, to reduce voters to crunched numbers, to be bland rather than bold, to court the money and marginalize the masses. In this view, perhaps Obama's victory of 2012 is a dismal return to politics as usual; from the electrifying heights of hope, change, and popular participation to the ugly pragmatics of what it takes to win. Equally, pragmatism is frequently opposed to ideological principle. Karl Rove, in particular, has become the whipping boy among Republican right-wingers, still astonished by the party's failure to topple a relatively weak incumbent beset by the worst economic crisis since the Great Depression. Rove wielded his considerable influence to promote the (relatively speaking) pragmatic candidate and marginalize or even attack the likes of Newt Gingrich, Sarah

Palin, Rick Perry, Herman Cain, and so on, those who were ideologically much closer to the party's base. Super PACs associated with Rove raised and spent many millions in support of Romney and selected Senate and House candidates, the vast majority of whom were beaten. "Congrats to @Karl Rove on blowing $400 million this cycle," tweeted Donald Trump. "What a waste of money." These are familiar lines of argument in election postmortems, and by no means exclusively in the United States. There are near-global concerns about the conduct of elections and their capacity to enhance democracy and serve citizen participation, while, even if the Tea Party has engendered a particularly intense debate in the United States, it is commonplace everywhere for losing parties to search their souls and question whether defeat was due to a deficiency or excess of ideological purity.

This book is located precisely at the intersection between pragmatism and idealism; or to put it another way, between the pragmatism of marketing practice and the ideals of democracy. It rejects a binary division between the two. Both in theory and in history, pragmatism and idealism may be often in tension but not easily separated. This connects to deeper underlying debates about the philosophy and practice of politics. Pragmatism, in the tradition of Charles S. Peirce, William James, and John Dewey, is sometimes hailed as America's great contribution to political philosophy (Westbrook, 2005). Although often criticized, the tradition survives, and at its best keeps a path between the "illusions of metaphysics" and foundational "god-like" truths, and the "illusions of skepticism" (Putnam, cited in Westbrook, 2005: 2). Suffice it to say here that there are two relevant ways of considering pragmatism in relation to the 2012 election. First is the idea that assertions of "truth" are always to be judged by their practical consequences on human lives and interests. Viewed from this perspective, the key judgment on Obama 2012 is not his (democratically questionable) campaign, but what he delivers over the next four years. If, as Professor Gerstle suggests, Obamacare becomes an achievement to rank alongside Roosevelt's social security, then the conduct of his campaign is rendered pragmatically necessary. The second idea can be called the "glass half full" argument; pragmatists have not abandoned ideals, but accept that change comes slowly. They choose to see partial achievement as the glass half full, rather than half empty. In both ideas, pragmatism and ideals can be thought of as bedfellows, albeit uneasy ones.

Political marketers, indeed marketers in general, might be considered the ultimate pragmatists, sometimes to the point where pragmatism, skepticism, and cynicism become horribly blurred. The realist "whatever works" imperative is not self-evidently an idealist or even improving project. It is no surprise then that when practitioners consider the "good campaign" question they focus on the effectiveness of strategies, tactics, and communication. However, even among themselves, the ideal, the democratic dimensions of a "good campaign," do register in intriguingly pragmatic ways.

Take, for example, the issue of "hate discourse." This was raised in a postelection discussion in the consultants' trade journal *Campaigns & Elections*. Republican consultant Tom Edmonds (2012: 41) urged his fellow professionals to address "the nearly total lack of civility in the campaigns." Negative ads can provide vital information, he argued, but "any objective analysis of the recent elections would have to conclude that ... we are quickly reaching a tipping point in civil discourse. The fact is, we've become a rude, mean-spirited, base society." Consultants, says Edmonds, have become addicted to the potency of negative campaigning and increasingly reckless about the truth of attacks on opponents. But in the wake of the 2012 results, and given the public dislike of negativity, it was clear that billions spent on negative ads achieved very little: "maybe political professionals will do the right thing simply based on pragmatism rather than principle."

Edmonds's argument touches upon a further aspect of the democratic dimensions of a good campaign: the quality of information. In fact, this became a major theme in postelection narratives of success and failure and offers a fascinating case of the blending of pragmatism and idealism. In this instance, criticism of the Republican campaign turned precisely on the relationship of pragmatism to the ideal; a pragmatic (realistic) strategy relies upon the use and quality of information, judged according to correspondence with ideal standards of objective facts. The Republicans' misplaced optimism signified more than simple errors in internal campaigning polling; it was indicative of a much broader Republican "alternate reality" in which any discordant information was dismissed as Democratic propaganda, including notably the poll analysis of *New York Times* blogger Nate Silver, who had consistently predicted an Obama win. With barely disguised schadenfreude, Democrat consultants Carville and Greenberg (2012a) described a Republican "war on science and facts" that had led ultimately to a grand self-delusion. Karl Rove, once again, was tagged as a major culprit and deluder in chief for his partisan punditry on Fox News. His infamous "meltdown" on election night when he refused to accept Fox's call of the Ohio results quickly became a YouTube hit and the subject of satire. "Math you do as a Republican to make yourself feel better," joked Jon Stewart on the *Daily Show*.

These issues, the quality of information and the alienating or welcoming character of political discourse, touch directly on the nature of the communicative relationship between citizens and politicians. They plainly matter for any assessment of what we might consider as democratically desirable campaigns, and more generally for a healthy public sphere. The point is not that the political marketers, left to their own devices, will remedy the ills of campaign practice. However, it is to say more than that the pragmatism of practice is not axiomatically at odds with democratic ideals. It is to say that there are possibilities, explored in this book, for finding means and ways to encourage political marketers to do well out of doing good. And that ultimately is the point; it is not enough to try to understand political marketing practice, and how it relates to underlying conditions of competition. The point is to change it.

Introduction

What does the title "Consumer Democracy" mean? At its simplest it suggests that politics are sold like commercial products, and that citizens judge, and are invited to judge, politics as commercial products. As such, "consumer democracy" is an unlikely term of praise. It cuts directly to our anxieties about the state of politics; about what politics should rightly be, and that politics should be judged, lived, and contemplated by standards of the public good. By contrast, purchase decisions are not held to such demands; they are somehow divested of the idea of the public, typically seen as private and individual matters or, worse, anti-public and, when entwined in the political arena, corrosive to the fundamental principles of the public good.

The point of the title is precisely acceptance of the idea that politics *are* sold in similar ways to products; similar but not exactly the same because this simple definition of consumer democracy masks layers of complexity about political activity and voter choice, consumer purchases, and indeed commercial marketing itself, which is a living and contested theoretical field with no simple single formula for selling success. However, the title does not imply that "consumer democracy" is necessarily a descent from high principles of proper politics. Rather, this book considers how marketing might enhance democratic politics, for parties and for citizens.

This may seem contrary given the evidence that we shall see of, for example, branding in politics in the cases of Tony Blair and George W. Bush. There is no doubt that marketing as it is practiced is often problematic in politics. It has been associated fairly convincingly as a contributor to two of the abiding crises of modern politics: the crisis of public communication (Blumler, 1995; Coleman and Blumler, 2009) and the crisis of citizen engagement (Cappella and Jamieson, 1997; Ansolabehere and Iyengar, 1997). Much contemporary political marketing is dull or ugly or both, avoiding the big issues of poverty, social justice, and climate change and reverting all too easily to over-simplification, robotically repetitive messages, and vilification of opponents (Scammell, 2003). Accepting this, is it possible that marketing might enhance democratic politics, make it more vibrant, responsive, and accountable? This book argues that it can. Complex problems of citizen engagement, of low levels of citizen knowledge and participation are not solved by simple, unidirectional, one-size-fits-all remedies. These are matters that involve fundamental questions about, inter alia, electoral systems, political cultures, media environments, the distribution of wealth, and educational opportunities. However, the case here is that marketing *can* contribute to solutions, instead of being part of the problem as it seems to be so often now.

An immediate difficulty with this approach might be that marketing in politics seems inherently suspicious. Political marketing raises concerns about manipulation, trivialization, and uneven relations of power between self-interested, well-funded, and often apparently beholden political actors and us as ordinary citizens negotiating our way through an information environment that is simultaneously overwhelming, inadequate, and biased. In fact, suspicion is the right starting place. Commercial marketing, despite its astonishing resources as an industry and despite our often willing compliance with its blandishments, struggles to justify itself as a force for social good. Even before the latest wave of consumer activism exposed brands' reckless disregard of human rights and their pillaging of "public and mental space" (Klein, 1999: 340), thoughtful practitioners admitted a problem of public legitimacy. Edward Bernays, the nephew of Sigmund Freud, is acknowledged as a founding father of promotional marketing; he infamously branded Lucky Strike cigarettes as "torches of freedom" to attract custom from the 1920s women's rights activists. He later reconsidered the power of marketing for good and ill, and devoted much of his career campaigning for the licensing of public relations professionals. PR was a field of great social impact, Bernays (1992) argued in a speech to the Association for Education in Journalism and Mass Communication. "Those persons who heavily influence the channels of communication and action in a media-dominated society should be held accountable and responsible for their influence...."

Skepticism, not to be confused with cynicism, is healthy for democracy. Modern democracies are founded on principles of distrust and the necessity to restrain those with the potential to abuse power (Warren, 1999). The good citizen is critical and will not invest trust in haphazard fashion in those who claim authority over society. If this is true for democracy, then skepticism is essential for the claims of marketing. Promotional marketing, after all, is often based on manipulation. Understandably the very word "manipulation" hoists the red flag for danger. However, of course, much manipulation is harmless; we often welcome and greatly enjoy it. We are eager accomplices in our own manipulation whether in "retail therapy" or in entertainment, most obviously in fiction books and films, which rely on the deft skills of the storyteller to draw us into compelling narratives. Moreover, emotional manipulation is enlisted for socially desirable aims, such as greener communities and fitter, healthier people: it is called "social marketing." However, commercial marketing is driven by self-interested motives, and is too often careless, as Bernays highlights, of its wider social impact. As such its manipulation *is* inherently suspicious; and crucially, unlike the fields of media, film, and literature, there is no developed and dedicated body of marketing criticism.

Thus, skepticism is the necessary starting point. But skepticism does not prejudge conclusions. It does not assume that all marketing is automatically bad, somehow inherently anti-democratic, antipublic, and corrosive of citizenship. Imagine that there was no place in politics for marketing. What might that look like: no market research, polling, or focus groups, no advertising, no razzmatazz, no slogans, no rhetoric, no news management counterweight to media power, and no image making? To flip the old adage on its head, can we really argue that promotional politics should be *less* professional than selling corn flakes? Politicians have a democratic right and duty to communicate, and one cannot, and more importantly *should not*, attempt to thwart effective correspondence and connection with citizens. One could Canute-like cry "halt" to the incoming tide only to demonstrate the limits of kingly intervention. Alternatively we can seek to channel the tide, protecting communities with sea walls where necessary while tapping its energy for socially beneficial ends.

So these are two main goals of this book: first, to consider how marketing might enhance politics; and second, to contribute to a debate about standards for criticism of political marketing as it is practiced, to differentiate the democratically good from the bad and to help develop a political marketing that is genuinely aimed at connection and correspondence with citizens and not merely at strategic and short-term tactical gain. Underlying this, and in the spirit of skepticism, will be the continuing theme of the relationship of marketing and democracy, and, more specifically, political marketing and democracy.

POLITICAL MARKETING: BETWEEN IDEALS AND PRAGMATISM

Any student of political marketing cannot help but be struck by mismatches between ideals and practice. On the one hand, there is democratic theory and from right and left critiques of the flaws of democracy and failures to meet the ideals of free, autonomous citizenries being the genuine authors of the laws that govern them; and on the other, there is the often grubby and petty reality of scrap, compromise, apathy, cynicism, triviality, and self-interest that characterizes much of the day-to-day reality. This sense of mismatch is evident abundantly among commercial marketers themselves when they come to think of politics. Normatively political marketing splits the field. There are those who take the managerial (management science) view that political parties and candidates are simply organizations like any other with something to sell. Surely, the specifics of the political marketplace are unique; it has its own set of ethical problems and its particular competitive structures and is peopled with producers and citizen-consumers with deeply held views that are often linked to fundamental issues of personal and social identity. However, many markets are unique; children's products, health care, financial and voluntary sector services each raise distinctive ethical questions and tap into consumers' most privately held anxieties and wider social views. The difficulty, from a managerial perspective, is not that politics is unique; it is to refine marketing theory to make it more valuable to politics in practice, to improve political efficiency, responsiveness, and ethical sensitivity. Philip Kotler (1981; Kotler and Kotler, 1999), the influential business management scholar, is a leading proponent of this view.

On the other side, there are those, also often from the business marketing discipline, who balk at the idea that politics may be considered a commodity or service like any other. Market values are not morally neutral, as political philosopher Michael Sandel argues forcefully in *What Money Can't Buy* (2012: 17); they cannot be applied with impunity to all walks of social and public life. Markets are valuable and effective tools for "organizing productive activity," but we must beware the social costs if all aspects of public life "are made over in the image of the market." Democratic politics is, or should be, about fundamental questions of social justice and the common good, and these cannot be reduced to simple questions of supply and demand. Therefore, encouragement of the notion that there is no basic difference between political and consumer choice is inherently troubling. It undermines the (normatively desirable) rationality of voter decisions, promotes selfish rather than public interest, and lends credibility to irrational motivations, which may be relatively harmless in daily shopping behavior but are much more threatening when applied to decisions that affect the common good. Above all, democracy provides the framework that legitimates and guarantees all rights and responsibilities, including those of producers and consumers. The risk of the marketing approach is that it may turn democracy itself into a product. I have sympathy with both sides of the argument. Political parties are not unlike other organizations operating in competitive conditions; strategic options, communication strategies, and even activist behaviors have broad similarities. However, the idea of politics as a commodity like any other is potentially frightening. "War and bigotry by consumer demand?" It is no stretch of the imagination. It feeds into contemporary nightmares about a slide into an instant e-voting "plebiscitary democracy" that "eschews significant deliberation and throws important decisions at an otherwise passive and propagandized public" (Barber, 2003: 36).

In part this gaping divergence reflects a difference of focus: the marketing advocates deal with the individual (party, candidate, and voter), while the critics are concerned with systemwide effects and broad principles: the former deal with the pragmatic within relatively short time horizons, the latter focus on the protection of democratic ideals and look to the middle distance. "Consumer democracy" stands at the intersection of the ideal and grubby reality. It takes seriously the ideals of particularly neo-pluralist democracy, as espoused by Robert Dahl, and deliberative democracy, as championed by Jürgen Habermas. If democracy is to aspire to the founding goals of autonomy, self-determination, liberty, equality, and the common good, it cannot remain indifferent to day-to-day practices that undercut these ideals. It must, therefore, be on its guard against political marketing and a win-at-any-cost, ends-justify-the-means campaigning practice. However, this account is also informed by historical reality in the sense that, even if consumer democracy falls way short of democratic ideals, it is not historically a fall from a state of grace, tumbling from a mythical golden age of public spirited politicians and citizens.

Histories of high politics and of campaigning demonstrate again and again that self-interested calculation, scandal, dirty tricks, and corruption are not inventions of modern times (Troy, 1991; Scammell, 1995; Schudson, 1999). From Cicero to our modern politicians, maneuvering, compromise, deception, manipulation, and backstabbing are familiar in political practice. Politics is a blood sport, in which, to paraphrase Winston Churchill, one may be killed many times. The tedious "narrative of decline" that underpins so much of our media and politics scholarship does more than simply glaze the eyes of thousands of students; it is insidious in that it fosters cynicism, offering no route to progress except, improbably, backward.

Possibly democracy, like sausage, is so much more appealing if one does not delve into the details of its making. Doubtless, the focus of this book will make politics appear unappealing to many, analyzing as it does the strategies and techniques of electoral success. For me, though, the reverse is true. It is part of the appeal of political marketing that it makes politics flesh and blood; it speaks the language that practitioners actually use; it reveals problems as they see them. It recognizes that political practice is also the story of driven human beings with all-too-human weaknesses working in complex situations not of their own making. In that sense, a sympathetic account of political marketing is underpinned by sympathy with democratic politicians. We impose upon them monstrous expectations of knowledge, commitment, and integrity, and then congratulate ourselves for our sophisticated cynicism when they inevitably fall short. We expect them to court us for our votes but are suspicious or even horrified if they are smart at it, and scornful when they are dull and clumsy. We want them to be in touch with that great intangible, the public mood, but accuse them of weakness and lack of principle if they too obviously pay close attention to polls and focus groups. An intuitive grasp of public sentiment is a political virtue it seems, while the study of opinion surveys is somehow a priori evidence of insincerity and absence of mission. We deride their inconsistency when they seem buffeted to and fro by media headlines, but then are intensely suspicious if they assemble mighty "spin machines," complaining that the "permanent campaigns" of many contemporary governments threaten basic principles of democratic accountability.

To put all this another way, we seem to want political leaders who are naturally – *authentically* – talented at the arts of marketing, but without the insidious apparatus of marketing, or the spinmeisters, the pollsters, the brand builders, in short the group of people we can call collectively "the political marketers." Collectively these are now the villains of popular political entertainment: witness Stephen Meyers, the corrupting press aide in George Clooney's *Ides of March*; Conrad Brean (played by Robert De Niro) in *Wag the Dog*, who is the unscrupulous political consultant who fakes a war in Albania to divert attention from the sex scandal engulfing the U.S. president; foul-mouthed Malcolm Tucker, in the film satire *In the Loop*, is overtly based on Tony Blair's powerful spin doctor Alastair Campbell, bulldozing senior politicians and civil servants to promote the war on Iraq; Bruno Gianelli, loosely modeled on Bill Clinton's strategist Dick Morris, is the brilliant and amoral counterpoint to the idealist activists of Jed Bartlet's *West Wing*. Kasper Juul is the morally dubious "spin doctor" (and yes, they use the English term) in the Danish political drama *Borgen*. These political marketers encapsulate much that seems wrong with our modern politics: the virtual reality of images honed for media consumption, the calculated self-interest, the fake sincerity, the lack of principle, the cynical manipulation of voters and media. To paraphrase Bill Clinton's erstwhile pollster Stan Greenberg (2009: 2), collectively consultants' reputation is akin to that of drug dealers: they tempt politicians into vice with poll pills to popularity and image quick fixes.

Precisely this group of people, the political marketers, and their work provide much of the subject matter of this book. It investigates this new class of political professionals and their world of "practical politics": what is distinctive about their contribution, how do they know what works, and how they are changing politics.

THE ORGANIZATION OF THIS BOOK

Chapter 1 provides the rationale for this book: why political marketing matters. It expands two of the arguments already alluded to: the importance of political marketing literacy and the theory and practice of political marketing in relation to normative ideals of democracy. It also proposes a third and more unusual reason why political marketing matters: the analytical value of the marketing approach. Typically accounts of political marketing, whether from practitioners or from political communication scholarship, focus on its strategic and tactical uses and normative consequences. It is commonly regarded as a kind of practitioner's tool set created from a complex of causes including resistance to media power, adaptation to communication technology, and submission to neoliberal hegemony. Thus, political marketing is normally considered as the object of explanation. It is more rare to see marketing theory used as the explainer, as a detached analytical approach to understanding contemporary campaigning (this sort of scholarship has been pioneered in the *Journal of Political Marketing*). Chapter 1 argues that the neglected analytical power of marketing is crucial for the development of political marketing literacy.

Chapter 2 examines the main protagonists, the heroes and villains of consumer democracy: the political marketers. The professionalization of political communication is a much-noted phenomenon throughout most of the democratic world. However, as a new class of political actors, the marketers are strangely understudied. This chapter explores the evidence to offer a portrait of who they are and what expertise they think they are bringing to politics in the light of underlying concerns about "politics lost" and "politics transformed."

The next two chapters examine branding as the most evolved form of political marketing. Lifted directly from the commercial arena, branding, including its methods and insights, provides a means to emotional connection with citizens. These chapters look at how branding works in practice, with the example of Tony Blair, and investigates its use-value as a tool for the understanding and critical evaluation of political communication, focusing on George W. Bush's 2004 campaign.

Chapter 5 cuts to the question that every student and every practitioner wants to know: what works? It examines how political marketers themselves assess campaigns and how, in parallel with commercial marketing, they rely on plausible narratives, case studies of success, and increasingly, marketing metrics. More fundamentally, it raises the question of what is a good campaign, and how we might judge that, not merely from the point of view of effectiveness, but in terms of democratic dimensions. It asks the question whether the imperative of winning is somehow antithetical to democratically desirable objectives.

This question is explored further in Chapter 6 in the broader context of markets (and marketing) and democracy. It argues that markets are twinned with democracy, but in a state of permanent tension. Marketing is simultaneously a lubricant of, a beneficiary of, and a threat to democracy; it requires democratic regulation and citizen surveillance, but at the same time it reminds us that active and rationally engaged citizenship is facilitated by rewards of pleasure and sociability. It offers a marketing critique of political marketing. This is not merely that substance and style, consumption and citizenship, emotion and reason can coexist in democratic harmony; it is that marketing encourages us to focus on the experience of politics and to consider how to make citizenship a pleasure as well as a duty.

A NOTE ON EVIDENCE AND CONTEXT

This book draws from a wide range of literatures, sometimes linked, sometimes discrete, and not usually put together: political science (democratic theory, voting behavior, campaign studies, democratic design, political psychology); propaganda studies (a mix of history, communication, and politics); political communication, which itself is a hybrid of political science and media studies; business marketing scholarship; political marketing studies, again a hybrid of commercial marketing and politics; and practitioner literature, including biography, insider campaign accounts, and general trade literature. This involves an exercise of interpretation and bridging, considering how, where, and why these various literatures relate to each other, and just as important, why they do not. Business marketing research, for example, is very rarely cited in mainstream political communication studies. Conversely, some political marketing research, normally originated from business disciplines, pays remarkably little attention to media. The media, so much the focus in political communication, are relegated to "instruments of promotion"; and hence media are the "dogs" that curiously do not bark in some political marketing models (Savigny and Temple, 2010).

The exercise of bridging was driven by a quest to be able to speak in general terms about political marketing, and this also requires international perspective. Over the past twenty or so years there has been a flowering of comparative research on campaigns, media, professionalization of communication, political advertising, and specifically political marketing. The book draws on this international evidence and argument throughout; however, it is important to note that precisely because of the broad disciplinary mix in this field, comparative frameworks vary and core definitions of key concepts (e.g., "Americanization," modernization, personalization, marketing) are themselves subject to interpretation and debate. Norris (2009: 322), in a critical review of comparative political communication research, claims it has not yet developed into "adulthood." Contrasted to political science, for example, it still lacks "theoretically sophisticated analytical frameworks, buttressed by rigorously tested scientific generalizations, common concepts, standardized instruments, and shared archival datasets." She complains, with some justice, that too much comparative research is driven by U.S. dominance, with international scholars diligently inquiring whether their own countries have become more or less like America, for good or ill.

Certainly, it is true that there is a scarcity of robustly comparative data sets around key aspects of political marketing, notwithstanding some valuable international surveys of consultants and content analyses of advertising. This book is informed by these data but does not claim to be driven by quantitative data. It is not a quantitative book. It is a work of interpretation of research in the field, viewed through the lens of political marketing, supplemented by the views of practitioners themselves, through their published campaign accounts, commentaries, and trade literature and by interviews with them and through observation of election campaigns over many years. It does not claim either to be *the* political marketing perspective on campaigning; this work is part of a growing field with vigorous debate about appropriate models. Moreover, inevitably, what follows reflects biases in the evidence base, and as Norris rightly says, the United States is by far the most studied country and without question tends to lead the world in the academic field of political communication. Furthermore, of course, many examples will come from the polity I know best, the UK.

Political Marketing

Why It Matters

This chapter highlights three particular reasons why political marketing matters. Two concern the study of political marketing: first, the importance of fostering political marketing literacy and, second, the use value of marketing as an analytical tool to understand developments in political communication. The third returns us to core ideas of democracy, in particular the theoretical relationship of marketing to models of democracy. All three are linked.

POLITICAL MARKETING LITERACY

The concept of *media* literacy is well established. It evolved through various paradigms throughout the second half of the twentieth century, including a critical effort to inoculate the working class against the ideological propaganda of the culture industries; the analysis of popular culture as the site of ideological struggle; and, more commonly now the educational paradigm, wherein media literacy is typically defined as the ability "to access, analyze, evaluate and communicate messages in a variety of forms" (Livingstone, 2003: 6). Many countries in Europe, North America, Australia, and elsewhere include media education as a standard part of school curricula. Notwithstanding continuing debate about the precise definition and purposes of media literacy, there is broad recognition that the ability to analyze critically media texts across a range of communication formats is part of the essential toolkit both for informed consumption and for citizenship in a mediated world.

There is no equivalent of political marketing. There are some eloquent pleas for literacy in the related fields of political propaganda (O'Shaughnessy, 2004) and public relations (Ewen, 1996: 412). Education, Ewen argues, "is pivotal since it has often been a casualty of public relations reasoning ... public relations is rarely intended to inform the population about the intricacies of an issue and is more often calculated to circumvent critical thinking." There are also relevant historical antecedents, most importantly for propaganda. The Institute for Propaganda Analysis (IPA) was created in 1937 precisely to educate the American public about the burgeoning use of propaganda, both abroad in the totalitarian states of Nazi Germany and Soviet Russia and at home, particularly in the hugely popular radio broadcasts of the pro-fascist Father Charles Coughlin. The IPA, a mix of journalists and social scientists, sought to spread propaganda education throughout schools and universities to equip the public with the critical skills to identify and analyze promotional political messages. The organization dissolved as the United States entered World War II; it had lost crucial support from publishers who were unwilling to foster critical examination of patriotic propaganda and, ironically, some of the IPA's professional critics were co-opted into the government's propaganda effort.

Intriguingly, while the academic study of propaganda has continued strongly, it has been marginalized from the mainstream of political communication inquiry. Propaganda is now identified mostly with the historical study of totalitarianism and warfare. By contrast political communication, as an independent field of inquiry, gathered momentum with the postwar rise of television as the dominant mass medium, and its core focus is on the relative power of media and politics to influence each other, and thereby impact public knowledge and citizen engagement. Clearly both fields are concerned with political campaigning and political messages, but with the exception of modern wars in which Western powers are involved, there is remarkably little cross-referencing.

However, propaganda analysis remains a necessary, if insufficient, component of political marketing literacy. It draws attention to the importance of language, the power of words and images, and the use of symbolism and myth in political communication (Hart, 2000; Nelson and Boynton, 1997; O'Shaughnessy, 2004). It highlights historical continuity. Harold Lasswell's (1927/1971) enduring examination of the propaganda strategies in World War I is relevant in wars today: the stoking of fear of demonized enemy leaders, the stratification of types of appeal according to the audience, heroic emotional language for the less educated on the home front, a more technical exposition of the legal justification for war to more sophisticated and neutral parties. Moreover, appeals to hope, national pride, and the everyday heroism of ordinary folk are standard emotional hooks of propaganda historically. These are evident equally in communist and Nazi propaganda, from all sides in war propaganda, and right to the present day are commonplace in electoral campaign language, as much from George W. Bush as from Barack Obama.

Clearly, there is overlap between propaganda and modern political marketing, rather more than is usually given credit by the ardent advocates of marketing as a perfect relationship of mutual exchange (see, e.g., Lees-Marshment, 2001). As long ago as 1928 Edward Bernays's book *Propaganda* urged politicians to adopt propaganda in ways that correspond closely to modern political marketing. Political campaigns, Bernays said, should involve (2005: 110):

the main business of studying the public scientifically, of supplying the public with party, candidates, platform, and performance, and selling the public these ideas and products. Politics was the first big business in America. Therefore there is a good deal of irony in the fact that business has learned everything politics has to teach, but that politics has failed to learn very much from business methods of mass distribution of ideas and products.

However, "propaganda" is insufficient for the understanding of modern political marketing. This is partly for the same reasons that Bernays failed in his quest to establish propaganda as an entirely benign concept. Propaganda became inextricably associated with deception following the exposure of blatant lies in the Allies' prowar promotion for World War I. Its sinister reputation was set in concrete subsequently by the Nazi's colossal propaganda machine. To this day, the word "propaganda" has remained a pejorative in common usage, despite the attempts of historians and war scholars to define it more subtly and neutrally (Jowett and O'Donnell, 2006; Taylor, 2003). Commercial marketing may be viewed as manipulative, but outright deceit is broadly unacceptable and contravenes marketing ethics and, on occasions, consumer protection regulation. More importantly, though, marketing proposed a distinctive response to massive societal changes. The broadening of democracy, the extension of the franchise, rising affluence, and education effectively shifted the balance of power from elites to populations. For democratic elitists such as Bernays, this created potentially a chaotic clamor for rights, special pleading of interests, and a paralysis of leadership in thrall to public opinion. "The great political problem of our modern democracy is how to induce our leaders to lead," he argued (Bernays, 2005: 109). Propaganda was to be the instrument through which leaders could be induced to lead; it enabled them to shape public opinion rather than merely follow it. Marketing, by contrast, approached societal change as a business opportunity. If consumers had become more powerful collectively, more affluent, educated, and aware of their choices, then their wants and needs should be put at the start of the production-consumption cycle. Produce what the customer wants, distribute it cost-effectively, and the result is "mutual satisfaction": happy consumers and profitable producers.

This simplified version encapsulates the essential difference between propaganda and marketing. Propaganda tries to lead public opinion; marketing to follow it. In reality, the two are often more difficult to disentangle. The skilled propagandist, of whom Bernays was an outstanding example, knows his or her limits, will seek to run with the grain of public opinion, and will rarely waste energy attempting to shift entrenched attitudes. Equally, innovative marketing can create wants where none existed; the profusion of hi-tech products – Sony Walkmans, smart phones, iPad tablets – demonstrates the continuing power of producers to lead public desires. The overlap of practice is why marketing can be accused simultaneously of two apparently contradictory vices: on the one hand, it is supposedly destroying the function of leadership, replacing statesmen with user-friendly personalities, whose principles are soft cushions, bearing the imprint of pollsters; on the other, through an ever more sophisticated arsenal to manage news and (mis)lead audiences, it increases the power of leaders.

However, in principle marketing is surely a democratic advance on propaganda precisely because of its essential element of reciprocity. Marketed politics may both lead and follow public opinion, but it must always attend to it, and grant some possibilities for public voice both in the communication and in the shaping of political programs. This is not to say that political marketing in practice cannot be misused, cynical and unethical, just as commercial marketing may be; but it is to say that marketed politics, as distinct from propaganda politics, is more or less permanently amenable to change, to the creation of shared solutions, and to the principle of reciprocal satisfaction. The "brand," it will be argued subsequently, embodies the principle of mutuality: it is effectively a cocreation, simultaneously top-down and bottom-up, between producers and consumers.

Ultimately, this is why political marketing literacy matters. It is not simply a matter of inoculation against the persuasive tricks of the trade, which was the driving concern of propaganda analysis. It is about creating a critical mass of critical citizen-consumers, who are neither so cynical that they assume all political marketing is a form of lying, nor so gullible that they cannot distinguish the promotion from the product. In short, it is about developing widely shared standards of critical evaluation of political marketing that can distinguish the democratically good from the bad, and that ultimately will impact the attitudes and behaviors of both politicians and citizens.

POLITICAL MARKETING: ITS ANALYTICAL VALUE

A prime attraction of political marketing is its descriptive and analytical power, disregarding for the moment concerns about its effects for good or ill on democratic practice. It is not just that the expertise and language of marketing is abundantly evident in political campaigning. More importantly, the marketing lens offers fresh insight into changes in political communication and campaigning. The analytical value of marketing is a key underlying interest of this book, as becomes clear especially in the chapters that deal with political image as brands; it is a vital component of the quest to develop standards of critical evaluation. It is a truly colossal task to compare and contrast marketing frameworks with the vast literature in political science and communication that explains campaign change primarily by the decline of ideological difference in modern society (Kirchheimer, 1966; J. Smith, 2009) or by the impact of communications technology, especially television and now the Internet (Meyer, 2002; Blumler and Kavanagh, 1999; Kerbel, 2009) or by cultural change (Wernick, 1991; Street, 2001) or by various combinations of these factors and general societal "modernization" (Swanson and Mancini, 1996; Norris, 2000; Farrell, 1996; Plasser, 2002). There is simply not space here to do justice to all these works.

However, Plasser (2002) valuably synthesizes the leading accounts of campaign change into one model (see Table 1.1). He draws on Farrell's (1996) typology of labor-intensive (low-tech, volunteer armies, mass canvass, public meetings) and capital-intensive (high-tech, TV-centered campaigns run by media and marketing experts, increased targeting of floating voters) campaigns; and Blumler and Kavanagh's (1999) three stages of political communication development, from the early days of television, through the period from the mid-1960s of television ascendency with campaigns fought primarily as TV agenda-setting battles and advertising wars, to the "third age" (1990s onward) characterized by complexity as audiences fragment across multiplying digital platforms. They highlight increasing politics-media tension as journalists react negatively to political

TABLE 1.1. *Modeling Changing Campaign Practices*

Phase	Premodern	Modern	Postmodern
Mode of political communication system	Party-dominated	Television-centered	Multiple channels, multimedia
Dominant style of political communication	Party messages	Sound bites, image management	Narrowcasting, targeted micro-messages
Media	Partisan press, posters, newspaper ads, broadcasts	TV news	TV narrowcasting, targeted direct mail, and e-mail
Dominant advertising media	Print, posters, leaflets, radio speeches and mass rallies, door-to-door canvassing	Nationwide TV ads, press ads, mass direct mail	Targeted TV ads, e-mail, telemarketing, Internet banners
Campaign coordination	Party leaders and staff	Party managers plus external advertising, polling, and media experts	Party campaign units and specialized political consultants
Dominant campaign paradigm	Party logic	Media logic	Marketing logic
Preparations	Short term, ad hoc	Long-term campaign	Permanent campaign
Campaign expenditures	Low budget	Increasing	Spiraling up
Electorate	Cleavage- and group-based stable voting behavior	Erosion of party ID, rising volatility	Issue-based and highly volatile voting behavior

Source: Plasser (2002: 6).

news management, political spin machinery expands to cope with twenty-four-hour news cycles across the ever-increasing range of political news outlets, and political news itself changes and is squeezed on national networks, expanded overall, and increasingly packaged as infotainment. Plasser incorporates these analyses within Norris's (2000) scheme of "premodern," "modern," and "postmodern" campaign. Norris's distinction between the "postmodern" and Swanson and Mancini's "modern" campaign rests on the technological capacity of cable, satellite, and digital to fragment audiences and thus transform campaigning from "modern" broadcasting to the nation to "postmodern" narrowcasting to target audiences.

Plasser's table is comprehensive in its categorization of campaign elements. Moreover, although it is not presented overtly as an explanatory model, it captures the dominant frameworks in that media and communications technology seem to be the main motors of change as we move from the era of "party domination" to the "postmodern" age of multimedia. It leaves us overall with a dramatic switch from parties in control of their campaigns to eras of media domination, with communications technology calling the tune, and parties responding with narrowcasting, micro-targeting, and "marketing logic." It would be a serious mistake to underestimate the importance of media, both in the sense of the transformative potential of technology characteristics and in the broader idea of increasing media power relative to politics. However, one is struck by what is missing from media-based accounts.

The glaring absence is competition. While, as Plasser's summary table indicates, orthodox political communication accounts explain "marketing logic" largely as a response to developments in media and communications technology, marketing theory seeks answers within the structure of competition. The distinction matters. For the former, marketing logic invades politics as an exterior influence; essentially an imported commercially tested means to manage the media and manufacture difference among ideologically similar parties. As such it comes laden with anxiety at the belittling or even depoliticization of politics itself.

For the latter, marketing logic is inherent in the structure of political competition. Marketing may be used more or less ethically, and put to more or less democratically desirable ends, but it cannot be somehow wished away or separated from the nature of competitive politics.

Business marketing theory argues that paradigms of salesmanship broadly correspond to competitive conditions: the structure of the market, the intensity of rivalry among sellers, the degree of consumer choice, the relative balance of power between producers and consumers, the taste and demands of consumer culture. It explains why producers, particularly service suppliers who are essentially selling *promises* to deliver future benefits, are utterly dependent on image: the credibility of those promises lives and dies by the reputation of the provider. It demonstrates that in conditions of oligopoly, rival competitors are highly interdependent, with consequences that are as relevant in politics as in business (see Table 1.2). Most important for our purposes, oligopoly competitors are particularly reliant upon and sensitive to marketing innovation. Small adjustments in market share may produce hugely significant effects upon profits, and thus there is a need for constant monitoring and instant responses to the marketing activities of rivals. The effect is to ratchet up the overall importance of marketing. Thus oligopoly, rather than more open competition, tends to provide the most intense concentration of marketing. Moreover, marketing scholarship demonstrates that in mature oligopolistic markets there is a tendency to product standardization, which in turn opens up gaps for niche providers with specialist or premium offers.

The parallels with politics are clear. Political marketing tends to be most intense and innovative in oligopolistic electoral competition. This is most obvious in the United States, but also evident in the UK, Canada, Australia, and other contexts, such as Germany and the presidential runoffs in France, that are dominated by two parties. Oligopolistic parties, just as companies, are particularly sensitive to the marketing efforts of rivals; innovation requires response, and the overall effect is to intensify the marketing process. In this process, political image is crucial, not just as an effect

TABLE 1.2. *Marketing, Competitive Structures, and Politics*

Perfect Competition	Imperfect Competition	Oligopoly
Many suppliers	Many suppliers	Few suppliers
Easy access	Barriers to access	Similar product
Equal resources	Unequal resources	High barriers to entry
Perfect information	Imperfect information	Competitor interdependence
No promotion	Brand differentiation	Promotion essential
	Promotional strategies	Branded products
Political activism/ interest market	Multiparty electoral markets	Restricted electoral markets
Many suppliers	Wide variety of electoral offers	Few (2 or 3) dominant parties
Easy access (via Internet)	Unequal resources	Similar policy platforms
Abundant information	Imperfect information	High barriers to entry
Little promotion	Variable promotion and branding	Competitor interdependence
		Imperfect information
		Branded parties/ candidates
		Promotion essential

of mediated politics, but as a decisive variable that determines the credibility of promises. The point is not to deny the importance of media, nor to suggest that political marketing innovation exists *only* in oligopolistic situations; rather it is to draw attention to the importance of competitive structures as highly significant and too often neglected driving forces of political marketing.

Typically, comparative political communication accounts of campaigning recognize the importance of electoral and media systems and regulatory environments (e.g., Swanson and Mancini, 1996). Trends to convergence around the "American model," with its characteristics of professionalization, personalization, and image-driven politics, are often said to be moderated by system features, for example these: candidate- rather than party-centered, statutory limits on campaign spending, and possibilities for paid political advertising. However, and again typically, this recognition has not extended to the incorporation of competitive structures in models of campaigning change. The absence is surprising given the weight of political science scholarship that links party behavior to competitive environments.

The importance of competition as a determining influence on political behavior is underscored in two of the most influential theories of democracy: Anthony Downs's economic theory of democracy (1957) and Joseph Schumpeter's theory of competitive democracy (1943). Downs provided the seminal economic model of how candidates must position themselves in order to maximize their chances of being elected. This is the median voter model, which says that a candidate seeking to optimize votes in a majority election must take a position at the median of a normal distribution of voters' policy preferences. Thus, logically candidates will gravitate toward the center ground where most voters are located; failure to do so runs the risk of being usurped by rivals who are closer to the median voter. Downs assumes instrumental (or economic) rationality on the part of both candidates and voters, in the sense that both seek to optimize the utility of their actions. The motivation is self-interest, and the assumption is that politicians and voters will act in such a way as to maximize the chances of fulfilling those interests.

In contrast, Schumpeter emphasizes the irrationality of voters. Schumpeter was notoriously pessimistic about the possibilities of public participation in politics. In reality, he argued, many people do not have the interest or knowledge in politics to make informed, reasoned choices. In order to make democracy work, parties must motivate voters to turn out at elections. What Schumpeter called the "psycho-technics" of electioneering (advertising, slogans, rousing music, and such) were not in his view corruptions of politics, but rather essential to mobilize the masses in the competitive struggle for votes (1943: 272–83). Thus working with a different set of assumptions about voter rationality, each came to the same conclusion: that the logic of competition renders "parties in democratic politics ... analogous to entrepreneurs in a profit-seeking economy" (Downs, 1957: 295).

There are obvious similarities with marketing analysis here. However, precisely because marketing is the dedicated theory and practice of sustainable success in competitive environments, it is both more dynamic than the classic economic theories of party competition and a more perceptive predictor of campaign change than media-based political communication alternatives. With due deference to the variety of theoretical standpoints in the literature (see Henneberg, Scammell, and O'Shaughnessy, 2009), it is a fair summary to say that shifts in marketing paradigms are driven by perceived shifts in the relative balance of power between producers and consumers. Broadly speaking, the more choice consumers have, the more affluent they are, the more discerning they are in their choices, the more power they have collectively relative to producers, and the more marketing paradigms insist on a (increasingly personalized) customer focus in the design, development, and delivery of goods and services. "Marketing," as opposed to general salesmanship, is a relatively modern concept. As a seminal text states (Baker, 2008: 3), "The enigma of marketing is that it is one of man's oldest activities and yet it is regarded as the most recent of business disciplines." What distinguishes "marketing" from older forms of selling is precisely the emphasis on customer wants and needs at the start of the production-consumption cycle. This is commonly known as the "marketing concept"; its grip as a central tenet of business philosophy takes hold from about the 1960s onward with the emergence of "affluent society" amid the postwar consumer boom. The burden of sales effectively shifted from postproduction activities – advertising and personal, often door-to-door sales – to preproduction research of the market and likely customer wants and needs.

In real-world complexity there is not a simple linear evolutionary path from "sales" to "marketing" (Keith, 1960). Innovators continue to design products first and then look for markets, and techniques of sales may change but are no less important, or even aggressive, than before. However, there is a consensus of marketing theorists that the general trajectory is correct: in broad terms business has moved from sales-oriented to customer-oriented approaches. It has done so because of a perceived shift in market power from sellers to buyers collectively; the spiraling costs of a purely sales-oriented approach became increasingly untenable amid intensifying competition and abundant consumer choice.

From the mid-1990s onward, marketing theorists examined the impact of the "new" economy of digital, global, and deregulated markets. The massive expansion of competition and choice produced a further substantial shift in the collective power balance in favor of consumers (Scammell, 2003). It led to the emergence of "consumer empowerment" as a key issue in marketing theory, with the rise of ethical consumption, consumer activism, and the Internet-enabled proliferation of customer review and price comparison information. Business theory responded to the new economy by moving from "marketing management" to customer relations and relationship marketing paradigms. The essential difference is that the latter emphasized the imperative to retain existing customers, to extract "lifetime value," since in conditions of high-intensity competition the cost of attracting new consumers is usually considerably more than the cost of loyalty-building strategies. Thus, we have seen the proliferation of loyalty marketing and brand-building, more personalized marketing strategies with product offers tailored to individual customer profiles (as, for example, Amazon or iTunes), and strategies to capitalize on consumer empowerment, such as "permission" as opposed to "interruption" marketing. In the former, consumers agree to be contacted about product offers; in the latter, typified by mass media advertising, promotion is experienced as an uninvited interruption. More radical examples of "consumer empowerment" include the rise of "prosumption," wherein the distinction between producer and consumer is blurred. The Internet especially abounds with examples of "prosumption": YouTube, Wikipedia, eBay, blogging and citizen journalism, and Apple's facilitation of consumer-created applications for the iPhone and iPad.

Clearly there are considerable similarities in the broad trajectories of salesmanship in commercial and political markets.
Political campaigning has moved from eras characterized at first
by personal contact, door-to-door canvassing, and political ral-
lies, through mass promotion via advertising and TV-centered
campaigning and increasingly research-driven issue platforms
and market segmentation, to our current period with its micro-
targeting, brand building, data banks of potential supporter
information, Internet-enabled permission marketing, and experi-
mentation with "citizen empowerment" strategies, evidenced in
the proliferation of "listening" initiatives over the past ten years:
most notably from Ségolène Royal's French presidential campaign in 2007, Hillary Clinton's various "listening" tours, the
UK Labour Party's "Big Conversation" in 2003, and Australian
Prime Minister Kevin Rudd's "dialogue" initiatives. Just as the
commercial sector has moved toward more "personalized" and
individually customized communication, so too has politics. This
is evident not just in technology-enabled communication via, for
example, mobile phone messaging and social networks, but also
in a revival of personal contacting on the telephone and on the
doorstep. As Nielsen (2012: 11–15) shows, "personalized political communication" (defined as "live interaction" between voters
and campaigners) has increased sharply in U.S. presidential elections: in 1992 about 20 percent of election survey respondents
reported a personal contact from one of the political parties; in
2008 that had increased to more than 40 percent. Recently we
have also witnessed attempts to involve voters directly as "pro-
sumers"; Howard Dean (2003–4) and, of course, Barack Obama
in 2008 are outstanding examples of campaigning cocreation.
Thus, the direction of travel of campaigning change echoes commercial markets: from sales-oriented to market-oriented to our
contemporary phase of adaptation to consumer empowerment.

Just as important, the motors for change are analogous to
commercial markets; a relative shift in power away from parties
(producers). The weakening of the dominant parties, declines
in membership, the erosion of the strength of party identification, loss of trust in parties as institutions, widespread declines

in voter turnout at elections; in short, the "crisis" of political parties is recognized nearly everywhere throughout the older democracies of Europe, North America, Australia, and Japan (Hay, 2007; Pharr and Putnam, 2000; Katz and Mair, 1994; Stoker, 2006). The crisis of major parties, the phenomenon of increasingly volatile electorates, the rise of "lifestyle" politics, and the emergence of new sectional and single-issue parties were trends even before the Internet-fueled new economy complicated matters (Bennett, 1998). The Internet provides near perfect competition for political interest, significantly boosting the opportunities for what might be called political "niches": single-issue and lifestyle politics, alternative activism, ideological extremists, and so on. These are everyday competitors for eyeballs, for political attention, monetary donations, and voluntary activism. Thus, the Internet, in politics, as in business, is contributing to a further relative shift in power away from the producers, conceived collectively.

If you compare Figure 1.1 to Plasser's summary table (Table 1.1) you will see many similarities in the details of campaign change. The big difference is the complete absence of media as a defining category in Figure 1.1. The absence is deliberate, but it is not to deny the importance of media as transformative agents (see Street, 2005, for a valuable overview). None but the foolish would do that. Rather, the point is to emphasize the neglected importance of competition as a key driver of political marketing and to highlight that some of the key characteristics of modern campaigning – permission marketing, personalized communication, empowerment strategies, and branding – are explained better by competition than by reference to communications technology.

One must be careful not to minimize the differences between political and commercial markets (Lock and Harris, 1996; Ormrod, 2007; O'Shaughnessy, 2001). Despite the marked decline in the strength of party attachments since the mid-1960s in virtually all the older democracies of America, Western Europe, and Japan, voting remains an act of social affirmation for many people. Party loyalty, even if declining, remains linked to social

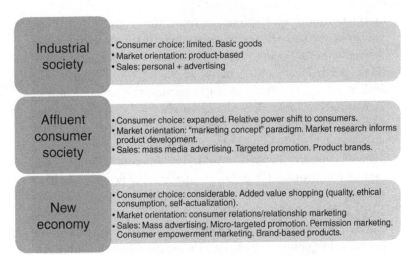

Industrial society	• Consumer choice: limited. Basic goods • Market orientation: product-based • Sales: personal + advertising
Affluent consumer society	• Consumer choice: expanded. Relative power shift to consumers. • Market orientation: "marketing concept" paradigm. Market research informs product development. • Sales: mass media advertising. Targeted promotion. Product brands.
New economy	• Consumer choice: considerable. Added value shopping (quality, ethical consumption, self-actualization). • Market orientation: consumer relations/relationship marketing • Sales: Mass advertising. Micro-targeted promotion. Permission marketing. Consumer empowerment marketing. Brand-based products.

FIGURE 1.1. Consumer choice and marketing paradigms: From sales to marketing

identity for many voters in a way that it is not for most consumption activity (Butler and Collins, 1999). Political markets, as Butler and Collins point out, contain "counterconsumers," a phenomenon not common in other markets, wherein people vote tactically to prevent a particular outcome rather than to support the candidate voted for. The political product is multicomponent, comprising a party, leader, or candidate, a set of values or ideology, and a package of policy proposals. Voters may like some and dislike others among the components, but are effectively offered all or nothing. Moreover, especially in proportional representation settings, the product is mutable. One may vote for one party only to discover that it is willing to sacrifice parts of its program for the sake of office in postelection coalition bargaining. Thus the political offer is far more complicated than is typical for commercial trading. Finally, and perhaps most important, political competition dynamics are shaped fundamentally by the periodic character of elections in contrast to the continuous or seasonal nature of most commercial markets. Particularly in the winner-take-all situation of first-past-the-post electoral systems the effect is to funnel marketing activities toward elections. The upshot is that in politics "all competition ultimately is focused on the election, so regardless of what happened in the past, the party or candidate needs to be in good standing come decision time" (Butler and Collins, 1999: 69).

The particularities of political markets prescribe caution before overlaying politics with too-simplified marketing schemas. We should not be surprised if many individual parties do not perfectly replicate ideal marketing models. Certainly, it is true that detection of the "marketing concept" in campaigns drove the rise of political marketing scholarship, as a discrete approach to understanding political communication. The term "political marketing" had been in occasional use since the 1960s and Jack Kennedy's celebrated presidential campaign, but it started to gain traction as a distinctive descriptor only in the 1980s with the successes of Ronald Reagan and Margaret Thatcher (Scammell, 1999). Although these two had strong ideological reputations, each was associated with pioneering political marketing, using experts from market research and advertising not just as ad hoc technical experts but as influential strategists (O'Shaughnessy, 1990; Scammell, 1995). It raised the question of whether political persuasion was moving from a propaganda (sales) orientation to a "marketing concept" orientation, in which the design of the political offer was shaped by a research-led analysis of the concerns and wants of strategically selected segments of the electorate. Bill Clinton and, following his example, Tony Blair's New Labour removed many doubts. They became commonly accepted as near-perfect exemplars of the marketing concept in politics as external market research was infused into the creation of leadership style, party image, and policy programs (Wring, 2004; Newman, 1994). These examples triggered a new wave of political marketing research with an emphasis less on the instruments of promotion (advertising, spin, media use, and the like) and more on the market orientation of parties. More or less clear instances of market-oriented campaigns were increasingly identified around the world, notably Helen Clark's Labour win in New Zealand in 1999, Gerhard Schröder's SPD campaign in Germany in 1998, Lula da Silva's win in the 2002 Brazilian presidential election and Kevin Rudd's campaign with the Australian Labor Party in 2007.

Some business marketing enthusiasts hailed a new dawn of responsive politics, directed externally to the views of the electorate, rather than internally to party disputes about principles and policy. Lees-Marshment (2001) is particularly associated with this claim, and she set out an ascending scale of product-, sales-, and market-oriented parties (see Coleman, 2007, for criticism of this schema). It sparked some comparative research, as scholars from various parts of the world examined whether their national parties matched the Lees-Marshment definition of "market orientation." Unsurprisingly, the main conclusion (Lilleker and Lees-Marshment, 2005; Lees-Marshment, Strömbäck, and Rudd, 2010) is that it is not so easy to clearly demarcate "selling" and "market" orientations in practice. Some parts of a party's program and brand reputation may be amenable to market-research led change and others not, while market-oriented campaigners sometimes become more sales-oriented once elected. In short, orientations are not fixed in aspic.

However, ultimately, the point is not whether individual political parties perfectly replicate ideal marketing types (in this case a rather rigid marketing-management model); rather, it is about understanding political campaign and communication change. Competition is inscribed in the democratic system; this very fact promotes entrepreneurial logic. It is no surprise, therefore, that political campaign trends have followed marketing; nor that commercial marketing theory and practice provide the sharpest cues to future development.

What's next for political marketing? Data mining the marketing potential of social media is one clear candidate: it enables "long-tail nanotargeting" of communities of interest (Greyes, 2011: 47). For example, mining Twitter hashtag and follower lists can help ensure the right messages to the right voters according to Democratic strategist Natch Greyes: "New media users post, repost, tweet, retweet, comment and interact with each other constantly. Users who feel a deep connection with a person or a brand are happy to show their public support and provide free marketing ... through their online activities." It can operate as a tool to create and sustain ad hoc networks of online volunteers. Another candidate is neuromarketing, the alliance of brain science with consumer personality profiling, which has created a commercial buzz in the past few years. It claims that by monitoring electrical activity in the brain it can identify subconscious triggers for sales that are not discovered by the normal techniques of consumers' self-reporting or focus groups. Its premise is a familiar one in brand research, that people are often not consciously aware of their motivations for action. To the extent that neuroscience can offer a deeper understanding of motivational processes, it will inevitably "impact all the channels of communication and discourse that flow through our society and economy: not just advertising and marketing, but education, public policy, political debate, and even medical treatments and therapies," according to neuromarketing firm Lucid Systems (2009). These are grand claims for neuromarketing, and they need to be subjected to the usual self-promotional discount. It is not yet clear that neuromarketing's "colorful brain maps" will lessen the need for the lower-tech skills of brand image researchers (Honan, 2009). However, "brain science" is more than one to watch in future campaigning; it has already started (Westen, 2008).

POLITICAL MARKETING AND MODELS OF DEMOCRACY THEORY

The case for the analytical value of marketing pays no regard to the normative consequences for democracy. However, clearly the analytical case is bolstered by reference to the validity of economic theories of democracy: Downs's essentially rational choice model and Schumpeter's competitive elitist model. Neither of these presents uplifting visions of democracy. Schumpeter's notorious lack of faith in ordinary citizens' interest in politics led him to a minimalist view of democratic possibilities. The grander ideals of participatory democracy were stripped down to the bare bones of a "democratic method," procedures for the peaceful and periodic transfer of power between elites, and mechanisms to ensure accountability and control their excesses. Schumpeter's legacy of competitive elitism remains durable partly because it compels attention to democratic design (see Chapter 6) and because of the considerable body of evidence that continues to show that, despite improvements in education, large minorities of populations in established democracies have little interest in or knowledge of politics. Delli Carpini and Keeter (1996) found that between 22 and 37 percent of respondents in Canada, France, the UK, and the United States could not answer a single question correctly on a simple five-question international current affairs quiz. The United States consistently scores particularly badly on political knowledge. Bennett's (2005) analysis of the 2004 American National Election Survey concludes that "most Americans were 'out to lunch' when it came to basic information about politics." There is no doubt that this dismal "realism" underpins the thinking of many leading campaign professionals, certainly in the United States (Scammell, 1997), and feeds their doubts about the questionable value of public opinion research on policy issues (Herbst, 1998). Practitioners, even if not political marketing theorists, embrace the legacy of Schumpeter.

Equally, rational choice models of democracy propose a dispiritingly "hard-nosed" explanation of political behavior (Stoker, 2006: 76). They argue, in essence, that both politicians and voters act "instrumentally to maximize the attainment of their preferences, and that in doing so they behave in a highly strategic manner, calculating a range of options before selecting the one that delivers the most benefits." It is essentially a view of democracy as the peaceful competition of self-interest. Political marketing, with its hardheaded calculation of possibilities, can be seen as the logical conclusion of this instrumentally rational (or "calculus") approach to politics. Especially in tight oligopoly competition "it is not difficult to show that it is rational for the parties to squabble over the centre ground in a race towards the median voter" (Hay, 2007: 119), with the outcome that policy differences are diluted. According to critics, such as Hay, this process of "marketization" is a key reason "why we hate politics." It dilutes the salience of elections, since parties are no longer competing on differences of principle. In that sense it is "profoundly depoliticizing," removing clear policy choices from public scrutiny; at the same time "it also serves to politicize a series of more ephemeral and non-policy matters – as personality contests replace the clash of competing policy trajectories in the determination of electoral outcomes." The more parties conceive of and appeal to voters as individual consumers, rationally calculating their own self-interest, the more likely these voters will "rationally disengage," since voting makes so little difference to policy outcomes.

Political marketing, indeed business marketing, theorists are only just beginning to grapple with the broader consequences of practice on democratic ideals. The comfortable assumption that ethical marketing is inherently democratic (Lees-Marshment, 2001) because it lubricates the process of choice and facilitates "mutual satisfaction" by delivering voters and consumers what they want is at last coming under sustained challenge (Henneberg et al., 2009; Yannas, 2008; Quelch and Jocz, 2007; Johansen, 2012). There is increasing recognition that political marketing, as theory and practice, needs to justify itself in democratic terms. For all its analytical realism, it is only just starting to do so.

CONCLUSION

This chapter has set out three reasons why the study of political marketing matters. The first concerns political marketing literacy and the importance of understanding the ways in which politics tries to sell itself to us. The significance of this includes but goes further than merely saying that citizens need safeguards against the persuasive "tricks of the trade." It is also that marketing, as opposed to propaganda, is distinguished by the essential idea of reciprocity. Thus, the development of literacy of political marketing not only enables understanding, but can also contribute to changes in political marketing practice. This point is argued more fully in Chapter 6.

The second and linked reason is a little more abstract. It says that marketing theory provides analytical tools to understand political marketing, and that these tools are vital complements to the more usual ways of seeing modern campaigning as a response to communication technology and media power. There are two key arguments arising from this: first that marketing of some sort is inherent in the competitive structures of democratic politics; and, second, that marketing theory itself can help us understand and indeed develop standards of critical evaluation for political campaigning practice. That is to say that the analytical power of marketing theory is essential for the development of political marketing literacy. The specific analytical value of a leading aspect of modern business theory – the brand – is put to the test in Chapters 3 and 4 and the political communication of Tony Blair and George W. Bush.

Third, this chapter admitted frankly that modern political marketing is wedded to economic theories of democracy. Both Downs and Schumpeter anticipate the selling of politics in ways that are analogous to commercial markets. It was also admitted that neither of these, often-called "realist," seminal thinkers offers inspirational views of the democratic project. Even if the practice of democracy is found wanting, the underlying aspirations of freedom, equality, and citizen sovereignty still retain explosive power (Habermas, 1996) and can mobilize populations as the Arab Spring of 2011 once again confirmed. Marketing generally, and political marketing in particular, needs to show that it can be an enabler, or at the very least no barrier to the more optimistic participatory visions of democracy. This book is a contribution to that debate and in Chapter 6 sets out some specifics of how marketing may enhance democracy.

The terrain of this book is now clear. It is concerned with the work of the people we can call collectively the political marketers; the people whose business it is to sell to us political parties and candidates. These are the men and women who pull "the strings in American politics" (Johnson, 2012) and increasingly elsewhere and whose work is heavily inflected with consumerism. It is about understanding this work, contributing to standards of critical evaluation and driving arguments that can progress democracy in our highly marketed, consumerized societies.

2

Political Marketers

Who Are They and What Do They Think They Are Doing?

The political marketers, or the "professionals" as they are often called – the advertisers, spin doctors, pollsters, strategists, and especially career political consultants – are totemic figures of modern political communication. Their existence at the top tables of political power is both symbol and proof of a transformed politics. They are the agents and evidence of what is sometimes described as "politics lost" or "colonized" by media and marketing logics (Street, 2005; Wring, 2004; Meyer, 2002; Wernick, 1991; Finlayson, 2003). They are commonly considered both an effect and cause of a depoliticized, nonideological, strategy-dominated politics (Kirchheimer, 1966; Panebianco, 1988; Franklin, 1994; Klein, 2006). They are cited as both effect and cause of the decline of long-standing parties, an all but ubiquitous trend among Western democracies (Manin, 1997; Sabato, 1981; Pharr and Putnam, 2000; Diamond and Gunther, 2001). Their methods and influence have spread beyond the electoral realm into all manner of interest groups, with the effect that issue publics are reduced to target audiences for strategic communication (Bennett and Manheim, 2001). Outside their own ranks there are few defenders of these professionals and their activities, and scarcely any who claim they could somehow improve politics by making it more vibrant, responsive, and accessible. At best, they are necessary functionaries in the complex and competitive world of modern political communication; at worst, they are catalysts of a reduction of politics to shallow and cynical power games.

Yet, curiously the professionals remain neglected figures in academic research, notwithstanding the eruption of interest in campaigns, political marketing, and political communication generally over the past fifteen years. There is widespread acknowledgment of the significance of their work, and in campaign studies especially names are named and roles described. However, there have been remarkably few studies of the professionals as a *class*, as a particular and new category of political actors. There is only a handful of studies even in the United States where the business of political consultancy is most advanced (Thurber and Nelson, 2000; Johnson, 2001; Luntz, 1988; Sabato, 1981; Johnson, 2012) and fewer still on international consultancy and the non-U.S. professionals (Plasser, 2002; Bowler and Farrell, 2000). There are even fewer attempts to categorize the specific knowledge that these professionals contribute to politics and whether it is mainly outside-in from the commercial world of marketing, media, and advertising, or homegrown from within the existing structures of party and issue campaigning (Thurber, Nelson, and Dulio, 2000; Plasser, 2002; O'Cass, 1996; Scammell, 1997; Johnson, 2012). The paucity of academic research contrasts with the proliferation of accounts from the professionals themselves (e.g., Stephanopoulos, 1999; Matalin and Carville, 1994; Morris, 1998, 2000; Gould, 1999; Gergen, 2000; Trippi, 2004; Napolitan, 2003; Blumenthal, 2004; Faucheux, 2003; Campbell, 2007; Plouffe, 2009; Greenberg, 2009; Price, 2010; Séguéla, 2011), who in increasing numbers are ever more willing to talk of their activities in campaigns and the corridors of power.

It *matters* what professionals think they are doing. This is not because they are the most objective and accurate definers of their own contribution, nor do their intentions circumscribe the list of potential consequences. It matters because it makes clearer how the conduct of politics is changing, if indeed it is, and in which direction. It helps us understand the driving forces of modern political communication; who is in command here, the parties, the leaders, the professionals, the media? It clarifies how and to what extent political campaigns and communication are converging across the democratic globe. Above all, it sheds light on the grander theories of politics lost, transformed, or colonized by media and/or commerce.

THE PROFESSIONALS: WHO ARE THEY?

First, how do we define the "professional" political marketer? This is fairly straightforward in the United States. It means typically the independent consultant whose specialist and/or general skills in communication and campaigns are available for hire to parties, candidates, and increasingly other organizations. The emergence of independent consultancy as a flourishing business is the commonest indicator of what has come to be known as the "professionalized paradigm" of political communication (Blumler, Kavanagh, and Nossiter, 1996). A defining characteristic of the professionalized paradigm is the shift in power from the old political elite of party managers and activists to the new elite of campaign experts. To paraphrase Weber (1946), it is the idea of "politics as a vocation" and involves a shift from those who live *for* politics to those who make their living *from* politics. U.S. political consultancy perfectly fits this bill: consultants increasingly have replaced the party bosses and staffers as campaign managers and strategists; and where once services such as advertising and polling were commissioned from agencies primarily engaged in commercial work, now political consultation thrives as a business independent from other forms of income production.

The origins of modern political consultancy trace to California and the emergence of firms such as Baus & Baus and Whitaker-Baxter in the 1930s (see Mayhew, 1997: 209–13). From slow beginnings, the business began to take its present shape in the 1970s, propelled by the dual impact of the decline of mass-member parties and the triumph of television as the dominant mass medium. The American Association of Political Consultants (AAPC) was founded in 1969, and only a few of people attended its inaugural meeting at the Lincoln Center, New York. It now has an active membership of more than eleven hundred and estimates that more than one billion dollars is spent annually on campaign communication. The political consultancy business has come of age and offers an impressive and ever-expanding range of specialized services from general campaign management to polling, media message development, advertising, speech writing, opposition research, voter profiling, direct mail, grassroots organization, campaign software, website creation, social media management, event planning, and fund-raising.

Consultancy boomed in the 1980s and 1990s fueled by the "superheated fund-raising activities of the national Democratic and Republican parties and the explosion of soft money and issues advocacy" (Johnson, 2000: 49). Despite repeated attempts at campaign finance reform, spending records continue to tumble. Polsby and Wildavsky (1996: 67) calculated that total campaign costs for all candidates at all levels of U.S. government rose from $425 million in 1972 to $3.2 billion in 1992. The upward trend accelerated into the new millennium. Spending on the 2004 presidential and congressional races alone reached $3.9 billion, according to the Center for Responsive Politics, a 30 percent increase from 2000. The Center for Public Integrity tracked campaign expenditure in 471 federal races in 2004 and found that $1.85 billion was spent on consultants. The cost of success, according to the center's study, was $7 million on average for a Senate seat.[1]

Campaign budgets spiraled again in 2008. "If 2004 was the gold-plated presidential cycle, 2008 is platinum," according to a report in the consultants' trade journal *Campaigns & Elections* (Duran, 2007). The journal reported a "presidential surge strategy" from almost all the major candidates for nomination, who by early to mid-2007 had already assembled fully fledged campaign

---

[1] The study, sponsored by the Joan Shorenstein Center on the Press, Politics and Public Policy, examined spending on 471 federal races during 2003–4, including the records of more than 900 candidates, major party national committees, and 90,527 organizations. The report is available at http://www.public-i.org/consultants/.

staffs, built voter and donor databases, and put in place elaborate grassroots organizations ready for combat for the following year's caucuses and primaries. The "surge" effectively started the nomination race about "half a year earlier than in previous election cycles." The lengthening of campaigns ensured abundant opportunities for consultants, despite predictions that the Internet would make money less relevant. Bill Clinton's former consultant Dick Morris (2007) was among those who argued that the Internet had changed the rules of the game. "Campaign media is shifting away from costly television advertising to the free or at least very-low-cost Internet," he argued. "YouTube, candidate websites and blogs offer an alternative media that costs little or nothing but has a huge impact." Certainly, the power of the Internet, YouTube, and social networking sites emerged as one of the major themes of the 2008 cycle, especially in the rise of Barack Obama, but not at the expense of consultants' pocketbooks. Moreover, the Internet, far from decreasing spending, turned out to be a potent tool for raising vast sums from small donations. As the 2012 primaries got under way, the Center for Responsive Politics was predicting yet another record year with spending on all national races set to top $6 billion.

The profusion of money in elections has encouraged the work of consultants to spread downward and outward. In the 1960s it was concentrated in presidential, Senate, and gubernatorial races. Now the hiring of consultants is routine in congressional contests and has filtered through to races at virtually all levels: state legislators, mayors, city councilors, and even school boards. Increasingly, as the business has become more competitive, consultant firms have broadened their scope to ballot initiatives, and to issues management for corporate and trade association clients (Johnson, 2000). It has been estimated that there are some three thousand political consultancy firms now operating (Johnson, 2002), with at least seven thousand people earning their livings in the business (Scammell, 1997). Most controversially it has become an international business. It is not yet huge but is lucrative and increasing, sometimes supported by federally funded overseas "democracy assistance" programs (Sussman,

2005), especially in the younger democracies of Latin America, Eastern Europe, and the Far East (Plasser, 2002; Bowler and Farrell, 2000). American consultants make hundreds of millions of dollars overseas, according to a report in *Campaigns & Elections* (Miller, 2011): "In Latin America, candidates often size each other up with the phrase, 'show me your gringo.'" The Arab Spring of 2011 opened up a new "developing market" for consultants in Tunisia, Libya, and Egypt, facilitated in part by money channeled by the State Department's USAID program.

So who *are* these consultants? The most comprehensive survey thus far was conducted by Thurber et al. (2000), and it questioned 505 U.S. political consultants. It discovered that almost all respondents were white (98 percent), male (82 percent), highly educated (only 6 percent did not have a college degree), normally well paid, and relatively young (78 percent younger than 50). Despite the high-profile contribution of women in presidential campaigns (e.g., Susan Estrich for Dukakis in 1988, Donna Brazile for Al Gore in 2000, Mary Beth Cahill for John Kerry in 2004, Mandy Grunwald for Bill and then Hillary Clinton), U.S. political consulting is primarily an educated white man's world. Male dominance is particularly marked in the elite races (Panagopoulos, Dulio, and Brewer, 2011). Brewer's (2001: 8) study of women consultants found that "women make up a smaller percentage of the population in firms that are winning big and landing the best clients: 13 percent compared to being 18 percent of the total industry." As Thurber et al. point out, the demographic characteristics of consultants closely match those of the people for whom they work. Demographically at least the professionals seem to bring nothing new to the party: the new elite looks like the old.

The sense of continuity, contrasted to the radical rupture as implied in the professional paradigm concept, is compounded by the enduring strength of party attachments. According to Thurber et al.'s survey, 69 percent of professionals say they work only for the Democratic or the Republican Party. The idea of the free-booting political gun for hire is not a media myth. A minority of consultants works for both Republican and Democratic candidates, most famously Bill Clinton's erstwhile adviser Dick Morris. However, the vast majority stays party-loyal. Consultants usually begin their careers as party staffers and stay ideologically aligned. The irony, given that consultants are commonly considered as contributors to the decline of party organizations, is that party organizations remain the prime source of recruits to the business, as yet far more important than the media industries or vocational courses in universities (Thurber et al., 2000: 13). The parties provide the future professionals with their first career steps; they train them and then rehire them at greater cost when they become career consultants. "As a consultant, I do much of what I did as a party staffer, only for more money," as Martin Hamburger (2000: 62) puts it.

THE PROFESSIONAL POLITICAL MARKETERS OUTSIDE THE UNITED STATES

As yet we have no equivalent portrait of the professionals outside the United States. This is partly for the good reason there is no equivalent elsewhere of the U.S. consultancy industry. There are a number of celebrated consultants and profitable agencies especially in Europe, Latin America, and Australia (see Plasser, 2002: 24–37), many of whom ply their trade internationally as well as domestically. Among the most successful was the late Lord (Philip) Gould, long-time consultant for the British Labour Party, who set up a partnership with former Bill Clinton and Nelson Mandela advisers Stanley Greenberg and James Carville, and who worked for Gerhard Schröder in Germany and in Greek, Dutch, Austrian, Scandinavian, and Palestinian elections. Lord Tim Bell, formerly advertiser for Margaret Thatcher, has worked for, among others, the Ukrainian president Viktor Yushchenko, Russian president Boris Yeltsin, and the sultan of Brunei. There are a number of celebrated European consultants such as Jacques Séguéla of Havas, former adviser to Francois Mitterand and latterly associated with Nicolas Sarkozy; Stephane Fouks, adviser to the French Socialists and head of the Paris-based Euro-RSCG group, which works in France, Spain, Portugal, and Africa;

Michel Bongrand, a founding father of political marketing in France, who also worked with African heads of state; German consultants such as Volker Riegger and Peter Radunksi and the Dutch consultant Jacques Monasch, who are noted for work in Eastern Europe as well as their own countries. Israeli consultant Ron Werber has worked extensively in Eastern Europe and won acclaim for his role in the Hungarian Socialists victory of 2002. There are signs of a fledgling mini-industry of consulting in Latin America and especially Australia, whose most famous practitioner, Lynton Crosby, masterminded four successive victories for Australian Prime Minister John Howard and was hired to manage the British Conservative Party's 2005 general election campaign. The UK Conservatives hired Crosby again, in 2008, to run Boris Johnson's winning campaign for London mayor.

However, this is relatively small beer compared to the United States. To give some perspective, the European Association of Political Consultants listed about seventy members in February 2012; the Latin American sister organization, ALACOP, had about eighty. The International Association of Political Consultants, founded in 1968 by Joe Napolitan and Michel Bongrand, now claims more than one hundred members, although about half of these are American. These memberships added together total only about one-quarter of AAPC's number. It is clear that consultancy is a growing business around the world. However, as yet, there is simply nowhere else that possesses the United States' particularly tempting mix of incentives: an abundant money supply, a relatively deregulated electoral environment, cutting-edge technology, weak party organizations, and an extraordinarily high number of annual elections for public office. In Western Europe, by contrast, there are normally restrictions on television access and often on paid advertising, greater state intervention in financing of parties and campaigns, and in some cases (e.g., France, Ireland, and the UK) limits on campaign expenditure. There are far fewer elections for public office. As Johnson (2002: 8) points out, "there are 513,000 elected public offices in America; no [other] country comes close." Of these, he estimates about 50,000 enlist the services of political consultants.

By comparison to the United States, Europe is characterized by relatively strong party systems, notwithstanding the long-term membership decline. Western European campaigns continue to be *party-* rather than *candidate*-centered, and party staffs, rather than consultants, are the campaign managers.

Harrop (2001: 54) doubts whether campaign "professionals" exist at all in the UK, in the U.S. sense of the term: external contractors who earn their living from selling campaign services. He says that "the common perception is that the influence of the campaign professional is like the AIDS virus: new, dangerous and spreading everywhere. However, that stereotype is false and worse, it obscures understanding." This is a step too far. True, professional consultants are few in number in the UK, but those few have been highly influential. Philip Gould is the best example; working for the Labour Party since 1985, he was a key architect of Tony Blair's New Labour and remained in the inner circle of advisers throughout Blair's premiership. "There has been no figure quite like him in British politics," according to Blair's biographer, Anthony Seldon (2004: 136). "He is more than just a pollster who provides research: he is a tireless proselytizer for what that research means. He inspired and encouraged Labour's change from a doctrine/tradition driven party to a values/market-driven one. A political advertising man has taken the place of generations of socialist philosophers."

The advertising agency Saatchi & Saatchi pioneered marketing methods for Margaret Thatcher's Conservatives and transformed campaigning in Britain. They changed the role of professional advertisers from mere technicians applying communications polish to predefined programs to strategists intimately involved in the development of campaign themes and messages. The agency spawned political consultancy careers: Lord (Tim) Bell, who became an international consultant, Lord (Maurice) Saatchi, whose enduring influence was recognized in his appointment as cochairman of the Conservative Party in the run-up to the 2005 election, and Steve Hilton, who was widely perceived to be the most influential adviser to Conservative Party leader David Cameron.

In addition, there is no doubting the influence of overseas consultants in the UK. The two major parties have hired foreign professionals for all the general elections since the early 1990s: Ronald Reagan's pollster Richard Wirthlin worked with the Conservatives in the beginning of the decade; Democrat consultants Greenberg, Bob Shrum, Mark Penn, and Joe Trippi have all advised Labour at various times. Shrum's relationship with the Labour Party continued into Gordon Brown's premiership. Most strikingly in 2005 the Conservatives enlisted Australian Lynton Crosby to run their campaign – the first time in Britain that overall campaign management has been outsourced to overseas professionals. There are signs that UK campaigning is professionalizing along U.S. lines.

However, Harrop is correct to emphasize the leading role of parties, staffs, and politicians in UK campaigns. In the main, hired advice has tended to come from general commercial polling and advertising agencies rather than dedicated political consultancies. This pattern is familiar in much of Europe. There are abundant signs of professionalization both of campaigning and government communication, despite significant individual country variations (see, e.g., Swanson and Mancini, 1996; Negrine et al., 2007; Maarek, 2003; Holtz-Bacha, 2002; Mellone and Gregorio, 2004; Yannas, 2005). Papathanassopoulos et al. (2007: 12–13) summarize the European transformation as one "in which 'a culture of marketing' has established itself at the centre of a party organization." Overall, the finding of European convergence on professionalized, centralized, personalized campaigning (Negrine et al., 2007) confirms trends first identified in the pioneering works of comparative political communication (Butler and Ranney, 1992; Swanson and Mancini, 1996). However, Western Europe and Northern Europe have not yet seen the power shift so evident in the United States from parties to hired professional campaigners. As Holtz-Bacha says of Germany (2002: 35), "Parties have hired outside expertise for specific campaign tasks since the 1950s, [but] they have had to turn to all-round agencies because there are no institutes on the market specialized in the selling of politics." In fact, Bowler and

Farrell (1992: 225) concluded that, if anything, the professionalization of campaigning has strengthened central party machinery in most European countries; that is, decision-making power has become concentrated at the head of the parties, at the expense of local organizational autonomy.

One might expect that the former Soviet Union and communist bloc countries would display a different pattern; a marked rush to embrace modern communication practices might inevitably lead to greater reliance on "outside" hired experts as these countries took their first steps in competitive democratic elections. Indeed, that does seem to be the case, at least at first. As already indicated, the collapse of Soviet communism opened up potentially lucrative new markets for professional consultants, aided in part by grants from the United States and other Western countries (Sussman, 2005). Moreover, Western European parties were often eager to volunteer advice for their ideological sisters among the fledgling parties to the east. It is notoriously difficult to accurately assess just how influential these foreign experts were, not least because it suited all parties to downplay their role. A perception of foreign meddling in domestic affairs does not sit well with electorates (Negrine et al., 2007). However, it seems reasonable to speculate that this outside influence has lessened over time. The professionalization process has continued apace, but expertise is increasingly homegrown, in-house, or linked to commercial polling and advertising agencies employed on ad hoc bases.

Data from Plasser's (2002) survey of 592 campaigners in forty-three countries reinforce the continuing hold of parties, notwithstanding a growing influence of U.S. consultants. Plasser reasonably interprets his data as showing a trend toward American-style professionalization, yet they also demonstrate that party-focused, rather than party-distant, campaigning is the more common everywhere but the United States. Moreover, 67 percent of the survey respondents said that national party organizations had become either more or no less important to campaigns, compared to 33 percent (overwhelmingly the external consultants) who considered them less important.

Overall, then, we can summarize this discussion by conclud-
ing that the single most striking quality of political marketers
and their work is partisanship. This is certainly the case outside
the United States, but even in the United States political consultancy is predominantly a partisan business. The strength and
closeness of party attachments significantly structures the way
that campaigners perceive their own roles. Almost as notable is
the uniformity of demographics. Neither Plasser's nor Bowler
and Farrell's (2000) surveys of international consultants provide
demographic profiles. However, examination of the membership
of the European Association of Political Consultants (EAPC)
reaffirms the findings for the United States: consultancy is overwhelmingly a white, male business. Twelve of the EAPC's sev-
enty-nine listed members are women (15 percent), concentrated
mostly in Russia, Eastern Europe, and Scandinavia, and there are
scarcely any nonwhites. By partisanship and demographics, the
new politics is no different from the old.

Thus far the conclusion might be "politics as usual": the
"political marketers" are recruited from the usual channels, for
the usual motivations, and demographically speaking they are
much the same people. Yet, if it is politics as usual, the professionals themselves see a changed and changing politics and that
their roles are both a response to transformed circumstances – an
attempt to manage change – and an impetus to change. Once
professionalization starts, it cannot be reversed. Even if it is politics as usual, it is not politics as *before*. The professionalization
process itself ratchets up the levels of specialist expertise necessary to compete for elected office, and more broadly for influence over public policy and public opinion. Politics increasingly
becomes an arena in which, in Johnson's telling phrase (2001),
"there is no place for amateurs."

WHAT DO THEY THINK THAT THEY ARE DOING?

How do the political marketers perceive their roles in relation
to the political elites whom they serve? This simple question is
not easy to answer in broad, generic terms. This is partly because

the campaigners themselves are more comfortable talking specifics: particular races and key tasks such as strategy development, research, communications, and so on (Scammell, 1997). It is also because professional politics is a "people" business; roles fluctuate between and within races and administrations, and depend crucially on the strength of personal relationships. One politician's technical adviser may turn into another's "consiglière" of Dick Morris's depiction in *The New Prince* (2000), while equally even for the same client erstwhile insiders find themselves out of the loop. Even George Washington University, which provides the world's leading academic center for the training of consultants, struggles to find a generic definition. The university's Graduate School of Political Management introduces its mission in terms of what it is *not*. It is *not* political science and the detached study of political behavior. It is *not* the study of public policy and public administration. However, the school's title, "political management," is the most common self-description of the U.S. professionals' field of work, which is loosely described as "practical" or applied politics.

"Political management" is preferred to the more common academic descriptors, such as "political marketing" or "strategic communication," which are noticeable by their absence in the U.S. trade literature (Faucheux, 2003). For the professionals both "marketing" and "strategic communication" overemphasize the "packaging" aspects of job, and underplay its more fundamental and distinctively political nature. Philip Gould, for example, was suspicious of the characterization of New Labour as a manifestation of political marketing. For most academics in the field New Labour offered a nearly perfect example of political marketing as the party rebranded itself in line with Gould's own research (Wring, 2004; Scammell, 1999; Lees-Marshment, 2001). However, for Gould the term "marketing" had been corrupted in popular use, equated pejoratively with cosmetics, spin, and surface appearance. Instead, Gould preferred "campaigning politics" to describe his vocation and said his main role was one of "connection." It is about connecting people and politicians, understanding voters' priorities and attitudes toward politics, to enable politicians to "connect through *their* [the voters'] issues, not our concerns."[2]

The idea of "management" conveys the distinctiveness about the modern professionals' activities. This is not because the underlying functions of political management are particularly new: Machiavelli's *Prince* bequeathed to us "practical politics" as pragmatic power game, while effective campaign management has been necessary for as long as politicians have needed to influence mass opinion. However, what stands out now is the conscious enlisting of ordinary commercial management conceptual frameworks to political goals. It is no exaggeration to say that the drive to apply and develop management skills has underpinned the entire professionalization process. The editorial of the inaugural issue of the consultants' trade journal, *Campaigns & Elections*, made the point plainly (Reed, 1980: 1):

Only one in six political candidates wins. Only one in six businesses succeeds. What makes the difference between winning and losing … ? In political campaigns and in business, it is management that makes the difference. Management of resources: money, media and people.

Early issues of the magazine included articles from business school theorists, most notably Philip Kotler (1981), international doyen of what is called the management school of marketing. Kotler has been a consistent advocate of the conscious application of marketing approaches and techniques in politics. "Marketing orientation means that candidates recognize the nature of the exchange process when they ask voters for their votes," he counsels (Kotler and Kotler, 1999: 3). "And candidates have to view their campaigns from the point of view of the outcomes for voters, constituencies, and financial donors, the consumers in political campaigns." Marketing cannot guarantee success, "but it will at least ensure that the campaign's planning is systematic, efficient and voter oriented."

Campaigners' language and actions leave no doubt as to the importance in politics of marketing approaches and techniques.

[2] Philip Gould, "The Empty Stadium: Winning Elections in a World Turned Upside Down" (lecture, London School of Economics & Political Science, December 5, 2003).

The techniques especially – what business academics call "marketing instruments" – are obvious: the increasing use of consumer-based research methodologies, the quest for ever more precise market segmentation, micro-targeting, and now nano-targeting of key voters, the emphasis on strategic positioning, the increasing tendency to both research and consider parties and candidates as competing brands. The evidence for this is so abundant, certainly in the United States and the UK, that it is reasonable to talk of a paradigm shift in campaigns: from the "media logic" of national campaigns designed for mass television audiences to the "marketing logic" of micro-targeting, narrowcast advertising, direct mail, telemarketing, e-mail, and text messaging (Plasser, 2002). Among the political marketing school of academics the change is commonly characterized as a shift from the "sales-oriented" party to the "market-oriented" party (Scammell, 1999; Lees-Marshment, 2001; Wring, 2004), as described in the introduction. Moreover, the few major studies on the subject confirm the significance of business and marketing knowledge for campaigners around the world (Scammell, 1997; Plasser, 2002). According to the Global Political Consultancy Survey (Table 2.1), campaigners say that these disciplines are second only to political and communication sciences as must-have knowledge. Their importance is particularly marked in the newer democracies of Latin America, Eastern Europe, the former Soviet Union countries, and South Africa. Management and marketing know-how supplies the fast track to modern campaigning.

Political management, much as business management, is goal directed: teaching and learning draw much from case studies, while the theory and models from the mother academic disciplines are useful to the extent that they may assist real-world decision making. The core curricula from leading business and political management schools have much in common:[3] strategy

---

[3] The American Association of Political Consultants lists ten university graduate programs in the United States that teach applied politics and campaign management, including the universities of George Washington, Yale, Suffolk, Florida, and New York.

TABLE 2.1. *Essential Sources of Knowledge for Professional Campaigners (in percentages)*

Q: What is absolutely necessary in order to be a professional campaign manager?

	United States	Latin America	Western Europe	Eastern and Central Europe	CIS	Oceania	South Africa	India	East Asia
Study political or communication science	64	84	50	92	94	66	92	50	98
Study business and marketing	53	70	33	59	67	40	79	42	NA
U.S. trade literature	52	63	56	47	56	50	50	23	64
U.S. elections	NA	50	66	52	35	53	48	27	58
Western European elections	18	31	NA	85	53	NA	57	15	43
Personal contacts with U.S. consultants	NA	35	40	42	33	18	27	0	29
Personal contacts with European consultants	14	NA	NA	NA	NA	NA	NA	NA	NA
Contacts with universities	11	58	32	50	60	11	59	28	50

Source: Global Political Consultancy Survey 1998–2000 (Plasser, 2002: 43).

development, research, data collection methods and analysis, project organization, leadership skills, fund-raising and budget control, communication and promotion, relevant law and regulation, and principles of ethical practice. Training centers on the definition and achievement of objectives; it is propelled by the idea of success. Commonly success is associated with the winning of elections, but especially as professional consultancy expands to issue management and lobbying, it could be defined more broadly as the *effective management of influence* on political decisions.

This leads to the question of precisely how professionals provide effective management; in short, what it is that they think they are selling. Three keywords recur in their self-descriptions: organization, strategy, and research. All three are linked and are deemed crucial to campaign success. Typically the needs of organization have meant strong central control and a clear chain of command. The professionals often describe campaign management in military terms: "campaigns should be run by dictatorships, not committees" (Sweitzer, 2003: 99). Veteran consultant Joe Napolitan (2003: 47) puts it wryly: "Running a campaign is not a democratic process. It is more like a military operation – at least if it is run right." Military metaphors such as "war rooms," "war books," and "attack" and "defense" recur throughout campaigners' accounts of their work (e.g., Matalin and Carville, 1994; Gould, 1998). However, this strictly hierarchical top-down organizational model has come under challenge in recent years. It is associated with the "wholesale" politics of the mass audience television era, when message discipline and the efforts to influence the news agenda were seen as the prime campaign tasks. Amid concerns of a crisis of citizen engagement, falling voter turnouts, and the fragmentation of TV audiences across ever-multiplying media outlets, campaigners reviewed the effectiveness of the top-down model and looked for new ways to energize supporters.

The 2001 UK general election returned a second successive Labour government but also recorded the lowest turnout since 1918; future campaigns "would have to change drastically to promote voters' interest" (Butler and Kavanagh, 2002: 242).

Philip Gould sought lessons from the commercial sector's efforts to "empower" consumers through inter alia permission marketing, as opposed to interruption marketing (where customers indicate a willingness to be contacted as opposed to the uninvited interruption advertising of television or pop-up Internet ads) and coproduction possibilities evidenced in "listening" initiatives and attempts to include supporters in the selection of promotional material. In November 2003 Tony Blair launched the "Big Conversation," proclaiming it the largest ever consultation with voters. Similar high-profile "listening" exercises have been incorporated in campaigns for among others French presidential candidate Ségolène Royal (2007) and Hillary Clinton's "Listening Tours" as prospective New York senator and again in 2007 as an early marker of her intention to run for presidential nomination.

However, Howard Dean's fabled "open source" campaign in 2003–4 presented the most radical challenge to the top-down model. It demonstrated the "democratization of creativity," capitalizing on "people's increasing savviness when it comes to media, marketing and communication," according to campaigner-turned-business marketer Graeme Trayner (2006). Dean's campaign manager Joe Trippi (2004: xix) describes the campaign in apocalyptic terms, providing lessons that can be "applied to every election, every product, every issue in America." Trippi's story is one of at first shock, then recognition of the extent of spontaneous activism coordinated via Internet social networking sites in support of Dean. His campaign encouraged and harnessed this "glorious explosion of civic re-engagement" to help propel Dean from rank outsider to front-runner, albeit briefly, for the Democratic presidential nomination. Viral communication on the Internet created a movement (Trippi, 2004: 103): "Howard Dean didn't create this movement. In many ways, the movement created the Dean for America campaign." Trippi later claimed that the "bottom-up" Dean campaign was the forerunner of Barack Obama's quest for nomination four years later. He told *New York Magazine* (Heilemann, 2008) "we were the Wright brothers proving that you could design something … that you could actually fly in politics coming from the bottom up and using new ways to communicate. Four years later ... the Obama campaign is landing a man on the moon."

While top-down is still the norm, campaigners are adopting new metaphors for organizational structure. Philip Gould (2006: 58), for example, used the idea of a central communications "brain"; "a nerve centre that has the speed, the flexibility, the responsiveness, the strategic capacity, the operational capability to deal with the communications flow in all its complexity and all its time spans." Gould described running an election campaign as an attempt to "create order out of chaos": politics is an ever-changing, ever-unpredictable flow and "political activity is the attempt to interpret and marshal these forces in order to reach intended outcomes."[4] The "political flow" includes the large and small, short- and long-term forces: the news cycle and media agendas, social and economic trends, moods and attitudes of public opinion, self-interest of the various campaign actors, relationships and alliances within campaigns, policy objectives, long-term values and vision, competitive responses of opponents, and the risks and opportunities created by unexpected events. The "political flow" is why Napolitan can counsel that "every campaign is different; every campaign is the same" (2003: 37). Every campaign has the same basic ingredients: research, strategy, message, advertising, organization, and fund-raising. Equally every campaign is unique and strategy must be freshly prepared for each occasion.

Time and again, consultants say strategy is the key to success (Scammell, 1997: 13): for Napolitan it is "the single most important factor" and "the most important lesson I've learned in 30 years" (2003: 26); the right strategy can thrive even if campaign communication is mediocre, "but even a brilliant campaign is likely to fail if the strategy is wrong." Dick Morris agrees (1999: 46): "it is strategy, not spin, that wins elections." Easy to say, political strategy is more difficult to define with any precision. Professionals often describe it as a statement of how and why

---

[4] Gould, "Empty Stadium."

they will win, who will vote for them, and why, or as Gould puts it, "Campaign strategy is the means by which a political party or candidate attempts to win power at the expense of others." The process of strategy formulation is as important as the outcome; it focuses energies, promotes clarity, and demands realism. It helps create organization out of chaos. Typically, strategic planning is built through the preparation of campaign war books, incorporating research of the political market and opposition, the brutally frank assessment of competitive strengths and weaknesses, the dissection of the ultimate goal (often but by no means always election victory) into its component parts of smaller achievable targets, and the matching of politicians' objectives and programs with the concerns and aspirations of the electorate. War books may go through several drafts, and expand into hefty tomes, before ultimately boiling down to a strategy statement that may be written on one page. If it cannot be condensed and expressed with such simple clarity, it is probably not a strategy.

Strategy crucially depends upon the quality and interpretation of underlying research. If one had to pick one single factor that distinguishes modern campaigning from its predecessors it would be the reliance on market research as the sine qua non of professionalism. The use of quantitative aggregate polls has a long history in campaigning, but increasingly over the past twenty years campaigners have incorporated the lessons of commercial multimethod surveys and qualitative research. While campaigners may object that commercial marketing is inadequate for the intensely scrutinized, highly adversarial, ever-changing demands of the political flow, they have become ever more in debt to its research techniques. Johnson's (2001: 96) examination of U.S. consultants finds that survey research is the one skill of political management that relies on "well-developed social science methodology."

However, typically the social science comes filtered through the applied "science" of shopping. There is, and arguably always has been, a two-way flow between political and commercial marketing expertise, certainly since the advent of mass propaganda in the early decades of the twentieth century (Scammell,

1995: 27–28). However, there is no doubt that the direction of the flow in modern political management is heavily from commerce to politics. This is most clear in two ways: the use of consumer-based models for market segmentation and voter identification, and the centrality of qualitative methods for strategy development and message testing. Consumer selling has a fifty-year-old history of research into the social, demographic, and psychographic correlates and determinants of shopping behavior (see Johnson-Cartee and Copeland, 2004: 75–108). The quest has been less to create consumer wants out of nothing, more to find ever more precise ways to target products and appeals to the most receptive audience segments.

Campaigners have drawn much from consumer research models. Richard Wirthlin, Ronald Reagan's pollster, pioneered a version of the commercially popular values and lifestyles (VALs) approach, which links demographics to self-perceptions, aspirations, enduring values, and lifestyle choices. Expanding on VALs, geo-demographic profiling incorporates census data to link VALs with neighborhoods, pinpointed by postal codes. PRIZM (Potential Rating Index for Zip Markets), developed for the Claritas Corporation, emerged as the major exemplar of this approach, and its underlying principles have provided rich pickings for politics. U.S. political consultancy Crounse and Malchow created a political counterpart, CHAID (Chi-Square Automatic Interaction Detection), to identify target voters by postal code (Malchow, 2003). By incorporating its own baseline poll with consumer and census databases, it claimed to predict with a high degree of confidence (95 percent) the likely voting preferences of any group or subgroup within an electoral population.

This type of statistical analysis reached full bloom in the U.S. presidential election of 2004. The Republicans developed the "Voter Vault," a colossal computerized warehouse of demographic and voting preference information on an estimated 168 million people, which it mined for detailed research for strategy preparation and micro-targeting during the campaign itself (Tynan, 2004). The Democrats countered with their own version, DataMart. To the delight of the UK Conservatives, Karl Rove donated the Voter Vault software free of charge prior to the 2005 general election. The Conservatives added UK canvass returns and consumer and census data and built a program that party cochairman Liam Fox claimed revealed "new parts of society that the party has not targeted before, but who could be persuaded to vote Tory" (cited in Thomson, 2005). Labour's response, an equivalent computer program called Labour Contact, led to the most intensively targeted general election yet seen in Britain. In the UK, as in the United States, the national-television-centered campaign is gradually being superseded.

The impact of the "science" of shopping is more marked still in the use of qualitative research. Market research is built into every aspect of commercial product design, brand development, promotional strategy, and customer satisfaction. It tests which words, tone of voice, colors, and shapes are most appealing; it seeks ways to build and sustain emotional connection between buyers and brands. The increasing use of similar techniques has become the hallmark of professional politics. It has moved way beyond campaigns into the permanent apparatus of governance, with Bill Clinton the exemplar par excellence of a trend that started long before him. David Gergen (2000: 331), White House adviser to Nixon, Ford, Reagan, and Clinton, notes the escalation: "All modern presidents have polled heavily – Haldeman [for Nixon] put three different pollsters in the field at a time and secretly paid for a fourth to keep an eye on the others – but no one before Clinton has taken a poll to determine whether he should tell the truth publicly (the Lewinsky case) or to use American ground troops (Kosovo)." Clinton, Gergen reports, spent nearly ten times as much on polling in his first year in office as his predecessor spent in two years. Focus group and public opinion testing guided "every public pronouncement" in the Clinton White House, famously even a decision about where to take a family holiday. Clinton "polls as often as he breathes," according to Dick Morris (cited in Johnson, 2001: 89).

The sheer amount of survey data is impressive in top-order races and increasingly in government. However, just as important and less remarked is the *type* of research. Politics has lifted directly from advertising the trend to research, position, and promote parties and candidates exactly as consumer brands. Political advertising has generated its own specific and considerable academic research literature; and paid advertising has come to be regarded as a characteristic of modern or "Americanized" campaigns. However, the focus on advertising content overlooks the more fundamental contribution of advertising, which is less its messages, more the process by which they are arrived at. Mass advertising, Gould (2006) claimed, is not central to most campaigns outside the United States anyway, since in many countries there are restrictions on campaign expenditure, and sometimes, as in the UK, bans on paid television advertising. Even in the United States, he says, mass advertising is dwindling in importance as audiences fragment in a multimedia environment and ever more precise targeting is the driver of campaigns. We are living in a "post-advertising age," he says. Gould says that Karl Rove admitted "privately that what mattered to him in 2004 was forcing the message through free media and connecting directly with voters through word of mouth and personalized communication. Advertising was not decisive any more." However, the *process* of advertising creation is vital. Its point is to distill into the most clear and simple language possible the essential characteristics of competing parties and candidates, to find points of emotional connection with voters. In short, it treats politics as brands (see Chapters 3 and 4).

THE PROFESSIONALS: POLITICS AND NONPOLITICS

It is sometimes startling to hear professionals discuss their work. They dissect elections in the language of management: tasks to be achieved and problems solved. Policies and issues, if not quite beside the point, are considered according to their strategic and tactical usefulness. Leaders, candidates, and parties are discussed in terms of brand attributes and values, and urged to modify their too overtly political selves for ease of consumption for a nonpolitical public. Yet, at the same time these political managers are usually intensely political people. Often the first self-defining characteristic is that they perceive themselves as political activists. The very same people who advocate "nonpolitical," personalized, brand-based campaigning are usually strongly party-aligned, and sometimes deeply ideological. The survey evidence of party attachment is supported more fiercely still by the professionals' own words. Political commitment is overt in Sidney Blumenthal's (2004) defense of Clinton's White House. Old-fashioned Democratic liberalism courses through the pages of George Stephanopoulos's (1999) sometimes tortured account of his years in the White House as senior adviser to Bill Clinton. An even more emphatic liberalism motivates another former Clinton adviser, James Carville, most explicitly in *We're Right, They're Wrong* (1996). A less strident but resolutely antiliberal Republicanism infuses Ari Fleischer's (2005) narration of his time as press secretary for President George W. Bush. There is no doubting the passionate conservative commitment of Richard Viguerie, the pioneer of political direct mail, in his book *America's Right Turn* (2004). Long-standing Democratic attachment is equally clear in David Plouffe's (2009) account of his much-praised grassroots campaign for Barack Obama. The list goes on.

Grand ideological designs to refashion the entire political landscape inspired the efforts of some of the most influential professionals. First, Lee Atwater and then his protégé Karl Rove, key advisers in turn for the two Bush presidents, strived to shift core bastions of Democratic activists and financial support into the Republican camp in a quest to refashion the political landscape. In the UK, Gould wrote about the "the Project": "a long-term radicalism, to ensure that progressive instincts become rooted in the institutions of the nation, just as conservative instincts were in the past ... New Labour may have won an election, but now it has to win a century" (Gould, 1998: 394). Peter Mandelson, formerly Labour's communication chief, describes the project in almost identical language as "enduring political realignment," which makes social democracy "the natural system of government" (2002: xlix). The motivation and work of these top professionals is not confined to communications advice and election campaigns. It is much more political than that.

Joe Trippi (2004: 15–17) describes his fellow professionals as "cynical idealists"; nothing they would not do for each other, nothing they would not do for a vote, driven by "irrational commitment" and sacrificing much for little reward:

Working day to day on a presidential campaign is unlike any other job on this planet. It's a thankless job, an outrageously difficult job, the most emotionally draining, physically taxing, stress-creating job you can imagine, and when it's done, it almost always ends in total, abject failure.

Trippi's portrait of the physical and emotional punishment of top-flight campaigning echoes time and again in the various insider accounts. His point, and it is often the first one that professionals make when speaking to outsiders, is that few would undertake such an ordeal and fewer still could take the pace unless driven by an idealism of sorts. Trippi's beguiling *West Wing*–style picture of self-sacrifice, caustic humor, and relentless high-wire juggling is hugely sympathetic and, much like the *West Wing*, is too good to be true. Professional campaigning has moved a long way since veteran consultant Stanford L. Weiner (cited in Scammell, 1997) proclaimed that he and most of his colleagues were in it for love. It is now a profitable business, and more than two-thirds of U.S. consultants reported an average annual family income of more than $200,000 in 1996–97 (Thurber et al., 2000: 12). Moreover, the prospect of book sales from insider accounts and/or lucrative spin-off work for media and corporate clients doubtless cushions the shock of ultimate failure for high-profile "celebrity" consultants, not least Stephanopoulos, Dick Morris, and Trippi himself. Money has clearly been a powerful motivation for the growth of the political consultancy business. It has provided incentives that have diluted partisan ties and spawned a significant minority of consultants who pick winners over parties. However, the evidence from surveys, practitioner accounts, personal observation, and interviews over many years is persuasive and consistent. As yet anyway, the financial rewards are simply not great enough, nor are career paths sufficiently secure, to lure a new cohort of bright young people away from the rival temptations of media, advertising, and public relations. The same stock of incentives that have been associated with political activism generally also motivate consultancy: personal ambition, expressive attachment, ideological commitment, enjoyment of the political process, and the potential for political influence. Campaigning, consultant Martin Hamburger (2000: 64) suggests, "is the preferred venue for our personal political action"; the impact of money has been to convert activism into career choice.

THE POLITICAL MARKETERS: POLITICS LOST?

What is implied in the phrase "politics lost"? There are several linked strands contained within this claim, some of which emerged in the introductory discussion of marketing and democracy. However, it is useful to recap the arguments. The first involves the idea that politics, properly speaking, should be about competing conceptions of the public good; ideology in short. The claim is that marketing has moved the basis of competition from ideology to other less political, more trivial differentiators. In broad terms it draws on the "end of ideology" debates that emerged in the 1950s and 1960s in the aftermath of the postwar consensus about the welfare state (see, e.g., Marcuse, 1964). Specifically, in relation to the work of the professionals, it boils down to the concern that the instrumental logic of marketing will lead parties to compete in the center ground where most voters are located, and where there are few genuine differences of ideological principle. Parties (like oligopolistic companies) become forced to manufacture difference out of personality and style because there is no real difference of political principle (Panebianco, 1988; Hay, 2007; Finlayson, 2003). Thus, politics is lost.

A second key strand concerns the importance of parties. Modern democratic politics assumes robust and socially rooted parties that represent sectors of society, aggregate interests, and facilitate compromise across interests, offer citizens possibilities of permanent participation in political discussions, link politics to communities, and train and select future leaders. As Norris summarizes (2005: 3), "At the level of the nation-state, political parties are indispensable to the practical workings of government. Indeed, without parties, modern representative democracy is simply unworkable." The long-standing fear about political marketing is that it weakens party organizations (Sabato, 1981; Swanson and Mancini, 1996): it centralizes policy and campaign decisions, thus disempowering local organization and activists; it displaces party workers with marketing and professional consultants; and it refocuses brand images around leaders and candidates rather than parties. Attempts to connect citizens to parties are increasingly focused on emotional connection with leaders, and thus the basis for party support is rendered inherently transitory and depoliticized.

The third related claim concerns the role of citizens. On the one hand, marketed politics slices and dices the citizenry into electorally amenable segments and target voters are tempted with policies and appeals designed to suit them. In this way, marketing treats voters as narrowly self-interested consumers, rather than as citizens concerned with the common good. On the other hand, marketed politics is acted out on a mediated stage, offering competing images to citizens who are kept remote from the decision-making processes of parties. In this way, citizens are reduced to spectators (Entman, 1989); representative democracy has become "audience democracy" (Manin, 1997) in which the participation of citizens is largely restricted to response to the offers presented on the political stage. Thus citizens become consumers and spectators, and "conclusion may be that the professional political communicators contribute to the development of democracy without citizens" (Hamelink, 2007: 182).

What light can we now shed on these claims? Starting with the ideology point, it is certainly true that the economic approaches to democracy (including political marketing analysis) do predict gravitation toward the center ground, or median voter to put it in Downsian terms. To that extent, clear ideological differences are blurred. However, political marketing analysis (as suggested in Chapter 1) rejects the idea that marketing is a kind of nonpolitical alien invader brought in to substitute for the

absence of politics. On the contrary marketing logic is inscribed
in the structure of competition. Thus, at a basic level it disputes
the implication that "market" and "nonmarket" can be placed
as though they were necessarily in opposition to each other.
It is not a simple equation: more marketing equals less politics. The consequences of marketing use are more nuanced and
contingent, not least on the structure of competition. Thus one
would expect a wider spectrum of ideological differentiation in
electoral systems that incentivize vote share rather than winner take all. However, even in the essentially two-party majoritarian competition of the UK and the United States ideology
continues to matter. Left/right, liberal/conservative distinctions
still exist and occasionally become polarized (as in Thatcher's
Britain or now in the rise of the right and the Tea Party in
the U.S. Republicans). For the political marketers ideology and
partisanship are often hugely important spurs to action; that
is the overriding conclusion from our overview. Equally, however, political marketers tend to be results-oriented and thus
practical people. They are fascinating precisely because of the
combination of high politics and nonpolitics; grand political
designs meet the methods and language of nonpolitics. Thus,
when one looks at real-world examples one can find many
instances of marketers advising parties/candidates to shed policies that do not resonate in the political middle. At the same
time, and sometimes from the same people, political marketers
advance strategies that seek to shift the entire political landscape, pushing the center of gravity left or right. Rove for the
U.S. Republicans and Gould for the UK's New Labour are outstanding examples of this.

It is a commonplace of political studies that parties are in
trouble around the world, losing public trust and active memberships (see Chapter 6). It is also a fair point that the tendency of professionalization, to centralize program, candidate
selection, and campaign decisions, marginalizes ordinary party
members and hence decreases incentives for would-be activists
to join parties. Equally, political marketers can and do argue
that their work not only is essential for party survival but has

rekindled once-struggling organizations. To take one example, Philip Gould's immodest boast in the title of his 1998 book was that the modernizers had "saved" the Labour Party, by rescuing it from extreme ideologues and repositioning it as a popular center-left candidate for government. That kind of claim is familiar, perhaps especially with Labor parties in Australia and New Zealand. Certainly, the more extreme activists are seen as a liability in marketing terms; and a typical reaction of European parties has been to seek state protection and funding, to overcome the difficulties of maintaining healthily active mass memberships and to avoid the whiff of corruption associated with private and corporate donations. At the same time, parties across Europe, in particular the French Socialists, the German SPD, and the UK Labour and Conservative Parties, have made reforms to encourage participation and to invite broader involvement from nonmember supporters by, for example, holding primaries for candidate selection.

The third claim, democracy without citizens, is also intriguingly nuanced. On the one hand, a kind of democratic elitism is often a foundational belief of political professionals. The evidence for this comes mainly from interpretation of trade literature and interviews, while Herbst's (1998) categorization of political actors' "lay theories" also lends support. It is common, perhaps especially in interviews with U.S. consultants, for them to assume that broad swathes of the electorate are not interested or knowledgeable. To that extent, "democracy without citizens" is merely a fact of life, and not necessarily a problem unless voter turnout falls below more-or-less acceptable levels. At the same time, the efforts to "empower" voters, the listening initiatives, the increase in personal contacting, the elements of open source campaigning as pioneered by the Howard Dean and Obama campaigns are all suggestive of some determination to reconnect with voters and encourage enthusiastic participation. However, in general, political marketers focus on the practical and the short term; where winning is the immediate goal, the longer-term desirables, such as knowledgeable and active citizenries, do not disappear but are removed to distant horizons.

SUMMARY

Campaigns around the democratic globe are professionalizing, and the evidence of political marketing accumulates with every new study (see, e.g., Lees-Marshment et al., 2010). Professional campaign consultancy, as a full-time career, is on the increase around the world also. It is most obviously developed in the United States, but there is a fledgling industry in Latin America and a growing, if still relatively small, group of campaign consultancies in Europe, Israel, and Australia. A strongly recurring characteristic of the majority of these consultants is partisanship and ideological affinity with parties and candidates for whom they work. There are consultants who sell to the highest bidder or who attempt to hitch their star to likely winners regardless of party or ideology; but these are in the minority. In the relatively strong party systems of Western Europe, Australia, and New Zealand, parties continue to be in command of campaigns even as they show increased willingness to hire in professional expertise in market research and promotion. The consultants tend to reflect the demographic characteristics of the people they work for, and thus political marketing offers new skills but not a new demographic profile for political elites.

Political communication has and is being transformed, and in its professionalization it has ratcheted up the skills and expertise needed to run campaigns and squeezed the space for amateurs. The military "high command" model is still the predominate way of running campaigns, even as some campaigners look to more flexible and inclusive ways of incorporating citizen initiative. However, this chapter rejected the claim that political marketing means "politics lost." It rejected the idea that markets and marketing can be assumed to be inherently in opposition to proper democratic politics, however we may prefer to define it. This kind of binary opposition is of limited assistance when we try to evaluate real-world campaigns in terms of fidelity to democratic ideals. The next three chapters come to grips with this task of evaluation as we look at political branding and the various academic and practitioner perspectives on "good" campaigns.

Finally, the terms "political marketers," "professionals," and "campaigners" have been used interchangeably in this chapter. It was noted that some practitioners do not like the term "political marketing" as self-description, preferring "political management" or "strategist" or such. Yet, their tasks as described here *are* political marketing; they are engaged in an attempt to sell parties, candidates, and political ideas and use and adapt methods and approaches pioneered in commercial marketing. To that extent they are political marketers; and that means more than "packaging," involving the design of the political product and not just its promotion.

3

Political Brands

The Latest Stage of Political Marketing and the Case of Tony Blair

By the summer of 2007 the presidential race in the United States was already moving into high gear and the commercial brand consultancy Chernoff Newman seized the opportunity to showcase its talents (Image 3.1). Picture Hillary Clinton as a car and she would be a Volvo, according to the agency's market research: "solid, reliable and there to get the job done, not make you fall in love." Barack Obama was a "BMW Z4 convertible, sporty, flashy and fun"; Rudy Giuliani, a Toyota crossover vehicle; John McCain was the all-American Ford pickup, and Mitt Romney "a Dodge Viper – it looks like it's built for speed, but is too unfamiliar to the average driver to know for sure." It is entertaining stuff, and it is an intriguing new way for agencies to advertise their work.

These brand analogies are not real, in the sense that they were neither commissioned by the campaigns nor designed to help candidate strategy. However, they are real in that they are drawn from market research and promoted to lend credibility and an aura of importance to an agency's broader brand-building approaches. Their political interest is less that they tell us anything particularly new about public opinion, but the *way* they do it; in condensed and striking fashion with the implication that voters are entirely comfortable with and possibly more honest in their assessments, when asked to compare would-be world

IMAGE 3.1. If the candidates were cars ...
Source: Chernoff Newman/MarketSearch

leaders with product brands. These cartoons are more or less amusing, but they do not seem absurdly inappropriate. We are now so accustomed to the use of marketing language in political campaigns that these images do not shock us. On the contrary, they are illustrative of the kind of work that actually happens in campaigns; candidates and parties are imagined, researched, and developed as competing brands. They reflect in part the way that professional campaigners increasingly perceive voters, as comfortable consumers whose political choices are infused with brand values.

We have become so used to the lexicon of branding in so many parts of our everyday lives that we are living in what Kornberger (2010) calls "brand society." Branding is massively exploited, but underinvestigated, and we hardly stop to question what branding means in politics. This and the following chapter examine this question. This chapter looks at an example of political branding in action, detailing the strategy to "reconnect the Prime Minister" with the rebranding of Tony Blair before the 2005 British general election.[1] It then examines the merits of the brand concept for political campaigners, operating in what they increasingly call a postadvertising world. It explains why branding has become the

---

[1] The discussion of the Blair brand reproduces material first published in Scammell (2007).

new cutting edge of political marketing; why the political brand has overtaken the older but related concept of political image as the means to develop political strategy. The following chapter examines the analytical power of the brand concept, investigating whether brand analysis adds any value to our understanding of the appeal of George W. Bush. More broadly, these chapters argue that branding is the new form of political marketing. If market research, strategic positioning, spin, and advertising were the key signifiers of marketed parties and candidates in the 1980s and 1990s, "branding" is the hallmark now. However, for all its ubiquitous usage the "brand" is still a fuzzy concept. It is necessary to consider exactly what a brand is.

BRANDS: WHAT ARE THEY?

While practitioners, journalists, and researchers have talked of political brands for many years, only recently have we seen sustained attempts to apply the concept analytically. Needham (2005), for example, makes a strong case that branding is the most appropriate way to understand the "permanent campaigns" of modern governments; Gareth Smith's (2009) use of brand personality offers a perceptive tool to understand voters' party images; White and de Chernatony (2001) applied brand principles to an analysis of the functional and emotional appeals of New Labour; while in this chapter we examine branding in practice (see also Scammell, 2007), showing how apparently small details – tone of voice and style of presentation – were crucial to the "re-connection strategy" of Tony Blair before the 2005 general election. This work reveals some of the analytical promise of branding. However, it also exposes potential confusions in the field, as each approach offers its own distinctive take on the brand. Effectively there are multiple brand models in use, and as yet we are only just starting to develop discussion between researchers about the most appropriate models for political marketing research (see, e.g., the special issue on branding in political markets in the *Journal of Political Marketing*, in press).

It is helpful, therefore, to start with what is commonly understood. There is broad agreement that brands are "intangible" assets that in the business world can translate into colossal financial value. The value of "intangibles" (roughly equivalent to the gap between companies' "book values," such as material assets, and their stock market valuations) rocketed in the last quarter of the twentieth century. Interbrand, a respected international consultancy, notes the transformation over thirty years, from a time when "brand" merely meant "logo," to the situation now when it can account for more than 50 percent of stock market value. The cash values are astonishing: Interbrand's league table of "best global brands" for 2011 estimated that Coca-Cola, the world's number one, was worth more than $71 billion; Google had a brand value at more than $55 billion, while Apple was the fastest mover in the top ten at more than $33 billion.[2]

All this intangible value resides in brand image. According to Grönroos (2000: 287), "The brand concept is always an image." In marketing literature it is often defined as "the psychological representation" of a product or organization, its symbolic and reputational value, which includes but is not reducible to its tangible use value. It is effectively a combination of "function" and "meaning," with a distinctive emphasis on the latter. Successful brands add a layer of emotional connection with consumers above and beyond functionality; the classic example, of course, is Coca-Cola. In blind tests two-thirds of respondents preferred the taste of Pepsi but two-thirds *asked* for Coke. This much is familiar in brand scholarship and is a commonplace of virtually every business school branding textbook. Beyond that there is wide agreement about the main brand functions: the brand signifies ownership, it acts as a symbolic representation, operates as a marker of quality and hence reduces risk for consumers, acts as a shortcut to choice, and so on.

Furthermore, and crucially, there is a consensus that brand images are shared projects. The "brand" emerges not simply

---

[2] These estimates of brand value can be found on Interbrand's website, www.interbrand.com.

from the marketing activities of owner companies but from the experience and perception of consumers, which in turn arises out of multiple and diverse encounters. As Kornberger (2010: 264) puts it, "Brands supplement the cold logic of transaction with the chatty logic of interaction." Ultimately the brand is only as good as consumers say it is. O'Guinn and Muniz (2010) develop this idea further: brands are not merely cocreations between producers and aggregates of individual consumers, they argue. They are social constructions, arising out of interactions between "multiple parties, institutions, publics and social forces." It is precisely this socially interactive quality that makes the brand concept so powerful. It is not just that it is a complex source of strength and weakness for producers, with the capacity to add billions to corporate worth on the one hand, and highly sensitive to even small shifts in consumer perception, on the other. It is not just, either, that this sensitivity created opportunities for the upsurge of consumer activism from the 1990s onward (Bennett and Lagos, 2007; Micheletti and Stolle, 2007; Klein, 1999). More fundamental than either of these points, it positions the brand at the heart of the entire citizen-consumer debate. It is at one and the same time claimed as the site of complicity, of citizen submission to the commercialization of public life (Barber, 2007); and, conversely, it is also the mechanism that promotes "ethicality of business" (Kornberger, 2010: 207), that precisely introduces public concerns into the commercial sphere.

In summary, there is core agreement on three brand dimensions: the brand provides symbolic value (functionality plus meaning), it impacts consumer choice, it results from producer-consumer interaction. However, thereafter, it can get confusing. Search the web and there are myriad competing ways to conceptualize brands. What are we talking about? It could be brand attributes, brand tasks, brand functions, brand personality, brand identity, brand image, brand equity, and on and on. However, I have found two particular approaches helpful in understanding the construction of political images. The first comes from Grönroos (2000) and his analytical separation of brand *identity* (the image that the marketer wants to create) and brand *image* (customer perceptions of the goods, service, or organization). The distinction is useful for political analysis, enabling us to examine communication design separately from voter perceptions. The second is drawn from James Donius's (in Woods, 2004) model of brand distinctiveness, which distinguishes between "boundary conditions" (the basic economic and functional performance of a good, service, or organization) from "brand differentiators" (the cultural, psychological, and social associations in consumer choice). The model is useful for two main reasons. It effectively categorizes all commonly accepted attributes of brands, and does this in a way that connects the imagined to the tangibly real. The idea of "boundary conditions" is precisely that an acceptable level of functional performance is a necessary condition for brand sustainability. Second, it demonstrates how in crowded consumer markets, where many products meet the threshold of acceptable functionality and pricing, competition is concentrated at the level of differentiators.

The boundary/differentiator division is not intended as a model of how brand images develop in consumers' or indeed voters' minds. Both political psychology (Marcus, Neuman, and MacKuen, 2000) and the concept of emotional intelligence (Richards, 2004) show that emotion and reason are entwined. Hearts do not automatically follow minds, as the old practitioner adage sometimes puts it; rather, emotion and rationality work together. Thus, in consumer perceptions the levels of the model interact, such that consumers' propensity to imbue a product with favorable psychological associations modifies assessments of product price and functionality; and vice versa, perceptions of functionality modify the possibilities of emotional association. However, the distinction is useful for analysis of brand appeal. It enables brand managers, for example, to disentangle problems of communication from "real" problems of functionality, pricing, and concrete experiences of customers (Grönroos, 2000: 294–96). The distinction is also valuable for the analysis of political image, differentiating between the levels of the substantive factors that drive reasoned voting (boundary conditions) and social, psychological, and cultural associations (brand differentiators).

TABLE 3.1. *What Makes a Brand Distinctive?*

Cultural	"Symbol of our society"	Brand Differentiators
Social	"Grew up with it"	
Psychological	"Says something about me"	
Economic	"Value for money"	Boundary Conditions
Functional	"Works better"	

Source: The Donius Model, adapted from Woods (2004).

The task of brand research lies in discovering how differentiators operate in consumers' brand images and finding patterns of differentiation. A common theme is that, while brand differentiators emerge from multiple and diverse experiences and psychological associations, they often work at a low level of consumer attention. Consumer psychology, drawing from cognitive psychology, calls this low-involvement processing (Heath, 2001). Moreover, "many of the encounters that each of us has with a brand are experienced beneath the radar of conscious attention. The tiny details that do contribute to brand image such as the quality of plastic carrier bags, the information on a till receipt ... sneak into our brains invisibly" (Gordon, cited in Burkitt, 2002). Hence the skill of brand research is to make explicit that which is normally unexpressed and to convert it into a prioritized order that can assist brand development and promotion.

Brand research is primarily qualitative, seeking of necessity to delve beneath the surface evidence of quantitative polling. Burkitt (2002) describes two traditions of consumer qualitative research: first, the behaviorist school, which seeks explanations through direct observation of consumer behavior, rather than through questioning respondents; second, the human psychology school, which is premised on the assumption that people can and do understand their own motivations, although they may need help ("moderation") to access and make explicit "views and values that people have not thought about in a very conscious way or do not normally admit to." The latter school is commonly equated with the focus group. It enlists enabling and projective techniques from counseling and self-development to uncover respondents' normally unspoken intuitive associations and hard-to-admit private feelings. Typical techniques include "mood boards" (collections of pictures/images that evoke emotional territories, lifestyle, and feeling), "concept statements," in which respondents are asked to write down their views before discussing them, and party-game-type associations, which are probably the best known among the brand researcher's devices. Hence questions that lead to the brand analogies referred to at the start of this chapter, such as "If product X was a car/fruit/ football team what kind of car/fruit/football team would it be?" Beyond this, and as we shall see in the case of Tony Blair, researchers call upon techniques of psychoanalysis to access respondents' most privately held or even repressed opinions.

"RECONNECTING THE PRIME MINISTER": POLITICAL BRANDING IN ACTION

The strategy to "reconnect" Tony Blair with disaffected voters prior to the 2005 UK general election offers a sharp illustration of the use and centrality of brand thinking. Labour, although consistently ahead in the polls, approached the campaign nervously, worried at their ability to mobilize their own supporters and concerned at the depth of anger toward Blair, especially among women voters. Moreover, Labour, as the party of government for eight years, was particularly susceptible to rising public cynicism. Politicians, Philip Gould said (2003), were talking to an "empty stadium"; voters felt powerless and ignored and were looking for a more interactive engagement with politicians. The 2001 contest had produced the lowest postwar turnout, at 59 percent, and Labour strategists feared that another record low rendered them vulnerable to a hung parliament or worse should the Conservatives motivate their base through their campaign of anti-Blair appeals and promises of tough immigration policy and lower taxes.

This was the context in which Labour, in January 2005, enlisted the services of Promise Corporation, a commercial consultancy specializing in brand building. Promise set out its approach, methods, and recommendations in an unusually frank and detailed paper for a Market Research Society conference (Langmaid, Trevail, and Hayman, 2006). The following account and quotations all come from their paper, unless otherwise stated. Promise came to Labour's attention in December 2004 through an article written by Charles Trevail, one of the company's founders, in the *Financial Times*. Trevail had argued that Labour was a "premium brand"; a high-cost, high-service product that, precisely because it raised consumer expectations to high levels, was especially vulnerable to credibility problems. This, said Promise, was "the pain of premium": premium products offered high quality to customers, and their very success brought with it the risk that consumers may "idealize these brands – they imbue them with lots of positive qualities they'd like them to have, and which they cannot always live up to." Trevail's argument was spotted by Shaun Woodward, former Conservative communications director, who had defected to Labour. Woodward arranged a meeting between Promise executives and Labour campaign strategists Philip Gould and Sally Morgan at Number 10 Downing Street in December 2004. Following the meeting, Promise conducted preliminary research for Labour, involving standard focus groups of Labour loyalists and former Labour voters who were now undecided. Although it mainly confirmed what Labour already knew, the party's campaign team were impressed, especially with the analysis of respondents' "relationships with Blair personally" and how these fed into overall attitudes. Promise was commissioned to devise a strategy to counteract the Conservatives and crucially to recommend ways to "reconnect" Tony Blair to the electorate.

Thereafter, Promise focused only on undecided voters, particularly groups of women who had previously voted Labour, and whose hostility to Blair and Labour "might severely damage their showing at the polls." Promise attempted to isolate the Blair factor through the numerical scaling it uses in its brand index, asking respondents to award marks out of ten to parties and leaders on the basis of two attributes: reputation and delivery. It then asked respondents to score Labour and Conservatives against their own set of ideal attributes driving their opinions of political parties (competence, leadership, teamwork, integrity, in touch, understand, interactive). "Worryingly for New Labour, the Tories outperformed them on all of the attributes"; and worse for the prime minister, he scored lower than his party. Overall, Promise concluded that the New Labour brand was undermined by constant media attacks, the Iraq war, and the perception that Blair had lied about weapons of mass destruction. A key finding was that Blair personally was crucial to brand perceptions and that there was a marked deterioration over time, from enthusiastic welcome of the young Blair to resentment and anger at the later tough Blair.

To probe further the link between perceptions of Blair and the party brand, Promise used expressive techniques, including asking respondents to write a letter to Mr. Blair, "to let him know what they thought and more importantly how they felt," assuring them that "we would place the content of their letters before him, as we did." Promise summarized the emotional experiences of Blair under three broad headings (see Table 3.2): "you've left me," "you've become too big for your boots," and "you need to reflect on what you've done and change."

From these broad emotional themes, they then drew on Gestalt psychology and the "two chair" exercise, asking a volunteer to act out both parts of a two-way conversation between herself and Blair. The conversation was reported as follows:

WOMAN VOTER TO BLAIR: I thought you were one of us. A people person. Yet you were more interested in sucking up to people more famous than yourself. To do that you even put our boys' lives at risk in Iraq even though more than a million people had marched against that war. Why didn't you listen? Why are you spending so much time away from us? Why didn't you come home straight away after the tsunami? How could you stay on holiday when our people were dying?

BLAIR TO WOMAN VOTER: I'm afraid you've only got part of the picture. From where I sit the war in Iraq was crucial to the cause of world peace. But I understand that it's difficult to see the whole thing for you (boos from the group!). You put me in charge and I must do what I think to be the right thing. I am sure that history will prove us right in the end."

TABLE 3.2. *Letters to Blair (from undecided women voters)*

Key Phrases	Underlying Emotional Experience	Desires/Wishes/ Direction
Theme 1: you've left me! "you should have come home" (tsunami); "your country needed you"; "where were you when the disaster happened?"; "all the promises you made that never came to fruition"	Abandoned and unimportant	Put us first Get back in touch Get more involved with us
Theme 2: too big for your boots/celebrity "a president with Cherie"; "globe-trotting holiday makers"; "celebrity hero worship [Bush]"; "thought you were a people's person, not a movie star."	His self-importance and global lifestyle leave me feeling inferior/ undervalued	Reorder priorities Get back to basics Get real
Theme 3: reflect and change "take time to think"; "how foolish you've been"; "you've lost sight of reality."	Not held in mind Uncontained Out of control	Think, reflect – are you still the bloke we elected; have you moved on to bigger things?

Source: Langmaid, Trevail, and Hayman (2006).

After group discussion of the imaginary conversation, the woman returned to the chair tasked to be Blair saying what she would like to hear from him. This is what she said:

BLAIR TO WOMAN VOTER: I understand you, feelings and I realize that there are many who do not agree with me over Iraq ... I still believe on balance that we did the right thing, though I have been shocked to appreciate the depth of frustration among those who disagree with me. I solemnly promise to spend more time at home in contact with our own people and to debate these issues more seriously before we launch on such an endeavor again.

It was a relatively small difference in Blair's response, but it produced an extraordinary reaction, one woman even shouting out "we love you." This was the crucial moment in the strategy to rebrand Blair. The women's anger toward Blair stemmed not just from opposition to the Iraq war, although that was deeply unpopular, but from perceptions of Blair's patronizing tone and self-justificatory response to criticism. Promise researchers had been taken aback by the "degree of aggression – even hatred" directed at Blair. Moreover, the strength of hostility was related to the warmth of their welcome to the younger Blair, who had seemed so "fresh," "approachable," "modern, progressive and easy to look at and listen to."

Promise concluded, "There appeared to be almost two completely separate Mr Blairs out there in the public's consciousness. The one, ideal, almost perfect as a leader and source of hope; the other almost equally mendacious, even wicked as a source of disillusionment and despair." Ideal Tony had become Terrible Tony. Respondents reacted to Blair "with the feelings of jilted lovers: he had become enthralled by someone else, a figure more powerful than ourselves, the resident of the White House.... Therefore feeling rejected ourselves we must start to reject him." The task, as Promise saw it, was to integrate the two Tonys, the young, hopeful Tony and the older, tough Tony, into a new "mature Tony"; and the two chair exercise suggested that it was possible to do this through communication style and tone.

Simultaneously with the Blair focus groups, the Promise team worked on a new brand model for Labour, approaching the issue "as they would any other large brand," exploring the environment in which the brand existed, how it was promoted, and most importantly what it meant to consumers. New Labour had emerged out of a sophisticated brand strategy, driven by "intimate contact with voters, the party's customers." But by 2005 it was badly tarnished: "The brand lens through which people viewed the party had become clouded by the Iraq war and constant media attacks on the government.... The research categorically stated [that] New Labour had a problem with their leader, but so influential was he as an icon of the brand, the party also had a problem that reached the very core of the brand." The New Labour brand, personified by Blair, had stopped listening, it was too reliant on him, but without him seemed lightweight, all spin rather than substance.

The depth of dissatisfaction on three core attributes, competence, integrity, and teamwork, "could not be reversed over the 12 week period before the election. However, we realized that the brand did have an opportunity to address issues of integrity and teamwork head-on.... We recommended a strategy that portrayed members of the Cabinet working as a team; something that was very much lacking for the Tories." Promise suggested the rebranding of New Labour as "progressive realists": passionate, friendly, and inclusive for the benefit of all. It needed to show strength in depth by promoting a greater range of spokespeople, show competence through highlighting management of the economy, emphasize public services ("this brand is about *we*, not *me*"), and emphasize communications that looked "in touch." For Blair this meant showing that he understood why people were angry, and that he should drop the much-resented "I know best" stance in favor of "we can only do this together."

The consultancy's analysis was presented directly to Blair in Downing Street in late January 2005:

He [Blair] was able to see the sense of much of the analysis, particularly the discussion of people's idealization of him in '97 turning to a more negative view in 2005. We characterized this broken relationship as much like a damaged love affair for women voters.... We then had a 45-minute discussion, his two concerns being how to deal with the press and how to create a moment of drama around the need to reconnect with the UK electorate.... He also told us how he had thought about the New Labour project as a brand back in 1997 and that Clause 4 was a brand moment that he created.[3]

---

[3] Clause 4 was the best known section of the Labour Party constitution and was printed on membership cards. It committed the party to public ownership and

FROM "TOUGH TONY" TO "MATURE TONY": THE
MASOCHISM STRATEGY AND THE 2005 GENERAL
ELECTION

The plan to "reconnect the Prime Minister" got its first airing two weeks later (February 2005) with Tony Blair's speech to the Labour Party Spring Conference. To the delight of Promise, sound bites chosen by the media highlighted the new "mature Tony" approach: "I understand why some people are angry, not just over Iraq but many of the difficult decisions we have made, and, as ever, a lot of it is about me," said Blair. "So this journey has gone from 'all things to all people,' to 'I know best' to 'we can only do this together.' And I know which I prefer. A partnership."

Promise's main recommendations appeared in Labour's campaign war book: "TB must connect with the electorate ... and make it clear that he has not abandoned them"; he should show greater candor, humility, and willingness to listen (cited in Kavanagh and Butler, 2005: 57). This emerged publicly as the "masochism strategy," in which the prime minister increased his appearances on television in the run-up to the election, deliberately seeking out aggressive interviewers and asking TV shows to find hostile audiences to question him. The strategy, with its underlying analogy of a rocky marriage, provoked considerable press interest and no little contempt as the prime minister was subjected to some humbling encounters. He was repeatedly lambasted over Iraq, while in the most excruciating confrontations a hospital worker asked the prime minister if he would be prepared to "wipe someone's backside for £5 an hour," and on the popular Saturday night show, *Ant and Dec's Takeaway*, a child asked him, "My dad says you're mad. Are you mad?" Much of the press did indeed think that the strategy was madness (Rawnsley,

---

equitable redistribution. One of Blair's first major acts as party leader was to urge the party to abandon Clause 4 and replace it with a less stringent pledge for social justice. This led to a party-wide debate and vote, which Blair won, ultimately fairly comfortably. The "Clause 4 moment" became acknowledged as a crucial symbolic victory for Blair and the modernizers and a key step in the rebranding of the party as New Labour.

2005): "The traditional campaign playbooks say that leaders should always be displayed among crowds of cheering supporters affirming their goodness and greatness. And predictably conventional reporting has depicted these TV trials as evidence that the wheels are already coming off a 'humiliated' Prime Minister's campaign."

However, the masochism strategy was central to Labour's campaign, as was the attempt to showcase a united leadership team. The reuniting of Blair with his chancellor, Gordon Brown, was signaled in the party's first election broadcast (PEB) of the campaign. Directed by filmmaker Anthony Minghella (*The Talented Mr. Ripley*), the PEB featured Blair and Brown chatting together about their common values and achievements; it was a "soft-sell about a 'partnership that's worked'" (Harrison, 2005: 111). Remarkably, this was the only PEB under Blair's leadership that had highlighted any Labour politician other than him. In general, Labour's advertising and promotional material was far less Blair-focused than it had been in the previous two elections; instead, the team theme continued with Brown repeatedly at Blair's side on the campaign trail.

As Labour's campaigners predicted, the Blair-Brown double act contrasted with the Conservatives' reliance on its leader, Michael Howard. It also went with the grain of commentary from the Labour-supporting press (such as the *Guardian* and *Daily Mirror*), which, despite considerable misgivings over the Iraq war, urged readers to vote Blair and get Brown-Blair (Scammell and Harrop, 2005). In the event, Labour's efforts successfully raised the team profile but could not protect Blair from brutal press treatment, with the Conservative tabloids repeatedly calling him a liar over the causes of the Iraq war. The concentration on him was extraordinary even compared to the normal leader predominance of recent elections; it was an intensely personal and hostile campaign for Blair.

However, ultimately Labour campaigners had reason to celebrate the success of their strategy. This was due not so much to election victory, which according to the polls was never in real doubt, and which in any case delivered a reduced majority.

Rather, it was because, unlike 2001 and 1997, Labour improved its poll ratings over the course of the campaign. Its preferred issues of the economy, health, and education increased in importance to voters as the campaign progressed, while Labour augmented its lead over the Conservatives as the best party to deal with them. Moreover, for all the hostility directed at Blair he managed to improve his advantage over Michael Howard during the campaign (Kavanagh and Butler, 2005: 89). Crucially there is some suggestive evidence that the reconnection strategy may have been effective with women. Unusually, the gender gap favored Labour rather than the Tories. This success, much like the election result itself, was qualified since there was an overall swing away from Labour. Nonetheless, the defection was significantly less among women than men (Worcester, Mortimore, and Baines, 2005: 224–26).

BRANDING: ITS VALUE FOR POLITICAL CAMPAIGNERS

Branding as a concept and research method has both particular and general value for campaigners. The particular value is demonstrated in the "reconnection strategy"; its general usefulness becomes clear in the evolution of political marketing thinking. The reconnection strategy was a strikingly different way to deal with the problem of leader unpopularity. Typically previously, as in the cases of Margaret Thatcher and former Labour leader Neil Kinnock, campaigners had made relatively little attempt to shift entrenched opinion; Kinnock was shielded behind a team while Thatcher ran relatively sparse campaigns that highlighted her strengths as a commanding leader but made no effort to counter perceptions that she was "out of touch" and "talked down" to ordinary people (Scammell, 1995). Neither course perfectly fitted the bill for Blair in 2005. It would have been impossible to shield him from the scrutiny of the press, much of which treated the campaign as a referendum on the prime minister (Scammell and Harrop, 2005: 131). The option of protecting him from the public, with a Thatcher-like presidential campaign, was also risky. First, being seen as in touch was the essence of the New Labour brand, and until the Iraq war had been personified by Blair. He personally and the party generally had more to lose than Thatcher had. Moreover, his closest advisers were concerned to bolster his authority in the party. The "Tough Tony" was largely responsible for the party's current image problems; he should be seen to be spearheading the solutions.

The general value of branding to campaigners is both conceptual and practical. It provides a conceptual framework to distinguish and fathom links between the functional perceptions of parties and leaders (the "boundary conditions") such as economic management, policy commitments and the competence to deliver, and the emotional attractions ("brand differentiators"), such as "one of us," authenticity, approachability, attractiveness to the ear and eye. It brings together the emotional and intellectual, the rational and irrational, the big and tiny details that feed into overall images. Branding is underpinned by the insight that these images are highly vulnerable, constantly changing, and rarely under complete control. The near permanence of change became a Gould mantra. One of his key criticisms of political science analysis was that it is "static"; it can explain admirably a moment in time but cannot capture the "messy unpredictable and often random nature of politics as it happens" (Gould, 2001). Thus "re-assurance" was a key task of the brand in 1997 as Labour's research demonstrated that target voters were unconvinced that New Labour really was *new* (and would not go back to the old ways of special interests and raising taxes). However, by 2001, reassurance had turned into perceptions of caution and excessive concern with opinion polls, and so Labour had to refresh the brand, be prepared to show bold leadership, be "less nervous of unpopularity," far less concerned with the press "and, dare I say it, opinion polls" (Gould, 2002). By 2005, *new* New Labour needed to change tack again and reestablish "Tough Tony" as the listening, caring, in-touch leader whom target voters thought he was when they first elected him.

This constant adjustment of image is why branding *is* now the permanent campaign. The original model of the permanent campaign, as first used by President Carter's strategist Pat Caddell

(Blumenthal, 1982), was characterized inter alia by continuous polling, intense news management, and constant attention to media images. This model, says Gould (2002), "has had its day." It may be an understandable reaction to a "relentlessly intrusive media," and, he admitted, it had characterized the early years of the first New Labour government. However, spin not only was insufficient to maintain political leadership, it ultimately "contaminated" the Labour brand and undermined public trust. Permanent *revolution*, said Gould, rather than permanent campaigning, was the "better label for what is happening in British politics today." Permanent revolution meant constant sensitivity to changes in the electorate's mood because yesterday's strengths can transform rapidly into today's weaknesses. This is a grand political euphemism for branding. What Gould describes is not "revolution" in any meaningful sense of the word; rather it is continual adjustment according to brand environment research.

Needham (2005) argues that the brand concept, rather than the permanent campaign, is the more useful to understand communication in the governments of Blair and Bill Clinton. She enlists a scheme of brand functions (differentiation from rivals, reassurance and the reduction of risk, values and emotional connection) to examine communication initiatives in both administrations. The permanent campaign, she argues, focuses on the instruments of media politics, the up-rated use of research and news management. However, the brand concept uncovers the underlying strategic concerns of efforts to maintain voter loyalty through communication designed to provide reassurance, uniqueness (clear differentiation from rivals), consistency of values, and emotional connection with voters' values and visions of the good life.

Part of the general attraction of branding stems from its practical familiarity. Branding uses qualitative research techniques, designed to tap into emotional connection, which are essentially an extension of methods long used for political advertising. However, the advantage of branding is that it provides a conceptual structure to link advertising insight into all aspects of strategic positioning, development, and promotion. Paradoxically given the shared methods, the marketing turn to branding has coincided with shaken faith in advertising itself as capable of encompassing all the details, big and small, that create brand image. As former Conservative vice-chairman and celebrated advertiser Lord Maurice Saatchi (2006), puts it, we are now living in a postadvertising world.

POLITICAL BRANDING: A CONSUMER MODEL OF POLITICAL COMMUNICATION AND WHAT IT MEANS

Branding is shifting campaigning emphasis away from a mass-media based model of political communication to a thoroughly consumerized and individualized model. This is evident not just in the reliance on brand thinking but also in the perception that voters' attitudes to politics are shaped by their experience of consumerism. There is a perfect circle: campaigners research voters as though they are consumers; and their research is finding that voters' attitudes toward politics are profoundly shaped by their experience as consumers. This is made clear in Gould's 2003 "brand environment" analysis, titled "The Empty Stadium: Winning Elections in a World Turned Upside Down,"[4] in which he argued for a new campaign paradigm. The analysis posited a fundamental mismatch between people's experiences as confident consumers, on the one hand, and insecure citizens, on the other. Affluence and a profusion of choice had empowered people as consumers, but the pace of globalization, threats of terrorism, and environmental erosion had led to insecure citizens. Individuals' sense of greater control as consumers exacerbated their sense of loss of control as citizens. Conventional politics was blamed for the rising climate of insecurity and social fracture, while simultaneously being considered irrelevant to a "new consumer world of empowerment, self-actualization" and personal values. Consumer power had led to a paradigm shift within marketing thinking, from "interruption marketing" (such as TV or pop-up advertising, unasked for, unwelcome) to "permission marketing"

---

[4] Gould, "Empty Stadium."

(anticipated, relevant, personal). All interruption marketing was resisted, said Gould, but political communication was the most resisted of all. He warned that "if we play the game as we have always done," the stadium will continue to empty. Modern campaigning required more personal and interactive communication and necessitated that politicians engage on the tough issues: asylum, crime, and social disintegration. "It is better to disagree with the public than ignore it."

Branding is not the elusive magic bullet to political success. Brand research does not provide automatic answers; its results and recommendations are negotiated by the relevant political actors much as any other research. It is not suggested either that branding provides a direct causal arrow from market research to concrete policy, although it certainly maps out broad territories for political attention. However, it does explain better than alternative accounts why and how Blair's Labour actually communicated. The masochism strategy, "mature Tony," and the attempt to reposition the party as "team Labour" all emerged from a brand-based view of the political market. The Labour example demonstrates a key principle of political marketing explanations of modern political communication. The prime driver of change in political communications practice is not the media, vastly important though they are, but campaigners' strategic understanding of the political marketplace, encompassing both the electorate and competitors. The reconnection strategy makes it abundantly clear that Labour viewed the electorate as citizen-consumers of a political brand.

SUMMARY AND CONCLUSION

The shift to branding, in politics as in commerce, turns attention to the "intangibles"; how and why brand images are as they are, and how the emotional, cultural, and psychological (meaning) connect with the tangible (the functional or boundary conditions). The example of Tony Blair shows how important were the insights of consumer psychology to his political communication strategy. This is a new level of market research in politics, well beyond the normal polling of issues or focus group research of image dimensions. Its implications go way beyond the production of the usual tools of political promotion, advertising, spin, and news management. Branding becomes the more or less permanent means of understanding and adjusting parties and governments' connections (and disconnections) with voters.

Branding in politics raises profound, if familiar, concerns for the health of democracy: the danger of misleading the public through an increasingly sophisticated understanding of consumer psychology; the elevation of communication style; the threat of depoliticization as politicians are encouraged to accent the personal; neglect of the wider public itself as research hones ever more precisely amenable target groups. As the Blair example shows, the "reconnection" strategy emerged out of research of a relatively tiny number of voters. Equally profoundly, branding encourages both politicians and citizens to import into politics, and give legitimacy to, the tiny details that differentiate brands and inform consumer choice. In the case of Blair, it was a relatively small detail – tone of voice – that was the key to unlocking the reconnection strategy. Branding in politics may be uncomfortable for those advocates who prefer to imagine that political marketing, properly speaking, is about responsiveness to voter issue preferences and delivery of policy promises. The rational economic model of political marketing becomes the consumer marketing model.

However, branding exposes opportunities as well as threats. The reconnection strategy reveals a determined effort to understand voters, to take seriously and not dismiss as irrational their emotional (dis)connections with politics. It revealed considerable maturity in these target voters; they understood and were willing to accept differences with their political leaders provided that their voices were properly heard and that they were not patronized. Arguably, too, this level of attention to the emotional intelligence of citizens is valuable not just for practitioners but researchers of politics. It directs attention to how rationality (both as utility maximization and deliberative reason) are connected to emotional responses; and it allows that these connections are "intelligent." Reason is not opposed to emotion, as though they were mutually exclusive. A minority but growing group of political communication researchers argue precisely for a redefinition of political rationality to include emotional intelligence (Pels, 2003; Corner, 2003; Richards, 2004; Scammell and Langer, 2006) to enable a more holistic understanding of the relationship between citizens and leaders.

Theoretically, then, branding may assist connection between citizens and leaders, and need not mean, and in the case of Labour in 2005 did not mean, the absence of substantial political debate. For Blair, it was the reverse, as he voluntarily sought out his critics and faced up to them. We have not yet developed ways to distinguish good (democratically speaking) branding from smart (effective) branding. We have some clues in the brand model itself with its analytical separation of boundary conditions and brand differentiators; and this point is explored further in the following chapter. This task is now urgent because political branding is here to stay. It is yet more confirmation that we live in the age of the citizen-consumer.

4

George W. Bush

The Ultimate Brand?

FusionBrand, a consultancy that claims Coca-Cola and Hitachi among its clients, tantalized its online readers with a short piece in February 2006 called "George W. Bush, Branding Guru?" in which company executive Nick Wreden attributed Bush's electoral triumphs to "superlative branding skills."

Wreden wrote,

Bush and his advisors understood that he could have never been elected as an ordinary candidate. He had run three businesses into the ground, and was associated with shady stock deals such as Harkin Energy. He slipped into the "champagne unit" of the Texas Air National Guard at a time when his peers were being drafted and dying in Vietnam.... He was governor of a state that was at the bottom of the rankings in education, healthcare and literacy. His verbal mistakes were – and are – legendary. So Karl Rove, one of the most brilliant political operatives ever, re-packaged Bush as a brand. Instead of a Yale graduate who was a scion of a blue-blood Connecticut family, Bush was presented as a straight-shooting Texan. Instead of showing off his 10,000 square-foot house on an estate that is larger than the Kennedy and Kerry compounds combined, Bush told everyone he lived on a ranch. Instead of defending his being the only presidential candidate ever convicted of a felony (drunk driving), Bush shifted the debate to President Clinton's adultery. While hobnobbing with Enron CEO Ken Lay, indicted Tom DeLay and influence-peddler Jack Abramoff, who has pled guilty to bribery of top government officials, Bush adroitly positioned himself as a drugstore, truck-driving man.

The Bush brand lessons were, said Wreden, the power of strong and positive visuals, consistent messaging, adroit naming, and "branding the base" – focusing sharply on core supporters and contributors. "Bush the brand guru" provoked a lively online discussion. "Stick to business issues," retorted one poster. "This piece is nothing more than your political rant couched (not so subtlety) as a study in branding." Another poster objected, "Excuse me fellas – since when has propaganda become branding? Good branding is what happens when a company (or person) does everything else right – and does it consistently. Bush's propaganda is finally catching up with him.... It's a modern media savvy version of 'the big lie.'"

This exchange exposes the big fault lines in the political marketing debate. For the first poster, politics (presumably *good* politics in his view) is not reducible to marketing; the "brand guru" claim is a political slur against Bush, a claim that his success is based on promotional trickery. The second poster provides the opposite view, raising the familiar complaint of commercial marketers that politics gives their profession a bad name; marketing (presumably *good* marketing) should never be confused with political propaganda and the latter's sorry reputation for disinformation and dirty tricks. The exchange gets to the heart of the matter of George W. Bush's communication and how we should make sense of it.

GEORGE W. BUSH: THE BRAND GURU?

The forty-third president offers a fascinating test of the analytical value of the brand concept. The question is, does considering Bush as a brand add anything to our understanding of his appeal and communication strategy? Was there a George W. Bush brand in any real and deliberate sense, or is his success better analyzed as good old-fashioned propaganda?

There is a strong case for the propaganda argument. Part of the wonder of Bush's communication was its uncompromisingly old-fashioned style. After the smooth, focus-group-tested, intimate, and publicly accessible style of Bill Clinton, George W.

seemed almost a throwback to an earlier era. If Clinton courted public affection, Bush seemed to thrive on enemies. Bush, as his many critics asserted, ruled through fear. It is an age-old technique of rulers: as Barker (2006) has shown, historically, "enmity narratives" supply a means for legitimating leaders' identities.

Bush reproduced, with eerie accuracy, the template for war propaganda first set out in Harold Lasswell's (1927/1971) seminal examination of World War I. Lasswell classified propaganda techniques according to aims and target audiences: the more distant (allies, neutral countries) and sophisticated (educated and questioning) the audience, the more propaganda should focus on rational justification for war: self-defense, proportionate response, and the upholding of international law. Mass home audiences, however, require more emotionally compelling reasons. Lasswell introduced the now familiar concept of demonization, only he called it more exotically and precisely "Satanism." This has two core aspects: the invocation of good versus evil and the personification of evil in one or a small group of identified enemy leaders. Both were essential to mobilize a population to suspend its own moral and religious codes and justify killing distant and unknown people. Propaganda should furnish a clear and easily understood target for hatred, the wicked enemy leader rather than the leader's poor subjugated people, and it must demonstrate that this leader is more than simply an illegal tyrant. He must be beyond the pale of civilized values. Looking back ninety years, much World War I propaganda seems laughably crude, with Kaiser Wilhelm caricatured, often literally, as the Antichrist. Yet, the propaganda genre Lasswell described, with its repertoire of rhetorical motifs, of righteous civilizing purpose on "our" side and personified evil and atrocity on the other, fits perfectly the Bush blueprint for mobilization against Saddam Hussein (O'Shaughnessy, 2004).

Polarized enmity narratives of good versus bad are staples of warfare throughout the ages, and one can find examples in the first Gulf War and the conflicts since. However, typically in modern wars involving democratic countries, the prime appeals have been to "just war" theory (Walzer, 1992), to self-defense, international consensus on the legality of intervention, and/or humanitarian motivation. The shock of Bush was less his 2002 reference to the "axis of evil," but the continued reliance on cru-sading rhetoric in which "concepts of cosmic war are accom-panied by strong claims of moral justification and an enduring absolutism that transforms worldly struggles into sacred battles" (Juergensmeyer, cited in Barker, 2006). It contributed to a danger-ous "abuse of evil," according to philosopher Richard Bernstein (2005: 10). Historically, our confrontations with evil promote *thinking*, Bernstein says; about what evil is, where it resides, how it is manifested, and about human nature itself.

But something different happened on 9/11. Overnight ... our politicians and the media were broadcasting about evil.... Suddenly the world was divided into a simple (and simplistic) duality – the evil ones seeking to destroy us and those committed to the war against evil.

What so disturbed Bernstein was that the rhetoric of evil was used, not as an invitation to think, but as a means to *stifle* think-ing: in the war on terror, "nuance and subtlety are (mis)taken as signs of wavering, weakness, and indecision." To question what it means to label our enemies as "evil" had become a near-unpatriotic act. However, what Bernstein describes is precisely the point of propaganda in Lasswell's classic schema. It is about mass mobilization, not public deliberation.

The overt enmity strategy of the "war on terror" was coupled with an aggressively partisan approach to the media and a cam-paigning logic inspired by the wisdom of warfare. Campaigning consciously perceived as a kind of bloodless warfare is a distinc-tive approach among U.S. consultants (Scammell, 1997), driven by the particular competitive conditions of the U.S. electoral market; winner take all in a two-party fight for vanishing vot-ers, in which career consultants' livelihoods depend on a track record of victory. Rove, following his mentor Lee Atwater (strat-egist for Bush Senior), is an arch exponent of campaigning as warfare: issues are used as weapons of attack and mobilization, and energy invested in tactics designed to "psychologically screw up the other guy," as Republican consultant Charles Black put it (cited in Scammell, 1997: 11). Rove watchers Moore and Slater (2006) detail the circumstantial evidence that links Rove (indirectly at least) to a trail of dirty tricks in campaigns conducted for Bush: the 1994 Texas gubernatorial race when Democrat opponent Ann Richards was victim of a homophobic whispering campaign; the 2000 Republican presidential primary in South Carolina when front-runner John McCain was rocked by rumors of mental instability and biracial adultery; and the 2004 contest when the negative advertisements of the Swift Boat Veterans for Truth derailed John Kerry's war hero status.

It is hard to know what shocked critics more: the conspicuousness of the propaganda ploys, the anachronistic style, or its apparent success as the "war on terror" reduced the Democrats to near impotency and swept Bush to new heights in public popularity. They cast about for a new way to characterize the Bush communication and settled on an old one: George Orwell's *1984* nightmare of doublethink and newspeak. *New York Times* columnist Maureen Dowd's (2004: 23–25) *Bushworld* exemplifies the tone, describing an Orwellian "alternate reality" in which what Bush says is the near-opposite of reality:

In Bushworld, you get to strut around like a tough military guy and paint your rival as a chicken hawk, even though he's the one who won the medals.... In Bushworld, they struggle to keep church and state separate in Iraq, even as they increasingly merge the two in America.... In Bushworld, we're making progress in the war on terror by fighting a war that creates terrorists.

THE BRAND CONCEPT AND GEORGE W. BUSH

In the light of all this, what does the brand perspective bring to the table? From across the ocean it was often difficult to understand Bush's appeal. He became a cartoon figure of derision around the world: "in frame one he is Ronald Reagan the B-grade cowboy, next he is Bonzo the chimpanzee, next he is the simpleton Alfred E. Newman" (O'Connor, 2005: 163). With his fabled "mispronuncifications," wild west "dead or alive" threats to enemies, and hand-wringing expressions of evangelical Christian faith, the difficulty was to parody Bush when he did it so well himself. Such is the depth of contempt for Bush that it is hard, as O'Connor admits, to write objectively about him, still less to fathom his "quite confounding" electoral success. The UK's popular tabloid the *Daily Mirror* gave its verdict after his 2004 reelection: "How can 59,054,087 people be so DUMB?" However, unless one is satisfied by the dumb and duped explanations, it is necessary to take Bush's appeal more seriously. This is where branding is useful as an analytical tool. It helps dissect the Bush appeal, its construction and coherence.

Donius's scheme of brand distinctiveness (Chapter 3) separates boundary conditions from brand differentiators. The boundary conditions (tangible use-value, value for money) are often considered the rational basis for consumer choice, while the brand differentiators (social, psychological, and cultural factors) provide the emotional motivation. Just to reemphasize the boundary/differentiator division is not intended as a model of how brand images develop in practice; the levels of the model interact, such that consumers' propensity to imbue a product with favorable psychological associations modifies assessments of product price and functionality; and vice versa, perceptions of reliable functionality modify the possibilities of emotional association. However, the distinction is valuable for the analysis of political image, differentiating between the levels of the substantive factors that drive reasoned voting (boundary conditions) and social, psychological, and cultural associations (brand differentiators).

However, the model needs modification for politics. In particular, the essentially economic idea of "boundary conditions" holds promise but needs reconceptualization. There are two linked ideas here: one of sustainability (functionality will determine sustainability in the long run) and rational choice (consumers/voters are "rational" and their choices will involve informed decision making). The idea of rationality contained within the logic of "boundary conditions" has a much stronger normative dimension in politics than in consumer markets. The legitimacy of elections as expressions of the people's voice depends in large part on notions of rationality. Democratic representation, in theory, relies on informed citizens voting for leaders who best represent their views; and each election is an exercise in accountability as leaders are judged on their performance in office. Even while we know that the determinants of voter choice are more messily multidimensional, the normative grip of reason and rationality remains strong. Hence for politics, the division between "boundary conditions" and "brand differentiators" could entail a sharp normative split.

Thus, a modified model of brand distinctiveness redefines boundary conditions as *substantive performance indicators*. These include specific policy proposals, record of competence and delivery of promises, credibility of promises, and demonstration of leadership qualities. Some of these indicators leak inevitably into areas that are sometimes deemed "image dimensions." Leadership qualities, for example, may include perceptions of "strength," "intelligence," and "trustworthiness." While these lack the factual verifiability of "record," they pass the test of rationality. The credibility of political promises depends on perceptions that leaders can be trusted to do what they say and that they have the necessary qualities to carry out their proposals. This point hints at the conceptual complexities that prevent neat separation of (normatively desirable) "substance" and (normatively suspicious) "image" in politics (see Langer, 2011, for a discussion of this). For this reason, the substantive performance indicators are split into two categories: the objectively verifiable matters of record, record of achievement, issue agenda, policy pledges; and the more subjective matters of performance attributes, such as leadership qualities and credibility of promises (see Table 4.1).

This model is not intended to suggest effects, or indicate the way brand images developed in voters' minds. Rather it is designed as a tool to shed light on campaign communication, in this instance George W. Bush in 2004. In particular, it enables us to dissect the image that Bush communication intended to project: his preferred "brand identity."

TABLE 4.1. *Political Brand Images*

Brand Differentiators	
Cultural	"Symbol of our society"
Social	"Grew up with it," "speaks to my sense of social identity"
Psychological	"Says something about me," "speaks to my sense of personal identity"

Boundary Conditions: Substantive Performance Indicators	
Record	Record of achievement
	Delivery of promises
	Issue agenda
	Specific pledges
Attributes	Leadership competence
	Credible policy proposals
	Trustworthiness
	Strength/intelligence

GEORGE W. BUSH: BRAND ANALYSIS OF HIS COMMUNICATION

Applying this scheme to Bush produces immediately some intriguing possibilities. A first look suggests that the positive promotion of the president relied overwhelmingly on brand differentiators. Bush's positive appeal was primarily emotional, all soft differentiation. However, attacks on opponents were much harder politics, to do with policy, competence, and record. Negative appeals, therefore, are located predominantly within the substantive performance indicators, competence, track record, and policy. The starkness of the contrast between positive/negative promotional strategies is striking. However, the closer one looks, the more evidence there is to support the contention.

Journalist Joe Klein, veteran presidential election reporter, uses different language but comes to a similar conclusion following decades of campaign observation and interviews with top consultants. Klein calls it *politics lost*. For Klein no one was more cynically nonpolitical than Bush's strategist Karl Rove, for whom there were only three basic questions that matter to voters: Is the candidate a strong leader? Can I trust him? Does he care about people like me? (Klein, 2006: 144–45). The triumph of Rove thinking is exemplified in Klein's description of Mark McKinnon's conversion as he joined the Bush media team; he turned from cultural Democrat not so much to "Republican philosophy but more to the Republican way of doing campaigns." McKinnon, says Klein, came to the "guilty" realization that the successful promotion of a candidate was not about policies and details of issues, it was about finding emotional character cues to answer convincingly Rove's three questions. The hard politics of specific issues were useful only as sticks to beat opponents or as illustrations of candidate values.

McKinnon was amazed that the Democrats had never quite figured this out. In fact, they had it ass-backwards. A guy like Stan Greenberg [Clinton's pollster] would take a poll to learn which issues people cared about…and then…figure out the best ways to talk about those policies…. The character of the candidate, they believed, would be inferred from the quality of his policies. How quaint. (Klein, 2006: 146)

The subjugation of policy to brand identity is argued also by Barberio and Lowe's (2006) comparative analysis of the presidential rhetoric of Clinton and Bush. They compared Bush's language, in speeches in support of "compassionate conservative" policies, such as No Child Left Behind, to Clinton's "service initiative" and AmeriCorps promotion. They coded rhetoric for its references to values (e.g., freedom, strength, responsibility), to explanatory content (how the policy would work, how and why it might bring benefit, how it compared to alternatives), and to symbolic content (references to historic figures and events). While both presidents made abundant use of value-laden and symbolic language (about 45 percent of all coded references in each case), Bush was markedly lighter on explanation than Clinton: 39 percent of Clinton's rhetoric was coded in the explanatory category, compared to just 22 percent for Bush. Particularly striking for the authors was Bush's tendency to link within the space of a few sentences disparate parts of his overall objectives into a single "branded rhetoric." Thus, for example, in a speech to a rally on "inner city compassion" (Cleveland, Ohio, July 1,

2002) Bush associated support for faith-based initiatives with the "war on terror":

Now out of the evil done to America is going to come some incredible good here. I believe it. I believe that our citizens, many citizens are now hearing the call that a true patriot is somebody who serves something greater than themselves.... A patriot is somebody who understands that life ... is complete when you make a sacrifice for somebody else. That certainly came home to a lot of Americans when Flight 93 was driven into the ground by citizens, normal everyday citizens, who realized the plane they were on would be a weapon.... They said a prayer, and they made the ultimate sacrifice for somebody else. That's the American spirit.... And that is the spirit exhibited every day in our country when people say "I think I want to mentor a child" ... when people help an elderly shut-in, when people deliver food.

Enduring parts of the Bush message are there in the references to evil, sacrifice, American community spirit, and optimistic patriotism. But, as Barberio and Lowe note, the speech provides no hard policy links between faith-based initiatives and the war on terror. It might have done, referring perhaps to recycling programs for the war effort, but it chose not to. Thus, the association was "superficial and arbitrary," in the authors' view. Barberio and Lowe's sample was self-admittedly small, a total of twenty presidential speeches and statements, but the evidence is clear enough for them to assert that "branding exists and that [Bush] has diligently pursued its use." As we shall see later, a similar "branded rhetoric" strategy is also evident in Bush's advertising. Viewed through the brand lens, the associations Bush used in the selected passage offer a good example of brand differentiation elevated over performance indicators. The appeal is not to the functional value of "compassionate conservatism" (its concrete success in, for example, alleviating poverty and distress) but to its psychological and cultural benefits. It perfectly replicates brand differentiators: offering symbols of society (American spirit, patriotism) and "saying something about me" (heroism, sacrifice) for the audience of faith-based volunteers. Thus, the associations, seemingly "superficial and arbitrary," provide emotional and cultural connections to the larger "product": Bush as national leader of the war on terror.

These themes are developed in the next piece of evidence, which comes from Mark McKinnon's account of the 2004 election campaign.[1] McKinnon, chief media adviser to Bush, argued that the U.S. press had mistakenly characterized the 2004 election as driven by hot-button "wedge issues," particularly abortion and gay marriage, to mobilize the anti-Kerry vote. In fact, McKinnon argued, this missed the broader underlying communication strategy, which was built around Bush's attributes and shared values: freedom, faith, family, and sacrifice. The key characteristics of the election itself were, McKinnon said, profoundly shaped by the 9/11 terrorist attacks, which had heightened fear and public demand for security but had also, and not so perversely, produced a "good community feel" as the country pulled together to get through the crisis. The promotion of Bush was designed to capitalize on positive public responses to his post-9/11 role as commander in chief, emphasize Bush's patriotic optimism, and match his perceived strengths as a family man of sincere faith with broader shared public values.

My analysis of McKinnon's presentation reel of twenty-six Bush-Cheney advertisements confirms his account of communication themes.[2] Table 4.2 shows that overall most ads contained specific policy and issue information, relying primarily on logical evidence, and that hope and patriotism, not fear, were the most common emotional appeals.[3] This conforms to the results

[1] Mark McKinnon, speech at "UK and US Elections: Lessons to Be Learnt" (Hansard Society Conference, Royal Geological Society, London, January 16, 2006).

[2] McKinnon's presentation reel contained twenty-six ads made by the Bush campaign, including three made by the Republican National Committee, and also two by the Swift Boat Veterans for Truth. Since the Swift Boat Veterans were formally independent, those ads were not analyzed. Many thanks to Mark McKinnon for providing me with the reel.

[3] This content analysis design used here was developed from Scammell and Langer's (2006) analysis of political advertisements, which in turn drew from Kaid and Johnston (2000). It followed Kaid and Johnston's categorization of types of proof (logical, emotional, and ethical) attached to persuasive messages. Logical proof denotes use of logical argument and/or factual support for messages; emotional proof is the association of messages with verbal and pictorial imagery (e.g., images of happiness/sadness, etc.), while ethical proof

TABLE 4.2. *McKinnon's Presentation Reel: Political Advertisements Bush-Cheney 2004*

	Count	Percentage
Positive	12	46
Negative	14	54
Total	*26*	*100*
Predominant proof		
Logical	16	61
Emotional	9	35
Endorsement	1	4
Total	*26*	*100*
Emotional appeal (coded if present)		
Happiness	1	4
Hope	9	35
Patriotism/national pride	5	19
Fear	9	35
Other/not clear	6	23
Specific policy/issue details	16	62

of Kaid's (2006: 41) analysis, which found that 85 percent of all Bush ads were issue, rather than image, focused.

However, breaking down the analysis into positive and negative groupings reveals with perfect clarity the performance indicator/brand differentiator split (see Tables 4.3 and 4.4). While Bush's positive ads highlighted shared values, hope, and national pride, they were also remarkably light on policy specifics. By contrast the negative advertisements battered Kerry repeatedly with details of voting record and policy flip-flops. The attack was carried overwhelmingly by what Kaid has called "logical" proof (the use of fact, even if selectively, to support argument; see Note 3). For the most part, and against expectations, the presence of fear in the negative ads was restrained, carried mostly in the background by the music.

typically uses endorsements from trusted figures/sources. The intercoder reliability for the content analysis averaged +.97 across all categories of the coding frame.

TABLE 4.3. *McKinnon's Presentation Reel: The Positive Ads*

	Count	Percentage
Predominant proof		
Logical	2	17
Emotional	9	75
Endorsement	1	8
Total	*12*	*100*
Emotional appeals (coded if present)		
Happiness	1	8
Hope	9	75
Patriotism/national pride	5	42
Fear	2	16
Specific policy/issue details	2	17

TABLE 4.4. *McKinnon's Presentation Reel: The Negative Ads*

	Count	Percentage
Predominant proof		
Logical	14	100
Emotional	–	–
Endorsement	–	–
Total	*14*	*100*
Emotional appeals		
Happiness	–	–
Hope	–	–
Patriotism/national pride	–	–
Fear	8	57
Specific policy/issue details	14	100

The positive promotion of Bush relied heavily on emotional proof. Thus, for example, America was "Safer, Stronger" (the first campaign ad that created controversy because of its images of 9/11), not because of any factual evidence, but because of the spirit of the American people "rising to the challenge," overcoming economic recession and the tragedy of 9/11. In the manner of the branded rhetoric characteristic of Bush's speeches, symbolic and rhetorical associations seamlessly link the war on terror to economic recovery in the space of seconds. In this and several other ads, shots of the president speaking and/or his voiceover are intercut with images of happy families and busy workmen, a terrorist gunman, and the heroes of 9/11, firemen, and U.S. soldiers, the heroes of war on terror. There is no logical proof in the form of argument, nor are any data presented, nor explanation of policy. It is about value association; linking Bush with a spirited people, rooted in happy families, who overcome troubles through enterprise and faith in themselves and the future. References to the war on terror are almost invariably devoid of any policy data or argument; rather the war on terror functions within the texts as a device to hail the American spirit, to associate Bush with it, and emphasize his strength as commander in chief. The war on terror, as McKinnon freely acknowledged, was a selling point for Bush in a way that the war in Iraq was not; "we tried to make the whole campaign around the war on terror." Iraq and Afghanistan are mentioned only once in these twenty-six ads, in "Victory," which welcomes these two countries as the world's newest democracies.

The imagery is strikingly ordinary across all the positive ads. We see Bush mostly as an ordinary family man, dressed casually, with Laura at his side, as he expounds his faith in the American people and his determination to keep the country safe; it is a significantly nonpartisan and almost nonpolitical portrait. Hope and patriotism are the main emotional appeals, buttressed by scenes of happiness signaled mostly by smiling parents and children. "Break," an ad aired toward the end of the campaign, is almost heroically happy and nonpolitical, given the context of predictions of a close contest. Sounds and images of aggressive anti-Bush political advertising give way to pictures of a smiling couple splashing their feet in water and to George and Laura happily admiring the view of a picture-postcard palm-fringed beach. "Tired of all the political ads? So we thought you'd like a break ..." runs the caption.

Across the spectrum of the positive ads, Bush's overtly presidential image is shown in scenes of him taking the oath of office ("I, George Walker Bush, do solemnly swear ...") and as

commander in chief pledging to protect his country. Highly significantly his strength and competence as commander in chief is the
overwhelmingly predominant performance indicator in Bush's
positive promotion, supported not so much by factual evidence,
but through emotional cues and argument, most notably in John
McCain's ringing endorsement ("First Choice"). Otherwise there
are no cues to Bush's political role as Republican leader or the
world's leading statesman. His portrayal is the embodiment of the
answers to Rove's questions: in touch, one of us, optimistic, caring, and strong in defense of family, freedom, and country. Even
the overtly religious language of "sacrifice" and "faith," obvious
cues for the Christian right, is accompanied with ordinary nondi-
visive images: of families playing and saying grace together at the
dining table and of ordinary heroes, firemen and regular soldiers.
It was a recurring technique of Bush rhetoric, embedding cues to
particular audience segments within a broader, inoffensive, uni-
fying language (Barberio and Lowe, 2006). Compounding the
ordinariness, the street corner diner, almost as much as the stars
and stripes, is the recurring image of nation.

Kerry's portrayal by stark contrast is intensely political and
policy dense; imagery and language connect him to Congress
and Capitol Hill as we are given an abundance of detail of how
his voting record will raise taxes, cut defense and intelligence
budgets, raise gas prices, and swamp health care in impenetra-
ble bureaucracy. Kerry's brand identity, as projected by the Bush
campaign, is located mainly within performance indicators. It
attacks his competence based on his record, his trustworthiness
to deliver a policy, and his weaknesses as potential commander
in chief. The brand differentiators attempt to show Kerry as
the typical equivocating Washington elite politico, distant and
out of touch as he tacks back and forth on his sailboard and
blows with the wind every tricky question. Kerry is more ridi-
culed than feared in the Bush ads, in contrast to the much darker
treatment of the Swift Boat Veterans, which bluntly questioned
Kerry's honesty, status as war hero, and claims to be a patriot.
The Swift Boat Veterans undoubtedly provided the outstanding ads of the campaign. Their notoriety, and apparent success

TABLE 4.5. *Bush Brand Identity*

Brand Differentiators		
Cultural	"Symbol of our society"	American flag, freedom, ordinary heroism, ordinary symbols of nation, e.g., street corner diner
Social	"Grew up with it," "speaks to my sense of social identity"	"American spirit," family values, "ordinary" Americans, "one of us"
Psychological	"Says something about me," "speaks to my sense of personal identity"	Hopeful, patriotic, heroic, religious, willing to sacrifice for others
Boundary Conditions: Substantive Performance Indicators		
Record	Record of achievement Delivery of promises Issue agenda Specific pledges	Commander in chief (kept America safe)
Attributes	Leadership competence Credible policy proposals Trustworthiness Strength/intelligence	Strong leader of war on terror

in wrong-footing the Kerry campaign, buttressed the common sense that Bush won through fear.

This chapter is about the usefulness of brand theory in understanding the construction of the Bush image. It stakes no claims to demonstrating communication effectiveness in terms of influencing attitudes and behavior, still less explaining all the factors that affected the election result. Thus, Table 4.5 shows not Bush's brand image (how people actually viewed him) but his preferred "brand identity" (how his communication *wanted* him to be viewed). Analysis of the ads show that Bush's brand identity was pitched heavily at emotional differentiators (hopeful, patriotic, in touch with ordinary Americans, religious and family oriented) underpinned by performance indicators that focused overwhelmingly on his record as commander in chief (strong leader of the war on terror, who had kept America safe and brought two formerly "terrorist" nations, Afghanistan and Iraq, into the family of democracies). In summary, the promotion of Bush as war leader was conducted not through reason and evidence but through emotional associations.

However, the brand identity constructed by McKinnon's ads show a Bush image quite distinct from the thesis of rule by fear and manipulated hatred of enemies. The communication is clearly designed to capitalize on the war on terror not through fear but through hope and national pride. It is an alternate reality, but it is a sunny, patriotic, optimistic one, driven by hope far more than fear. In this respect, Bush had more in common with Clinton than first meets the eye. Bush was hugely less likely to talk details of policy, but his appeal relied just as much on the projection of hope and being in touch with ordinary folk. However, Bush, even more than Clinton, was the common man in his presentation: he was the street corner diner to Clinton's Starbucks, to use the brand research imagery, the down-home and ordinary American to Clinton's fair trade, global brand.

Recent research in political psychology emphasizes that which campaigners have long held to be true: that emotional connections are crucial for voters' judgments and participation (Marcus et al., 2000). Moreover, comparative analysis of voters' assessments of candidates in the 1996 and 2004 presidential races highlights the neglected importance of hope (Belt, Just, and Crigler, 2005). While political scientists have concentrated on messages of fear and increasing campaign negativity, the authors' analysis of election survey and panel data suggests that "hope, above all other emotions, is essential to the formation of a candidate image that will translate into votes." Bush, their analysis finds, was a "lightning rod for emotions"; he aroused high levels of fear and anger in respondents (afraid: 44 percent for Bush, compared to 23 percent for Kerry; angry: 53 percent for Bush, compared to 31 percent for Kerry). However, he also elicited significantly higher levels of hope and pride (hope: 55 percent for Bush, 46 percent for Kerry; pride: 61 percent for Bush,

policy and issues is the fare of real, wholesome politics. Politicians can survive on brand differentiators for only so long. That is the moral of the Bush story, at least according to some Democrat campaigners. Bush in 2004 ran a near policy-free campaign and thus effectively had no policy mandate for his radical conservative agenda (Greenberg and Carville, 2004). Privatization of social security, the centerpiece of his domestic program, collapsed amid considerable cross-party opposition even before Hurricane Katrina exposed Bush to increasingly urgent criticisms of cronyism. By 2006 Bush was no longer the brand guru for Republican campaigners and more the cautionary tale. According to Tom Edmonds (2007), Republican consultant and vice president of the International Association of Political Consultants, "zealous rhetoric" was alienating Middle America and weakening the Republican brand on its core reputation of fiscal responsibility and pragmatism. "Democrats won in '06 because they weren't Republicans," he wrote. "And the Republicans? We lost because we weren't Republicans either."

Nonetheless, Bush offers a striking example of promotion heavily weighted to brand differentiation. Hope, national pride, faith, ordinariness, and ordinary heroism were the consistent, and apparently resonant, brand values. These factors have tended to be neglected by accounts that emphasize narratives of enmity. The point here is not that the propaganda thesis is wrong; its claims are particularly strong for understanding political communication that led to the war in Iraq. The point is that brand analysis helps complete the picture. For a while there, George W. Bush was the sunshine brand.

SUMMARY AND CONCLUSION

The Blair example demonstrated how branding is applied in practice; this chapter has explored branding from a different angle, as an analytical device. It used a model of brand distinctiveness, with its analytical split between brand differentiators and boundary conditions, the latter modified to incorporate substantive performance indicators (record, policy proposals, issue agenda, etc.). It tested the model on a sample of George W. Bush television advertisements in the 2004 presidential campaign. The purpose was limited to discovering if the model provided any fresh purchase on Bush's preferred brand identity, told us anything we did not already know, or cast any new light on the already familiar.

The conclusion was that it did. It directed our attention to the use and weighting of brand differentiators and how these were linked (or not) with the boundary conditions. It revealed a sharp split between positive and negative advertising. The positive Bush promotion was pitched overwhelmingly at brand differentiators, connecting Bush with optimism, national pride, and ordinary heroism. Virtually only one – and highly significant – substantive performance indicator emerged, his record as commander in chief, and even this was promoted primarily through emotional associations with the ordinary heroes of the war on terror – firefighters and soldiers. Thus, the brand identity did indeed capitalize on the war on terror, but more through hope and pride than fear.

Brand differentiation was applied here for analytical rather than normative purposes. However, it is plain to see how it connects to some of the troubling normative questions of professionalized political communication research, specifically the debates over positive/negative advertising and substance contrasted to political image. Underpinning these debates are two normative claims: that campaigns should provide sufficient appropriate and accurate information for citizens to make informed choices (the rationality principle) and that campaigns should mobilize citizens into voting (the participation principle). Since Ansolabehere and Iyengar (1997) first argued that negative advertising demobilized voters, the debate has revolved around these two normative claims (see, e.g., Jamieson, 2000; Geer, 2006). Critics claim that negative ads demotivate voters by promoting cynicism about politicians, while defenders champion their virtue on the grounds of substance; negative advertising tends to be issue-dense, while positive promotion is often image puffery.

The brand differentiation model of itself cannot resolve these claims, but it comes at them from a slightly different angle. It assumes that successful brands will both meet the boundary conditions and provide emotional connection. It invites us to ask not if, but *when*, we should be wary of political identities that rely wholly or heavily on brand differentiators. The model gives us the basis for assessment, by drawing attention to the balance and interconnections between substantive performance and differentiators. However, it does not assume that substance-weighted party communication is "good" normatively, as though it necessarily indicates a healthy conformity with democratically desirable goals of the informed citizen. This is partly a matter of the quality and relevance of the information, but it is also because, in order to mobilize, campaigns need to matter to us at an affective level. It may be that a campaign that pays no attention to emotional connection (differentiators) is as deficient as one that ignores the substantive indicators (boundary conditions). In short, the political brand distinctiveness model does not supply the normative answers; the work of evaluation is a task to be conducted on the basis of clearly justified democratic principle and contextualized possibly case by case. However, it does contribute to assessment, by asking us to consider what it is we expect and want from campaigns. Precisely what constitutes a good campaign is the task of the following chapter.

5

Campaigning Effects

How Do They Know What Works?

This chapter addresses three questions: What is a good campaign? How do professional campaigners deal with the problem of evidence? What is the independent verification from social science that campaigns matter at all?

WHAT IS A GOOD CAMPAIGN?

One can trawl through the vast expanse of trade literature and speak with dozens of consultants and arrive at the same answer: winning is the most important criterion of a good campaign. Winning is the essential condition even if campaigners recognize that it is not sufficient. As U.S. consultant Peter Fenn (2003: 79) notes,

We have all seen terrible campaigns that have, nevertheless, emerged victorious and we have seen great campaigns, great polling, great strategy and research, great media that have come up short. But few people talk about losing campaigns or mistakes, except to complain or put the blame on someone other than themselves. Even fewer people dare to write about a loss.

Fenn's article is one of the few in the twenty-six-year history of *Campaigns & Elections* that does dare to write about defeat. However, even he talks within the predominant frame: losing campaigns provide valuable lessons but primarily as case studies of mistakes. It is exceptional for losers to provide models of good campaigning, Howard Dean's Internet-fueled primary race in 2004 being one of the rare examples. There are at least two good reasons why this is so. First, in the competitive world of political consultancy, management of a losing campaign is a dubious recommendation to future clients, no matter how smart the strategy or disciplined the organization. Second is the problem of evidence. It is notoriously difficult to isolate and measure with any precision the impact of particular aspects of organization, strategy, and tactics in any given election. Thus campaigners must provide credible explanations of how their actions may influence election results; and since there are only two possible results, win or lose, consultants naturally link their work with winning.

However, if winning is the public yardstick of good campaigning, some wins are clearly better than others. The trade literature recognizes this through a classification of degrees of difficulty. The four main factors consistently contributing to difficulty are incumbency, previous party control, competitiveness judged by expenditure, and office visibility. *Campaigns & Elections* publishes a biennial scorecard of consultants' performances, which it weights according to these factors. Top points are awarded for a challenger win against an incumbent in a high-visibility race (presidential, governor, or Senate), followed by switch of party control in an open race. The easiest race to win is for an incumbent in a low-profile contest against a poorly funded opponent. Thus the classification focuses on the structural features of elections: the historical context of the race (incumbency, party control), the degree of public and media interest (for which office visibility is a proxy), and campaign funding. The first assumes that change is more difficult to accomplish than stability, while the latter two are crucial for determining the possibilities for campaigns to influence the media environment and keep control of key messages and issue agendas.

The scorecard provides a widely recognized indicative benchmark, and it is a reasonable assumption that the toughest wins are likely to have coincided with the smartest campaigns. Consultants' reputations can rocket on the back of a difficult win. Thus James Carville, who according to his own publicity has managed more races "than anyone in history" (Carville and Begala, 2006: 352), built his reputation by running Harris Wofford's victorious U.S. Senate campaign against a seemingly invincible incumbent Richard Thornburg in Pennsylvania (Johnson, 2001: 9–10), before achieving the ultimate tough win, with Bill Clinton against the incumbent president George H. Bush in 1992. The "architect," Karl Rove, moved toward his later awesome mystique by helping Bush Junior oust incumbent and favorite Ann Richards in the 1994 Texas gubernatorial election. The Davids – Axelrod and Plouffe – achieved ground-breaking status with their 2008 presidential nomination campaign for Barack Obama against the overwhelming favorite, Hillary Clinton. Lynton Crosby achieved his international "Wizard of Oz" renown by managing in 1996 an apparently impossible victory for the Australian Liberal John Howard against the incumbent Labor prime minister Paul Keating.

However, the scorecard tells us nothing directly about how well campaigns may or may not have been run. It does not specify the elements of a good campaign. Despite the growing professionalism, there is no general theory of campaigning, still less a blueprint for success. Consultants tend to be far less comfortable talking generalities than the specifics of particular races, and some elevate this tendency to a "law" of campaigning. On both sides of the Atlantic it is not unusual to hear campaigners say something similar to this comment from Ron Faucheux (2003: 20), himself at various times a candidate, consultant, and editor of *Campaigns & Elections*:

The first rule of political campaigning: there really are no rules. Although events, strategies, successes and failures of past combat may be highly instructive ... each campaign has its own heart and soul.... There are no magic wands in the campaign management business; there is no supernatural formula.

Ironically, Faucheux's "no rules" introduction to *Winning Elections* is followed by a chapter titled "Napolitan's Rules: 112 Lessons Learned from a Career in Politics." The second chapter, by the editors of *Campaigns & Elections*, lists another set of rules: "50 Things You Should *Never* Do" in a campaign. The course of each campaign is unique and often buffeted by unpredictable events. However, it is clear from our Chapter 2 discussion of what consultants sell to clients that there is a core body of transferable skills, most importantly in strategy, research, and campaign organization. The entire political consultancy business is predicated on the premise that political management expertise is transferable from race to race, and indeed from country to country. Moreover, if not a magic formula, there are discernable patterns of collective wisdom on the most important factors for success, strategic approaches and persuasive appeals. Some of these reflect consistency over time and place; others show variation according to political culture and system, and indeed the influence of particular campaigns that have become "paradigm busters" in campaigning folklore.

Clear strategy, disciplined organization and messaging, concentration on target voters, effective field operations, and get-out-the-vote activities were the commonly cited success factors in U.S. campaigns, according to my analysis of trade literature (a content analysis of issues of *Campaigns & Elections*, 1980–96).[1] These general indicators of good campaigning are supplemented by increasing attention to finance and budgets. Money on its own does not necessarily equal a "good campaign," but the ability to raise money is indicative of effective organization. Johnson's (2012) survey of some 250 U.S. consultants emphasized the point; money and message discipline were most commonly cited factors impacting chances of success. Internationally, the Global Political Consultancy Survey

[1] Articles in *Campaigns & Elections* from the first issue in 1980 to April 1996 (excluding 1994) were analyzed by headlines, descriptions of contents, and analysis of all articles geared to *general* lessons of campaigns, as opposed to details of individual contests. A total of 1,107 items were categorized according to the following subjects: persuasion, 6 percent; electoral law, 8 percent; money and fund-raising, 4 percent; specific campaigns, 18 percent; other, 39 percent. The "other" category includes all news items, personal profiles, reviews, and special reports on issues, countries, regions, demographic groups, and historical articles.

(Plasser, 2002) questioned consultants, party campaign managers, and staff members about decisive campaign. Their answers are reported in Table 5.1.

These data are suggestive of clustering of opinion and some regional differentiation, notwithstanding the caution that needs to be applied, especially to the smaller samples for some countries and regions. The importance of money is clear, and it is ranked as the first or second top factor in all but Western and Central Europe, New Zealand, and Australia. The exceptions are fairly predictable and may be explained by the greater frequency of spending limits, on national and/or constituency campaigns, in these countries. Strategy, as expected, is the second or third most cited factor in the areas commonly accepted as having the most professionalized campaigns: the United States, Western Europe, and Oceania. Overall, it is striking how strongly candidate personality and image rates, as a top three factor in all but Oceania, and considerably higher than issues in all but India and Oceania. Candidate image might be expected to feature prominently in countries that have presidential systems and in newer democracies where parties are establishing roots. However, it is fascinating to see how highly image is ranked in Western Europe, with its relatively strong party democracy. It is no shock though. It reflects the tendency that researchers have noted in political advertising, to sell parties as personality-led brands, most obviously Gerhard Schröder's Social Democrats in 2002 (Holtz-Bacha, 2006), Tony Blair's Labour, and before him John Major's Conservatives, which were promoted by Tory strategists explicitly as a personality brand (Scammell, 1995: 240). Silvio Berlusconi's Forza Italia is an iconic example of a party created entirely around personality (Mazzoleni, 2006), as was the extraordinary Lijst Pym Fortuyn in the Netherlands, while Campus (2010) shows how Nicolas Sarkozy's personalization strategy closely resembled Berlusconi's.

The one slight surprise is the relatively low ranking U.S. consultants put on personality, compared to their European counterparts. Personalization is a trademark of American-style campaigns, and has become accepted as a defining indicator of

TABLE 5.1. *Success Factors of a Campaign*

Q: How do you evaluate the importance of the following factors for the success of a campaign? ("very important" in percentage)

	Budget/ Money	Strategic Position	Candidate Personality/ Image	Issues	Target Group Data	News Management	Total *n*
United States	86	77	63	47	43	29	105
Latin America	72	63	84	36	69	41	64
Western Europe	34	63	79	41	43	60	122
Eastern and Central Europe	49	34	77	43	54	58	69
Russia	69	43	60	7	47	30	30
Other CIS	80	33	71	21	33	31	49
South Africa	69	54	65	35	62	31	26
Oceania	55	56	48	65	40	59	40
India	65	43	50	68	43	52	31
East Asia	54	34	70	13	34	54	56
							592

Source: Global Consultancy Survey Plasser (2002: 287) *Global Political Campaigning.*

trends toward Americanization elsewhere (Swanson and Mancini, 1996). However, it is in line with analysis of political advertising in U.S. presidential elections, which, contrary to expectations, has found consistently that the predominant focus is issues rather than image, where image is defined as the personal characteristics and qualities of candidates (Kaid and Holtz-Bacha, 2006). In general, emphasis on candidates' personalities has been on a downward path since the Reagan and Bush campaigns of the 1980s, and the Bush campaign of 1988 was the last presidential race in which either of the main contenders promoted personal image over issues. Kaid and Holtz-Bacha's (2006) comparison indicates a strikingly strong U.S. issue emphasis in political advertising compared with seven other democracies. They concluded that issue focus, rather than candidate personality, is characteristic of most countries, Turkey and South Korea being the exceptions. The particularly prominent issue focus in the United States reflects in part at least the dominance of negative advertising in America. A succession of studies on U.S. advertising has found that negative spots tend to be more issue-dense than positive ads (West, 1993; Kaid and Johnston, 2001; Jamieson, 2000; Geer, 2006). In its reliance on negative advertising, the United States continues to be the notable exception internationally.

The intriguingly *de*personalized portrait of U.S. campaigning also conforms to my reading of the trade literature. The candidate emerges as an ambivalent figure and is rarely mentioned as the key to a good campaign. The candidate is considered a "campaign input" whose contribution is scrutinized through polls and focus groups in terms of assets and liabilities. It is clear from interviews with international consultants that a strong, respected, attractive, personable candidate is universally considered a colossal asset. Indeed there are consultants who make personality emphasis a rule of campaigning. Rove's three key questions ("is he a strong leader, can I trust him, does he care about people like me?") lead inexorably to a personality and character focus. However, consultants are just as likely to talk of candidates who damage campaigns as improve them. Johnson (2012) concludes from his survey that U.S. consultants rank "hard work" and message discipline as the most important candidate traits, above personality and integrity. In our media age, when we are so accustomed to "natural" television performers, it is remarkable how many candidates, and leaders, fail to fit the bill. It is counterintuitive but true, and not just in the United States, how often the dull and media-awkward are the prime contenders for office. However, in addition, it appears that U.S. consultants have a low opinion of many of their clients. The U.S. political consultant survey, conducted under the auspices of the Improving Campaign Conduct project (Thurber et al., 2000: 14–16), found that 48 percent of the 200-strong sample rated their congressional candidates as "fair" or "poor"; 42 percent claimed to have witnessed a decline in the quality of candidates during their professional careers, while 44 percent said they had helped elect a candidate whom they came to regret seeing in office.

Thus, it is not so paradoxical that professionalized campaigning has simultaneously a personalizing and depersonalizing character. The degree and style of personalization is contingent and selective, promoting or suppressing aspects of private life to fit strategic needs. Candidates must be adapted to the strategy, at least as much as the other way round. The shoehorning of politicians into poll-driven strategic moulds has been a recurring complaint of campaign trail journalists who witness politicians turning into on-message robots day after day. Joe Klein's (2006: 240) *Politics Lost* denounces consultants precisely for draining the authentic, human qualities out of the politicians they serve: "They've put democracy in a Styrofoam cage. And the politicians – who tend to see caution as an aphrodisiac – have gone along."

The contingency of personalization is as evident in the now highly professionalized UK campaign environment as it is in the United States. The focus on leaders, as opposed to other party spokespeople, is a marked trend over the past twenty years, but if the leader is not considered an asset, she or he will feature little or hardly at all in advertising material (see Figure 5.1). A similar pattern has also been found in Germany (Holtz-Bacha, 2006).

One further noteworthy clustering revealed by Plasser's (2002) Global Consultants Survey (see Table 5.1) concerns the

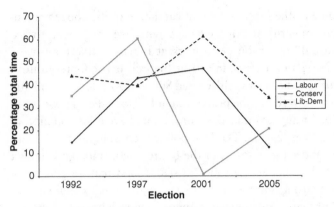

FIGURE 5.1. Party leader speaking (percentage of total time in party election broadcasts), UK general elections 1992–2005

importance of news management, defined as the control of topics and frames of reporting. Once again the regional pattern appears logical, related to the degree of regulation on media systems, restrictions on paid political advertising, and the presence of public service broadcast services. Broadly, the more reliant campaigners are on news media to deliver their messages, the more spin control is a determining success factor. Thus, in Western Europe, where many countries prohibit paid political advertising on television (e.g., Belgium, France, Portugal, Spain, the UK) campaigners invest proportionately greater energy into news management. In contrast, in the United States, despite providing for the world the term and concept of "spin doctor," paid advertising, rather than "free" media, has been generally considered the more important campaign communication vehicle. However, in all cases the purpose is much the same: agenda setting. Whether through ads or news media, campaigns are seeking to raise the public profile of issues and themes that are most favorable for them and least favorable for opponents, in the hope that this will translate into increased salience in voters' minds and hence ultimately influence votes.

The agenda-setting battle is commonly accepted by campaigners and academics alike as the core of parties' media campaigns and is underpinned by "issue ownership." In the fashion of brand image, issue ownership is determined by a combination of candidate principle and voters' perceptions as signaled by opinion research. It is central to strategy development, leading to marked tendency to narrow campaign agendas to a few themes and issues deemed decisive to voting decisions; and it is also a key element in assessments of campaign success. Election postmortems typically include appraisal of the various contenders' efforts to highlight or diminish certain issues, to frame them in particular ways and to improve public opinion rating in these areas. Typically, verdicts on agenda-setting success turn on the evidence of opinion surveys, and while there may be agreement on bottom-line results there is considerable scope for interpretation about which elements of the campaign were most effective. Thus, for example, communication consultant Mark McKinnon depicts the 2004 presidential campaign as a battle to keep voters' minds focused on shared values (family, faith, freedom, sacrifice) and the "war on terror," for which Bush had public approval, rather than the war in Iraq, where his standing was far less assured. Democratic consultants Stan Greenberg and James Carville (2004) acknowledged the overall success of the Bush campaign, but argued that it was mainly due to attacks on "flip-flop" Kerry and the use of wedge issues such as gay marriage and abortion; these led to a late and decisive shift toward Bush among white, rural, less-educated voters, they claim. The Kerry campaign, they say, failed to nail the agenda on the issues that might have swung it for him, especially the economy and health care. Thus Bush managed to persuade sufficient numbers of people to "vote their beliefs and feelings, rather than judge his performance or ideas for the future."

Contests of interpretation inevitably follow elections, among both campaigners and academics. Even with polls and increasingly sophisticated opinion measurement there is a relatively wide margin of uncertainty about precisely which campaign events turn elections. Ultimately, one or a few of the most compelling interpretations becomes accepted as the common wisdom, and feeds into the stock of campaigners' knowledge for future contests. This is essentially political folk wisdom (Scammell, 1997).

It boils down to intelligent and compelling narratives of success that may shift over time. In this, political campaigning shares much in common with commercial marketing and it leads to the abiding problem of evidence.

THE PROBLEM OF EVIDENCE

David Ogilvy's *Confessions of an Advertising Man* (1963) contained one of the enduring quotes of his profession: "Half the money I spend on advertising is wasted, and the trouble is I don't know which half." Ogilvy sums up in a sentence the problem of evidence for the persuasive industries. It captures the widely held and plausible sense that advertising in general has considerable effects. At the same time it reveals the doubt about the detail. How much advertising is necessary? What will work, with whom, and for how long? Ogilvy's sentiments, and the questions he raises, are equally relevant to commercial marketing and political campaigning. Despite the apparent triumph of marketing as the modern philosophy of business, despite the colossal value of brands as intangible assets, marketing still struggles to find a wholly satisfactory answer to this question: *does marketing pay?*

Commercial marketing, much more than its political variant, is theoretically developed, through business schools, postgraduate education, and a history of research in consumer behavior. Commercial marketing's claims to professionalism are far more advanced than political consultancy. It has developed broad consensus around basic tenets of what is called marketing philosophy, most importantly that market orientation can anticipate customer needs, that it can identify target markets, that knowledge of marketing theory and practice results in greater commercial success, that marketing is in its fourth stage of development, the latest being social responsibility. Yet, as Enright (2006: 107) argues, none of the basic tenets "is proven fact by virtue of universal applicability. Organizations that claim a marketing orientation still have failures." *Selling* is a fundamental commercial activity, says Enright, but *marketing* remains clouded with doubt that it is any more than "the extravagant complication" of a basic function. This makes it vulnerable: in hard economic times its inability to prove conclusively connection to the bottom line (ROI – return on investment) squeezes marketing budgets for research, advertising, and general promotion. This vulnerability of commercial marketing has spawned a mini-industry of effects seekers over the past forty years. The 1960s saw the PIMS effort (Profit Impact of Market Strategy), which attempted "to bring law and order to the wild west of marketing by quantifying and defining unambiguously the effect on profit caused by advertising, quality, market share, sales volumes and other marketing strategies" (Gummesson, 2002: 227). Ultimately, PIMS fell short, measuring covariation rather than showing causality. It was succeeded by a variety of other measurement regimes, from operation research, management science, and latterly micro-econometrics. The latter has provided a recent buzzword of effectiveness research, "metrics." It uses statistical analysis and cross-sectional and time-series data about individuals, households, and firms' marketing activities. The resulting flood of data raises new sets of problems, overwhelming marketing managers with spreadsheets that can cut a hundred ways the details of inter alia expenditure, advertising, sales, customer satisfaction, website traffic, and regional variations. Gummesson, a leading theorist of the increasingly fashionable relationship marketing approach, dismisses much of the quest for precise metrics as "irrelevant elegance." Marketing accountability, Gummesson's preferred alternative to effectiveness evaluation, directs attention to value creation, and the development of "management processes" to drive marketing value creation higher and higher. Ultimately, there is no single route to establish marketing's return on investment; clearly the statistics are vital, but number crunching it is not a simple matter.

By comparison with commerce, political marketing's measures of accountability are in their infancy. The raison d'être of *Campaigns & Elections* is to help make campaigns more effective, yet for all the many checklists it provides, and the lists of dos and don'ts, there is no clear consensus around standards of evaluation. In fact, there are remarkably few articles that broach the subject at all (see Faucheux, 2003). Specialists in some aspects such as fund-raising, direct mail, and voter registration may track their effectiveness against benchmarks provided by historical record and competitor achievement. However, by and large, the success of campaign activities is measured by covariation: correspondence of opinion poll change with particular messages and themes, achievement of audience ratings points for advertising aimed at target voters, increased turnout in targeted constituencies, focus group approval of style and messages, and day-to-day successes in news agendas. Covariation provides useful indicators and is a valuable guide to whether a campaign may be having any impact at all; but it is evidently an imprecise tool to isolate the effectiveness of any particular tactic or technique.

However, Karl Rove's "metrics" were a quantum leap in political marketing standards of evaluation. Rove's metrics became famous after Bush's 2004 victory, as stories circulated that his measurements, rather than the exit polls, provided the more accurate prediction of the result. What were Rove's metrics? Ken Mehlman, campaign manager for Bush-Cheney 2004, describes them as a precise set of predetermined benchmarks that enabled constant monitoring of the effectiveness of campaign tasks:

> You know ... a lot of people who are in politics and business and elsewhere say, "We're doing this; we hope it works." Well, the question is, how do you know if it's working? And [Rove] believes ... in having benchmarks that you agree on up front that will tell you if it's working, and measuring those benchmarks on a regular basis. By measuring those benchmarks, you're in a place where you can know whether you're successful or not. So the 2004 campaign did that for everything. We did it for raised dollars; we did it for voter registration; we did it for number of visits we wanted to make to different places around the country; we did it for polling; we did it for number of people [we] wanted to book on television. (*PBS Frontline*, "Karl Rove: The Architect")[2]

Rove's political metrics, much as business metrics, require the collection and measurement of huge amounts of political and commercial data. Most important was the creation and constant

---

[2] The transcript for Mehlman's interview is available at http://www.pbs.org/wgbh/pages/frontline/shows/architect/interviews/mehlman.html.

refinement of lists of potential Republican voters in target areas and experiments to check the most effective means of communication to their targets, testing, for example, the relative merits of mass media, telephone and personal contact. The metrics, *Washington Post* reporter Thomas Edsall told *Frontline*, began in 2001 and resulted in a long-term multimethod targeting of individual voters:

What kind of messages would work? Do you do it over Fox News? You do it through Fox News. You do it through direct mail. You do it through ... getting someone who's a member of their gun club to call them, all this stuff. They collect lists and lists and lists of local gun clubs, of local churches, and they would try to find Bush supporters in a given church, in a given gun club, who would be willing to actually become what amounted to precinct chairmen.

Political metrics operate not just as a tool of measurement but as an intellectual organizer: they force precise thinking about what matters in a campaign. They helped create what according to Mark McKinnon, Bush's media consultant, was less the typical ad hoc six months to one year election campaign, more a long-view marketing operation:[3]

Campaigns are usually ... pretty messy ... they are sort of instant corporations that you're trying to draw people together ..., creating a group of working individuals in parts that are supposed to create an outcome. And it's just usually pretty darn messy. The thing that was always amazing about a Rove campaign was he was just a juggernaut. Everything worked with precision and planning, meticulous. There was nothing messy about him. It was just well organized, well planned, no detail untouched.

Metrics cannot provide a magic formula, any more than any other campaign approach. Acclaimed after the 2004 presidential win, they were derided following the Republicans' heavy losses in the 2006 midterms, when it appeared that Rove's confidence was misplaced. Metrics are liable to the same drawbacks

---

[3] McKinnon interview on *Frontline*, PBS, "Karl Rove: The Architect." The interview is retrievable at http://www.pbs.org/wgbh/pages/frontline/shows/architect/interviews/mckinnon.html.

suffered in commercial marketing. Their value depends on the quality of data input, analysis and interpretation of that data, and, crucially, assumptions about what should be the key metrics in the first place. However, Rove raised the game for election planning and evaluation. His 2004 campaign for Bush has entered the campaign canon as a paradigm buster, shifting the conduct of campaigns, at least in the money-rich top-flight contests. Obama's indebtedness to metrics is made abundantly clear in Plouffe's (2009: 379) account of the 2008 campaigns. Whether it was fund-raising, voter registration, local press footprints, filling volunteer shifts, or voter turnout goals, metrics monitored the progress of the campaign, and in Plouffe's view they were of "chief importance," providing clear direction and enabling corrective action as appropriate, "based not on subjective measures but on clear, well-defined, objective ones."

DO CAMPAIGNS MATTER? THE EVIDENCE FROM POLITICAL SCIENCE

Despite the vast amount of money and energy poured into campaigning there are still plenty of political scientists who scrutinize elections as though campaigns were irrelevant or at best marginal and whose results are determined by longer-term factors such as economic performance and partisanship determined by the social identification of voters. Thus, for example, the post-2004 presidential election symposium in *PS: Political Science & Politics* examined the accuracy of a variety of voting models based on economic indicators, incumbency effects, and presidential approval ratings, with scarcely a nod in the direction of campaign impact. The same journal repeated the formula for the 2008 contest. Thus, even Obama's historic 2008 presidential victory can be explained largely as a consequence of long-term demographic trends and shorter-term noncampaign factors, such as the economic crisis and the unpopularity of President George W. Bush. As Abramowitz (2010: 111) summarizes, even with a perfect campaign, it would have been difficult for any Republican to overcome "such a toxic political environment."

Elections and voting behavior are probably the most studied fields in political science. However, only in the past twenty years has campaigning (as distinct from individual elections) come in for intensive scrutiny. Since Lazarsfeld's pioneering study (Lazarsfeld, Berelson, and Gaudet, 1948) the consensus bordering on orthodoxy has been that the main function of campaigns is to reinforce existing dispositions. Thus campaigns have a mobilizing function and may be useful to activate latent dispositions; but only exceptionally will campaigns do any more than tweak the margins of victory and defeat. Bartels's (1992: 264–65) review of U.S. electioneering over forty years typifies the skepticism: "Most changes in candidate support ... can be accounted for nicely – without any reference to campaign wizardry – ... on the basis of three principles": underdogs gain ground, economic prosperity advantages incumbents significantly, and heavily outspending opponents will be rewarded with a percentage point or two in vote share. According to Bartels's cold water verdict even the smartest campaign against the dumbest is likely to result in no more than a 1 percent residual vote shift.

If it is true to say that "limited effects" is still the political science default position (e.g., Bartels and Zaller, 2001), there has been sustained and comprehensive challenge over the past fifteen years fueled by three developments. First is the changing consensus about voting behavior driven by the decline of party identification. Most democracies in North America and Europe posted declines of more than 10 percent from the 1970s to the 1990s (Hague and Harrop, 2001: 142). This induced a shift from the idea of the voter as part of a social group, with choices highly constrained by social-demographic circumstances, to the idea of the voter as an individual, rationally calculating self-interest. The transformation is summarized as a paradigm shift: from the "dependent" voter to the rational or "judgmental" voter. Thus, as voters appeared less wedded to party allegiances, so greater possibilities for campaign impact were prized open. Moreover, in the newer democracies, especially those from the Soviet Union, the concept of party identification was barely relevant at all in some cases.

Second, and roughly over the same period, media research also began to dispute the "minimal effects" orthodoxy, which had effectively reduced media impact to reinforcement rather than change (Klapper, 1960). The most significant challenge here came from experimental studies that argued the importance of media as an agenda setter, famously influencing what people think *about*, even if not what they think (Iyengar and Kinder, 1987; McCombs, 2004). Closely allied to agenda-setting studies, research drew from experiments in psychology (Kahneman, 2011) to highlight the significance of media "framing" and "priming" for organizing not only what issues voters think about, but how they think about them, "encouraging citizens to understand events and issues in particular ways" (Kinder, 2003: 359). Following Goffman's pioneering *Frame Analysis* (1974), framing, defined as a schema of interpretation that promotes particular problem definitions and explanations at the expense of possible alternatives, has become arguably the leading theoretical approach to understanding media influence. Frames, as Goffman put it, organize our experience. Thus, as Holbrook (1996) argued, a major problem with the limited effects consensus was exactly *method*. Most of the analysis was predicated on models of voting behavior designed to elicit the importance of issues or partisan identification, and therefore any campaign or media effects were perceived as residual, after controlling for these other primary influences. These methods could not capture *indirect* effects on voting, influences upon opinion that feed into voters' decisions, knowledge, and attitudes to issues, parties, leaders, and candidates. They could not account for what is now often called "mediation," the idea that media are the constant presence in shaping our everyday experience of the world.

Third, and this was the most radical change, campaign research broadened its entire focus. It rejected the idea that the only significant question about campaigns was if they change individuals' votes. Instead, the new set of questions ranged from the large and general – how campaigns matter for the democratic process as a whole – to the particular – which specific campaign

TABLE 5.2. *How Campaigns Matter: Types of Effects*

	Intentional	Unintentional
Micro	Knowledge gain Perceptional change Mobilization Persuasion Activation Reinforcement Conversion	Knowledge gain Perceptional change (De)motivation Support/alienation
Macro	Electoral success Agenda setting Framing debate Public knowledge	Decline of elite responsiveness (De)legitimation (De)mobilization Elite transformation Party transformation

Source: Farrell and Schmitt-Beck (2002: 13).

activities are associated with knowledge gain, persuasion, and mobilization of individual voters.

Farrell and Schmitt-Beck (2002) categorize the range of effects according to levels of analysis (macro and micro) and by whether impacts are intentional or simply a by-product of the campaign process, whether intended or not. Table 5.2 summarizes the potential effects of campaigns according to these categories.

Macro effects refer to national-, system-, and aggregate-level impact and raise crucial criteria for judgments about good campaigns. The premise of macro concerns is that elections are critical to the health of democracy: they select rulers, shape policy, elevate conflict to the plane of discussion, and cement the connection between the public and its leaders. Voting at elections is the prime formal mechanism for public legitimation of politicians' policy programs and is the main act of political participation undertaken by most citizens. Thus, as Swanson and Mancini say (1996: 1):

> The manner in which democracies conduct their election campaigns is in some ways as important as the results of voting. The concept of democracy rests, after all, on a view of appropriate procedures for selecting representatives and making political decisions.

Hence, it matters greatly for the quality and nature of representation whether campaigns provide sufficient and accurate information about future policies and past record to enable informed choices. It matters for elite responsiveness that campaigns deal with the issues of importance to citizens and that campaigns mobilize rather than demobilize voter participation. As a consequence, much campaign studies research is dedicated to examining the quality of campaign discourse, both within the news and from the contenders. In the main, it returns an anxious verdict under the combined weight of professionalized campaigning and an increasingly depoliticized media (Cappella and Jamieson, 1997; Patterson, 2002; Coleman and Blumler, 2009; Negrine et al., 2007). It has noted the absolute decline in substantive political prime-time news at elections (Scammell and Semetko, 2008), and within the diminishing news hole a shift to softer, more interpretative news, highlighting the horse race, candidate personality and performance, and polls and strategies over the harder news of policy and issues. It has reported with alarm the tendency, particularly marked in the United States, to go negative (Ansolabehere and Iyengar, 1997), feeding voter cynicism about politicians and potentially demobilizing voters. While there is dispute about the methods upon which the evidence rests (Jamieson, 2000), the results, and their interpretation (Pippa Norris, for example, argues consistently for a "virtuous circle" of attention to news and participation), there is no doubt that these are fundamental issues for judging a good campaign. They take us beyond the obsession with success, which is such a feature of campaigners' assessments, or even the narrow political science focus of impact on voting behavior. It is not uncommon for campaigners to lament their opponents' use of negative tactics or exploitation of voters' base emotions of greed and fear (Scammell, 1995). Occasionally, as was the case with Bush in 2004, consultants such as Greenberg and Carville (2004) argue that a candidate's (Bush's) policy-free promotion had left the winner "with no mandate for his policy agenda." These complaints connect with basic principles of democratic representation, but as yet they scarcely feature in consultants' discussions of ethical conduct, and not at all in their judgments of a good campaign.

The micro category may be grouped into three key areas: political knowledge, persuasion effects, defined broadly to include changes in perception of issue salience (agenda setting) and attitudes toward the contenders as well as the ultimate voting decision, and mobilization. There has been an outpouring of research on these aspects over the past thirty years, focusing especially on the influence of media, advertising, and specific campaign events such as televised debates on public agendas, citizen learning and attitudes, and voter mobilization. The list of significant contributions is far too long to detail here (for brief overviews see Norris et al., 1999; Vavreck, 2009; Farrell and Schmitt-Beck, 2002; Iyengar and Simon, 2000; Holbrook, 1996). However, it is fair to conclude that the new consensus is that campaigns do matter, and can have a significant, even if not decisive, impact upon citizens' engagement and understanding of candidates and elections. In summary, attention to campaign news is associated with knowledge gains (Norris, 2000; Norris and Inglehart, 2009); campaign intensity affects citizens' propensity to engage (Popkin, 1992); citizens' affective (emotional) engagement with campaigns impacts their propensity for learning and action (Marcus et al., 2000); agenda setting has been found to be variable but significant across a variety of campaigns, while framing and the tone of news (negative or positive) continues to be a productive source of research (Just et al., 1996, Norris et al., 1999; de Vreese and Lecheler, 2012); and political advertising effects, even if variable and highly contested (for an overview, see Kaid and Holtz-Bacha, 2006), are certainly significant. As Vavreck (2009: 166) concludes in her examination of U.S. presidential campaigns, "the message matters"; the economy continues to be the great backdrop, but "the scenery is important ... as Shakespeare said, 'the play's the thing.'"

SO WHAT IS A GOOD CAMPAIGN?

The new consensus now among academic researchers and practitioners is that campaigns are important, and arguably more important than ever. However, beyond that, we can draw out two broad and distinct, even if overlapping, perspectives about why they are important: one is concerned with effectiveness, and the extent to which campaigns directly and indirectly impact voting decisions; while the second comprises democratic dimensions, and the ways in which campaigns impact desirable democratic goals. It is this second perspective that returns us to a driving concern of this book: the development of criteria by which we can judge political communication performance in the light of democratic ideals.

Extending the discussion of macro impacts, we can see that campaigns may affect the fundamentals of democratic politics. They affect the quality of the linkages between elites and citizens, raising issues about the responsiveness of elites to public concerns as well as accountability of elites for the past and present behavior. The communication environment provided by campaigns may impact the quality of vote decisions and the extent to which they are truly informed, and "correct" in the rational choice sense that vote decisions accurately match subjective judgments of voter interests (Lau and Redlawsk, 2006). Campaigns may foster or hinder participation. Elections provide system legitimacy, and thus campaigns are continuing tests of the fairness of electoral competition and of public perception of the democratic process overall. Mobilization is a key function, both intentional and unintentional, of campaigns. It is the major reason why, almost irrespective of the quality of information, it is possible, with Popkin (1992) and Schumpeter (1943), to champion pageantry, showbiz glitz, and adversarial clamor as essential lubricants of the electoral process.

Drawing on these points, Table 5.3 sets out the key criteria for judging a "good" campaign from a democratic perspective. Few of these criteria are likely to be controversial from an ideal perspective. Just two differ slightly from the macro effects as set out in Table 5.2: the importance of affective investment, which draws on earlier discussions of political brands and the significance of affective (or emotional) intelligence in participation and decision making; and the separation of the ideas of responsiveness and accountability. The significance of the latter is that these two processes are not the same, as Manin, Przeworski, and

TABLE 5.3. *Democratic Dimensions of a Good Election Campaign*

Democratic Dimensions	
Civic Dimensions (Micro)	System Dimensions (Macro)
Encourage political learning (about policies, issues, parties and candidates, and political processes)	Increase public knowledge (increase the stock of political knowledge across the electorate as a whole)
Encourage affective investment (promote individual sense that election matters to them by, e.g., drumming up enthusiasm, offering hope, raising anxiety about key issues, etc.)	Promote accountability (provide scrutiny of parties/candidates records/promises)
Increase sense of efficacy (promote idea that individual vote matters and can effect change)	Promote responsiveness of political elites (encourage elites to match programs with public concerns)
Activate citizen mobilization (convert interest into action, e.g., voting, campaigning)	Provide system legitimacy (overall satisfaction with democratic process as a fair contest and representation of public opinion)

Stokes (1999) argue in their account of representative democracy. Elite responsiveness is indeed a desirable function of elections; a fundamental characteristic of democracy is that elections ensure that contenders for office must be at least periodically responsive to citizen preferences. Accountability involves a separate dimension; it is the notion of a sort of contract between rulers and voters. The idea is that candidates are elected on the basis of promises, and if they honor those promises, the contract will be renewed. Thus accountability requires accurate and critical scrutiny not just of candidates' records, but, if that contract is to be meaningful, of the credibility of their promises and competence to deliver.

However, the objection can be made that these criteria are too ideal; that in practice the winning imperative too often conflicts with these desirable norms. Campaigns will inevitably distort information to spin the best possible case for candidates, and the worst for opponents. At the same time, disciplined messaging is a hallmark of modern campaigns, and this often seems to require the avoidance of scrutiny and restriction of public and media opportunities to question candidates. By the same token, campaigns may seek to limit future accountability; they either make promises so small and incremental that they are easily satisfied or so large and impossibly general that they could never be held to a standard of objective judgment. Responsiveness, surely, is signaled by the proliferation of politicians' "listening" initiatives and the willingness to tailor programs according to voter research; but equally such responsiveness is often partial, ignores vast swathes of the electorate, and concentrates on target voters deemed essential for success. A similar point could be made with respect to mobilization; it is not just that campaigns concentrate only on battleground territory, it is also that it may be in campaigners' interest to demobilize opponents' supporters. Such tactics are familiar in the negative campaigning of the United States but also are evident elsewhere; the UK Conservatives, for example, followed such a strategy in the 2001 general election. Beyond all this, there may be the objection (explored further in the following chapter) that campaigns do relatively little to generate enthusiasm and interest, except among the small core of the already committed.

In general terms all the objections have some force. However, the larger point is whether the winning imperative somehow inherently or inevitably clashes with these desirable norms. The answer to that question is a reasonably confident "no." The confidence springs partly from real-world examples of campaigns that do generate enthusiasm, encourage participation, enable scrutiny, and demonstrate responsiveness. The outstanding instance of this is of course Barack Obama's 2008 campaign; hailed as brilliant by its opponents for its sharp strategy and disciplined organization, it also energized activism, provided emotional connection, encouraged participation, and (although more arguably) enabled accountability through a clear policy agenda.

"Centuries from now, books will still be written about the 2008 extravaganza," says Sabato (2010: 31). It is possible, and does happen, that campaigners can do well out of doing good; and the task now is to find ways to encourage that.

SUMMARY

This chapter's purpose was to understand and define what is meant by "good" campaigning. It proposed that there are two key elements here: effectiveness and democratic dimensions. It provided an overview of academic and practitioner perspectives and found that, while there is some overlap, there is a sharp distinction in emphasis. Campaigners overwhelmingly stress the issue of effectiveness, while increasingly academics look to the democratic dimensions.

We paid a good deal of attention to problems of evidence. Much of this was about how practitioners claim effectiveness for their activities. However, it is also important to note that researchers too have difficulties with evidence in a field where comparative study is still in its infancy. Thus, making sense of what campaigners around the world think is rather like building a patchwork quilt built out of multicolored material: surveys, interviews, various individual analyses of campaigns internationally, content analysis of campaign material, political media, and trade literature. Much of this reflects the situation in the United States; this is simply where the most abundant evidence is. However, there have been some important internationally comparative studies, about campaign managers' opinions, about use of advertising, and about campaigning generally. In short, there is enough evidence now to be confident that our patchwork quilt shows some interesting patterns.

Results and effectiveness drive campaigners' work. The key factors in effectiveness are money, strategy-driven consistent messaging and agenda setting, and candidate qualities. It is reasonable to assume, and indeed the evidence suggests, that the weighting of these factors varies across countries, and is strongly conditioned by electoral and media regulation. These factors are all to be expected and flow logically from the earlier discussion (Chapter 2) of campaigners' self-assessments of their work. Perhaps the one surprise to emerge from comparative opinion surveys was the relatively high ranking of candidate image in the nonpresidential elections of Western Europe compared to the United States, the apparent epicenter of personalized politics. It was suggested that this was not because candidate qualities are unimportant in the United States; far from it. However, there is the tantalizing implication that the more professionalized campaigning is, the more candidates come to be considered as just one among a few key campaign inputs. In a good campaign the candidate follows the strategy at least as much as the other way round.

Overall, the discussion of campaigners' views highlights the connections between political and commercial marketers' assessments of effectiveness. This is strongly indicated in the political move to "metrics" to organize and benchmark campaigns. The direct evidence for this was drawn from the United States – Karl Rove's pioneering campaigns for George W. Bush and, following that, the key role of metrics in Obama's organization. The significance of metrics has generally been overlooked in accounts of Obama's campaign, which have understandably focused on its ability to generate colossal enthusiasm and supporter initiative especially through the Internet. However, the account of Obama's campaign manager, David Plouffe (2009), leaves no doubt about the importance of metrics. Although we do not yet have evidence of the international spread of this American-born campaign technique, it is a reasonable assumption that it will do so. America, if not the model, provides the archetype of modern campaigning for the world (Swanson and Mancini, 1996). Campaigners generally, with their obsession with effectiveness, inevitably will be drawn to techniques that seem to promote efficiency.

The academy too has never lost a concern with effects, although the trajectory of research has moved from direct to indirect impacts with increasing focus on agenda setting and framing, advertising impacts, media use, and citizen knowledge and assessment of candidates and parties. In general, the significance of these moves has been to change that old question, "do campaigns matter?" to "*how* do campaigns matter?" The emerging consensus is that campaigns matter way beyond direct influence on votes to what we can call the democratic dimensions. This is the idea that elections are still the most important single moments of participation for most citizens and are crucial to the health of democracy. They shape the nature and quality of our representation, and thus it matters greatly how they are conducted and reported in the media.

Finally, this chapter took a leap. We moved from discussing the general macro and micro democratic functions and effects of campaigns to propose a model of how we might evaluate the democratic dimensions of a "good" campaign. This brought together the two key elements that recur in just about every normative assessment of campaigning: the issue of mobilization (do campaigns mobilize or demobilize voters?) and the quality of information (is it sufficiently accurate, appropriate, and substantive?). This model does not counterpose substance and style as though they were opposites; rather it suggests that both are necessary for citizen motivation and rational choices. A good campaign will both encourage affective investment, and this may well be through image and style, and promote accountability, and that will require appropriate and accurate information. Campaigns in practice doubtless often, maybe usually, fall short of these ideals. However, on many of these dimensions they often also partially succeed. Judged by these standards, there is nothing inherently antithetical about campaigning practice and democratic ideals. The next chapter explores how marketing insight can help us find ways to bring closer the fit between ideals and practice.

6

Citizen Consumers, Political Marketing, and Democracy

This chapter concerns the third task of this book: to consider whether and how marketing might enhance democratic politics, for parties and for citizens. Political marketing not only is compatible, but is predicted by economic theories of democracy (Schumpeter, 1943; Downs, 1957). However, it is one thing to recognize that marketing of some sort is inherent in competitive democracies, it is another to claim it as a potential force for good.

In part, as suggested in the introduction, the risk is to be too dependent upon dispiriting "realist" theories of democracy: Schumpeter's elite competition in which the largely uninterested public exists primarily as a body to be mobilized at election times; and Downs's view of instrumental rationality in which political actors calculate self-interest. Both theories explain the existence of political marketing, if not its precise form in practice. Moreover, these theories, even if widely criticized, have enduring analytical power and influence on practice (Hay, 2007; Shapiro, 2002). They direct us to the importance of political structures, particularly the design and regulation of electoral and media systems. The significance of democratic design has become a key area of contemporary political science research and is crucial to the development of a democratically controlled political marketing. However, both theories fall into the category that Barber

(2003a) calls "thin" democracy; that is, they are relatively minimal models, seeking effective procedures for the protection of rights and the peaceful transfer of power between competitors for government, but have little to say about the encouragement of a more participatory democracy.

Increasingly, political marketing scholarship is uncomfortable with the routine linking of marketing to elite theory. Partly this is because there are a variety of marketing models in theory and practice, some which show a more natural affinity to more participatory visions of democracy. Relationship marketing is the preferred candidate here (Henneberg et al., 2009; Johansen, 2012; Yannas, 2008). It is also because, when examined in practice, "instrumental political marketing management" may not be doing what elite theory seeks: the election of those most fit to rule. The threat to leadership is one of the most common complaints against political marketing if competent but media-awkward candidates are sidelined in favor of celebrity and the political offer is rendered cautious, determined by polls and focus groups. Ultimately, however, judgments about the potential of political marketing as a force for good will be shaped by attitudes to democracy itself, what it is and what it should rightly be. Equally, though, it is important to recognize that neither is marketing one thing and there are a variety of models in practice and theory, related to the specifics of particular markets.

However, the main point here is not to advocate a particular model but to examine the ways in which commercial marketing generally might provide lessons for political practice, specifically how it can point us in the direction of a more ethically responsible, democratically controlled, and participatory political marketing. Underpinning this is the concern that, even assuming the most well-intentioned efforts of political marketing practitioners to connect with voters (see, e.g., Mattinson, 2010), we are living in an era consumed with anxieties of "democratic deficits" and "crises of democracy" (Norris, 2011; Pharr and Putnam, 2000). Around the democratic globe there is a broad trend to increasingly "critical" citizens, more detached from parties and politicians and less impressed with their performances. The point here is not that political marketing is a major culprit – although it certainly stands accused (Hay, 2007; Henneberg, 2004) – nor that it can provide simple solutions; rather it is that if marketing's main function is mobilization (à la Schumpeter) and that its primary justification is connection, it is clearly failing on the job. In short, how can political marketing be part of the solution rather than part of the problem?

COMMERCIAL MARKETING AND DEMOCRACY

Marketers in practice typically concern themselves narrowly with their own company's interests, and tend not to consider their broader impact on society and democracy. Marketing textbooks, if they address the subject at all, offer something along the following lines: marketing creates "value for society" by providing an efficient flow of goods and improving standards of living (Quelch and Jocz, 2007). It is a neat circle. Effectively, marketing activities oil the machinery of markets; markets provide the economic bedrock of democracy; therefore, marketing is automatically democratically beneficial. Simply by being legally compliant, avoiding fraud and deception, marketing contributes to public well-being.

There are influential theoretical underpinnings for this, notably liberal economist Milton Friedman, who distinguished sharply between economics and politics. Famously, Friedman (1970) argued that the only social responsibility of business was to increase profits through "open and free competition without deception or fraud." The job of allocating economic resources for social ends was a *political* – not a business – task. Therefore, he concluded that pressure for corporate social responsibility (CSR) amounted to "an assertion that those who favor taxes and expenditures ... have failed to persuade a majority of their fellow citizens to be of like mind and ... are seeking to attain by undemocratic procedures what they cannot attain by democratic procedures."

This strand of thinking typifies the conservative view in a debate about business and societal responsibility that extends over centuries (Carroll and Shabana, 2010). The call for responsibility has traveled through various manifestations from general social philanthropy to our contemporary wave of "ethical" business and global corporate citizenship. However, it was not until the 1990s upsurge of consumer activism that Friedman-like hostility received sustained challenge. The clamor for corporate citizenship now comes from virtually all directions; from on high from the United Nations, the European Union, the World Economic Forum, and the World Trade Organization, and from below from consumer activism and NGOs campaigning about human rights and the environment. Marketing has been forced to respond. However, typically, practitioners have focused on the "business case" for CSR; that ethical business reduces risk, enhances reputation, and leads to competitive advantage. Business bookstores are now awash with titles advising how to do well out of doing good; as leading marketing academic Philip Kotler counseled, social responsibility was the means to do "the most good for your company and your cause" (Kotler and Lee, 2004). As a matter of interest, Steve Hilton, a brand consultant and a leading architect of David Cameron's UK Conservatives with their small-state "Big Society" project, was prominent among these advocates for ethical business: "good business," he argued, was the best means to make profits and "change the world" for the better (Hilton and Gibbons, 2002).

Precisely because the business case for CSR is self-interested, albeit enlightened, it is easy to be skeptical of its grander claims of creating a fairer, more democratic world. As Benjamin Barber (2007: 303) notes, corporate citizenship is a "no brainer" when it results in increased profits and even when "profit neutral, it makes for good collateral marketing." The real test is whether business is prepared to sacrifice profit in the cause of public good, and Barber sees little sign of that in a world where "radical inequality is simply assumed" and "11.5 percent of the world's population controls 60 percent of the world's consumer spending" (p. 10). A danger of the business claims for CSR is the illusion that we can have it all; we can make profits, pursue the high comforts of affluence, and make the world a better more democratic place, all at the same time and without any real cost to ourselves. This is part of the process that Barber calls "infantilization." As *Harry Potter* tops adult reading lists and escapist adventure dominates the Hollywood box office, according to Barber, modern consumer capitalism fosters a juvenile me-more culture of instant gratification without wider consequences, in contrast to the "adult" recognition of public interest and social outcomes of individual actions.

The "civic schizophrenia" Barber describes, between the me-more childlike consumer and the public-aware adult, is observed also in politics. Deborah Mattinson (2010: 298), pollster for more than twenty-five years for the UK Labour Party, describes a "Peter Pan" phenomenon in her focus groups of undecided voters. Respondents often admit, says Mattinson, that they want to "have their cake and eat it"; they know that in reality they cannot, yet they "buy into promises that they suspect cannot be kept and then point the finger of blame when it goes wrong." The voter has become accustomed to being "indulged like a spoilt child by politicians desperately seeking their favor. They are offered gifts, made promises, sometimes lied to. Peter Pan politics creates a never-never land where politics is something that is done by politicians to voters, with voters only needing to take responsibility for casting their vote – and sometimes not even bothering to do that." Mattinson observes that her respondents, in romantic, almost childlike fashion, yearn for superheroes: "ideal" politicians, such as Nelson Mandela or the pre-presidential Obama, who are driven by noble aspirations, public service, and "never personal gain." Politicians, she argues, should try to "harness" this yearning. However, the superhero yearning has downsides. It is hardly surprising that most politicians, judged by such high standards, fall dismally short. Moreover (and although Mattinson does not say so), it may also increase perceptions of the distance between voters and politicians and decrease the possibilities of participation; since few of us consider ourselves superhero material, how can we make a difference in a political world peopled, as we imagine, by the ambitious, devious, and unscrupulously self-serving?

It is important not to overestimate the possibilities of CSR to bring about substantial democratic change. Equally, one should not *under*estimate the achievements of consumer activism (Micheletti and Stolle, 2007; Cohen, 2003; Glickman, 2009; Hilton, 2009). Citizen consumers have wrought significant beneficial changes in corporate behavior; "shopping for human rights" has forced the issue of ethical business into the mainstream and into the boardrooms. They have expanded the parameters of corporate reputation to include civic dimensions beyond legal compliance, honesty in product claims, and reliability of performance. They have forced a broad debate in business practice and theory about socially beneficial marketing. These are not trivial achievements. And this is the first lesson that commercial markets can offer politics; a critical mass of critical consumers can make a difference and arguably are essential catalysts of change. If political marketing is to become part of the solution to the democratic deficit it needs something similar: a critical mass of critical political marketing citizen-consumers who can force politicians and campaigners to consider how they can do well out of doing good. A crucial step in this process is political marketing literacy; the critical ability to differentiate between honest promotion and empty spin, between a genuine commitment to connection with voters and a shallow massaging of message. In short, it requires the development of critical standards of evaluation of political marketing.

At the same time, citizen consumerism is not enough on its own. There is, inscribed in the logic of markets, a tension with democratic aims. This is the tension described some thirty years ago by those towering figures of pluralism, Robert Dahl (1985) and Charles Lindblom (1977). Both accepted that the market is the twin of liberal democracy; markets thrive best in democratic society, and conversely liberal democracy has not survived anywhere without markets. But equally markets can inflict harm if left to their own devices. As Dahl put it (1985: 60), without restraint from government, the logic of profit threatens the welfare of citizens and engenders a mighty corporate capitalism that brings about "severe violations of political equality and hence of the democratic process."

Harvard Business School professors John Quelch and Katherine Jocz (2007: 275) offer an intriguing advance on the usual "citizen brand" advocacy precisely because their approach is informed by Dahl's critique. They examine marketing as a social force (rather than individual company practice) in the light of ideals of Dahl's rights-based democracy. "Does marketing undermine democracy?" they ask. Albeit unwittingly but precisely because of its success, "the answer may be yes." Marketing has contributed to a culture of materialism and individualism, and it has been able to capitalize on the forces of modernization – increasing affluence, social fragmentation, and complexity – in a way that civic society has not. While membership of traditional social-trust-inducing institutions, such as churches, political parties, and trade unions, has declined, brands have competed "successfully for an even bigger share of the finite level of loyalty that each of us can bestow." Marketing, with its colossal resources dedicated to motivating brand loyalty, is able to create and sustain bonds of trust in contrast to the apparently dwindling trust in civic life. Viewed from a macro perspective, it appears that the stock of social trust has shifted from civil society to consumption. And so, the authors concede, that arch-critic Barber has a point when he argues that marketing "is sucking up the air from every other domain to sustain the sector devoted to consumption" (Barber, 2007: 212).

Thus, and in line with Dahl's view, Quelch and Jocz agree that marketing must be subordinated to democratic control, or citizen sovereignty, as they call it. Marketing, they argue, "should be more conscious" of its deep social impact (p. 272), and not just narrowly concern itself, Friedman-like, with individual company profits. Thus marketing needs effective regulatory frameworks to ensure a fair consumer marketplace and entrench citizen sovereignty. Good marketing, from a societal point of view, requires many elements: regulation of markets and promotional claims, consumer protection, reliable information, ethical standards, consumer choice, activism, and mutual respect between buyers and sellers. Marketing, just as markets, thrives best in democratic society: "Without citizen sovereignty over societal institutions, including marketing, consumers – and many businesses – will be less well off" (p. 276).

However, Quelch and Jocz insist, marketing is democratic in its essential characteristics. The authors examine marketing in the United States set against Dahl's (1998) five conditions of ideal democracy: effective participation by citizens, equality in opportunity to vote and equal counting of votes, enlightened understanding on the part of citizens, the opportunity for all citizens to control and choose the agenda, and inclusion of all adults. Judged by these measures, the consumer market outperforms the political marketplace in the United States, they suggest. It is more inclusive, provides greater possibilities for choice and agenda control, and is more encouraging of participation. Consumer markets have in-built incentives to increase consumption and therefore reach all sectors of society, even the relatively poor. Huge profits are there for companies that combine high volume, low prices, and reliable quality. By contrast in U.S. politics – and arguably in most first-past-the-post electoral systems – the value of voters is governed by geography, and the relative importance of constituencies, states, and districts for determining results; or, as in the presidential primaries, by positioning in the calendar. The first-past-the-post voting system and the monopoly of the two major parties reduce incentives to increase political "consumption"; rather they encourage parties to perform ever more intensive targeting of those citizens who are most likely to vote in the key states and districts. Given the strong correlations among poverty, low education, and nonvoting, there is a strong case that the U.S. political marketplace is less inclusive and in that sense less democratic than the consumer equivalent.

The act of exchange (buying and voting) offers a telling example of how politics can learn from marketing. Consumer business attempts to make buying a relatively efficient, convenient, and pleasant experience, conducted normally within a spirit of mutual trust and civility. By contrast U.S. politics seems almost determined to make voting difficult: "The patchwork of state and local regulation of voting registration is not conducive to universal participation" (Quelch and Jocz, 2007: 191). The procedures of registration are sometimes cumbersome, same-day registration is rarely allowed, and eligibility to vote varies from state to state, some permanently denying votes to convicted criminals. The act of voting itself is often conducted in makeshift and unattractive venues, while voters are confronted with unfamiliar and diverse voting methods including punch cards, lever machines, and paper ballots. For consumers accustomed to automated cash machines, it is a throw-back experience, especially when countries such as "Brazil, India and Mexico have leapfrogged the United States in the use of sophisticated electronic voting" (p. 193; see also Brady and McNulty, 2011).

Quelch and Jocz's arguments can be condensed into two main factors, even if they do not put it this way themselves: first, the importance of the structure of the marketplace, and its propensity to offer choice and fair competition and encourage participation. In this their conclusion runs with the grain of contemporary political research into democratic design, including electoral systems and regulations. Second is the experiential dimension, and the importance of attending to people's enjoyment of the experience of participation. The latter may be marketing's most distinctive contribution. The idea of emotional (affective) involvement has become a leading strand in political psychology research, but the notion of enjoyment and that citizens might find pleasure in the experience of citizenship is hardly explored. These two dimensions – structure and experience – are the keys as we focus more closely on political marketing, its relationship with democracy, and its cues for politics.

THE IMPORTANCE OF STRUCTURE

Attention to democratic design has increased enormously over the past thirty years, triggered by real-world events. The emerging democracies of Eastern Europe, Latin America, and Asia sought new democratic constitutions, while following a period of some forty years of remarkable stability in electoral systems some older democracies embarked on substantive reform. The modern doyen of electoral systems research, Arend Lijphart

(1999), noted only one major reform (France) of the electoral systems in the years 1945–90 in twenty-seven established democracies. Since then there have been fundamental changes in Israel, Austria, Belgium, Japan, New Zealand, Italy, and the UK (Norris, 2004). These events, coupled with mounting global concern about participation and a crisis of democracy, have fueled an explosion of research into the links between electoral systems and particular outcomes, such as voter participation and satisfaction, representation of women and minorities in parliaments, trends toward oligopoly or multiparty systems, and so on (Gallagher and Mitchell, 2005).

In broad terms there are patterns of difference associated with the two major categories of electoral system, proportional representation (PR) and first-past-the-post or single-member plurality (SMP) constituencies. Compared to SMP systems, PR tends to produce multiparty competition, greater numbers of women elected to office, and higher voter turnout. However, the precise causes of these patterns are less well understood. Norris suggests two broad explanatory perspectives. The first, rational-choice institutionalism, claims that "formal electoral rules generate important incentives that are capable of shaping and constraining political behavior" (Norris, 2004: 7). These rules include the legal framework covering elections, but also constitutional conventions, codes of conduct, and administrative procedures and regulation, including fairness and balance rules, of the media information environment. Political actors and voters, as rational self-interest optimizers, will respond to incentives and thus modify their behavior. The second perspective, which Norris calls "cultural modernization theory," states that rational calculation of reward is constrained significantly by cultures and ingrained habits of behavior, "habits of the heart, rather than the strategic calculation" thus limits the capacity of rule reform to alter patterns of behavior, at least in the short term.

These hypotheses underpin the fifteen-year Comparative Study of Electoral Systems (CSES) project, which coordinates data from fifty national election studies across the world in an attempt to discover which "sort of electoral arrangements best serve popular representation" and to promote accountability, participation, and satisfaction with the democratic process (McAllister, 2005). The findings thus far support both of the underlying explanatory perspectives. Political culture, reflected in voters' "beliefs about representation," profoundly affects overall satisfaction with democracy (McAllister, 2005). However, the type of voting system also has a significant independent impact. Wider choice, associated with forms of PR, shows a statistically significant correlation with voters' satisfaction with the way democracy works. In short, the evidence from a growing number of studies confirms that structure affects outcomes: proportionality promotes greater choice, greater likelihood of multiparty competition, and greater prospects that citizens' views will be represented; first-past-the-post elections are associated with single-party governments and a more clear-cut chain of accountability.

Two key points emerge from this with respect to political marketing and democracy. First, structures affect the competitive conditions in which parties operate, which will in turn impact marketing strategies and behavior. Second, possibilities are constrained by the political cultures in which they operate. Both these points are in line with research in comparative political communication and electioneering, which has begun to blossom over the past twenty years (Plasser, 2002; Swanson and Mancini, 1996; Bowler and Farrell, 1992; Butler and Ranney, 1992; Esser and Pfetsch, 2004; Strömbäck and Kaid, 2008; Lilleker and Marshment, 2005). However, system distinctions typically are made between candidate- and party-based contests, and the thrust of the comparison is usually to discover whether "country X is or is not becoming more like the United States (for good or for ill)" (Norris, 2009: 2)

Occasionally researchers have applied marketing theory to electoral settings, and the most promising of these is Collins and Butler's (1996) application of marketing theory to party competitive positioning. They note that PR effectively increases the range of strategic options compared to SMP. For example, PR encourages "niche" marketing strategies; it offers the prospect of long-term sustainability for parties that may have no ambition to become market leaders but are content to hold market share, appealing to voters on the basis of ideology, region, ethnicity, or other minority interest. Equally, parties with ambitions for office have a variety of options: they might attempt to swallow other nichers, or enter alliances with other parties, or challenge the market leader directly, often by assimilating the more attractive parts of the market leader's offer, and so on. The last option, copying the marketing leader, is a typical strategy for challengers in oligopolistic competition, especially when incumbents have served two or more terms. Thus, in politics, just as in commerce, "product" standardization is a characteristic of oligopoly; and this, of course, was predicted by Duverger's famous law (1964) which states that first-past-the-post electoral SMP systems tend toward two-party oligopoly, with relatively minor policy differences as each attempts to command the center ground.

Collins and Butler's competitive positioning approach dovetails with political science approaches to political systems and electoral strategy. Norris (2004) summarizes the latter as "bridging" and "bonding" strategies. "Bridging" arises typically where systems present high hurdles to election and is associated most closely with the SMP model where parties need a plurality or majority to win in each district. Thus, they are incentivized to pursue median voter strategies, focusing on issues of most concern to the broadest swathe of voters. This is the "catch-all" strategy, associated with Kirchheimer's (1966) postideological parties. Bridging parties, because they need to aggregate interests, tend to create "cross-cutting allegiances" across faiths, regions, identities, generations, and ethnicities. Hence, they are relatively loose umbrella organizations, "highly permeable ... characterized by easy-entrance, easy-exit among voters rather than fixed lifetime loyalties" (Norris, 2004: 10). By contrast, bonding strategies are enabled by the lower electoral thresholds associated with PR systems; parties can win significant numbers of seats in parliaments on relatively small vote shares and thus do not have the same imperative to cast wide their nets. Thus, they can bond with particular relatively homogenous sectors of society, whether by religion, region, ethnicity, ideology, and so on. Bonding parties, Norris suggests, "are sticky organizations, promoting the interests of their own members and developing tightly knit social networks and clear 'one-of-us' boundaries."

Marketing scholars may recognize in these descriptions of nichers and bonding parties some affinity with relationship marketing, a paradigm of increasing interest for both commerce and politics. Relationship marketing has been the main challenger to the managerial or "instrumental" marketing school; the former was traditionally identified with the selling of services, the latter with fast-moving consumer goods. The main differences between them are that relationship marketing relies for profit on long-term trust-building interactions with customers and stakeholders, while managerial marketing conceives of exchange as discrete transactions with customers of relatively short duration with sharply distinct beginnings and endings (Morgan and Hunt, 1994). Relationship marketing has reshaped the field of business marketing in recent years primarily because, in conditions of heightened competition in digital, global, deregulated markets, the cost of attracting new customers is disproportionately high compared to the cost of retaining business. Hence, business has increased incentives to develop strategies to retain existing customers, to extract "lifetime value" (Scammell, 2003). Relationship marketing has attracted the interest of political marketing scholars because, with its emphasis on cooperative networks of stakeholders and long-term relationships built on trust, it appears more suited than instrumental marketing to address contemporary political concerns of declining participation, dwindling party membership, and lack of trust in political institutions (Henneberg et al., 2009; Johansen, 2005, 2012). It "inherently invites dialogue" and emphasizes core relationships with members, supporters, and other stakeholders and thus "provides incentives to develop political interest and engagement on an enduring basis" (Henneberg et al., 2009: 179).

The irony is that the "bonding" parties may be practicing, whether they know it or not, a more sustainable and participatory form of marketing than the more ostentatiously market-oriented "catch-all" parties, with their voter data banks, micro-targeting, and focus grouped messaging. The much-noted crisis of parties throughout much of the world is too deep and widespread to be attributed to single causes (Diamond and Gunther, 2001). Mair and van Biezen's (2001) analysis noted a major decline in party membership, both in absolute numbers and as a percentage of the electorate, across all the long-established European democracies in the period 1980–2000. They did not find a simple systemic difference between PR and majoritarian countries, although it is true that membership/electorate ratios were highest in countries operating varieties of PR (e.g., Austria, Finland, Norway, Greece, Belgium), while France, with its two-round system, and the UK, with a first-past-the-post system, were among the lowest. Political parties, they suggest, like other hierarchical organizations such as churches and trade unions, are impacted by trends of modernization: individualization and declining willingness to rely on hierarchical aggregator institutions to articulate increasingly "particularized" citizen demands. However, as they note, parties have "their own specific story," and part of this is that parties operating media-centered professionalized campaigns have had fewer incentives to recruit and maintain mass memberships. It is generally accepted now that the growth of political marketing – as typically understood to mean research-driven, professionalized, and mediated – has marginalized party members.

Sooner or later, the major parties under any system will have to reconsider their relationship with members if they want to remain sustainable mass-member parties. Passive memberships may suit leaders' short-term objectives, allowing freedom of policy and positional maneuver, and central control of messaging and campaigns. However, a reduced role as mere checkbook members or occasional cheerleaders for the leadership is unlikely to attract politically interested citizens who were once the life-blood of parties and gave them physical presence and enduring personal connection in the local communities of wider society. In short, it may be that dwindling memberships will provide the incentive for leaders to consider relationship marketing; they will have to "bond" as well as "bridge."

It is tempting to conclude that PR, in some variety, offers the superior system by broadening competition, increasing voter choice and participation, enabling more demographically representative parliaments, and increasing incentives for the politically interested citizens to work within the formal institutions of politics. Lijphart (1999) is unequivocal about this: the "consensus" democracies of the PR systems of Northern Europe have produced "kinder, gentler" democracies than the adversarial two-party systems of which the Westminster model is an archetype. His advice to young democracies is even more precise: consider the Danish PR system, which is closest to Lijphart's ideal of high proportionality and relative simplicity of operation. A review of expert opinion (Bowler, Farrell, and Pettitt, 2005) shows that most favor either the mixed systems of, most notably, Germany and New Zealand, or PR single transferrable vote systems, while the SMP systems of the United States, Canada, and the UK rank lowly but have strong supporters because of their enduring simplicity and propensity to produce stable governments.

Electoral systems have been emphasized here precisely because they tend to be neglected in political communications accounts. However, the overriding point is that rules matter, and because of this it should be possible to subject marketing in general and political marketing in particular to democratic control, or citizen sovereignty, as Quelch and Jocz have it. A powerful instrument of control is the presence of fairness rules in the campaigning and information environment. The power of money to distort fair competition in the political marketplace is well known and extends beyond campaigning into governing and policy-making processes. "The difficulty," Shapiro (2002: 246–47) notes, "is that, particularly in the United States, politicians compete in the first instance for campaign contributions and only secondarily for votes." It is reasonable to assume that "the proposals politicians offer are heavily shaped by the agendas of campaign contributors: why else would they contribute?" Mechanisms to create a more level playing field vary across countries and sometimes within countries. They include expenditure ceilings on national campaigns (e.g., Ireland, UK, Spain), public funding for parties and campaigns (apart from the UK most European countries provide public campaign funds, as do Canada, Israel, and also the United States, although at the discretion of presidential candidates), formal limits on campaign periods, and restrictions on paid advertising on television and/or the provision of free airtime for parties. There is also, of course, the question of media systems, the degree of media freedom, and competition and regulation on key matters of fairness and balance as between the reporting of parties. We know, for example, from comparative studies of election news that the degree of regulation and competition in media systems affects the fairness and balance of coverage, and encourages or inhibits the news to focus on substantive issues as opposed to the "horse race" and personality (Strömbäck and Kaid, 2008; Semetko et al., 1991; Strömbäck and Dimitrova, 2006). Broadly speaking, less regulation and more intense media competition are associated with less election news, more infotainment, and less substantive policy/issue news and analysis. We also have suggestive evidence that relates citizens' political knowledge with media consumption, finding higher knowledge scores associated with public service media use (Curran and Iyengar, 2009; Holtz-Bacha and Norris, 2001). Ultimately, then, there are many possibilities of democratic control. The likelihood of any rule changes and the impact of rule-based incentives are tempered by specific cultures, but this is clear: we do not need to merely lament the state of current political communication. We can examine, compare, and debate in concrete terms alternatives for change.

THE EXPERIENTIAL DIMENSION

On the one hand, we know that political activism is bound up with pleasure. For example, the pleasure of sociability is a continuing motivation for participation, as studies of parties and their members have shown repeatedly (Whiteley, Seyd, and Richardson, 1994; Bruter and Harrison, 2009). In fact, Bruter and Harrison found that sociability was the prime motivation of about 34 percent of young party members in six European democracies. Equally, history shows us repeatedly that pleasure goes hand in hand with popular participation: consider the grand pageants of the British women's suffrage movement at the turn of the twentieth century, the mix of politics and carnival in Gay and Lesbian Pride around the world, or more recently the exuberant outpouring of fun among the youthful pro-Obama activism of 2008. The examples abound. Schudson's (1999: 145) history of American civic life describes an era (1865–1900) when Americans "enjoyed" elections: the torchlight processions, the towering liberty poles, the glee clubs, musical bands, singers, and offerings of food and drink. He is struck by the commonplace intermingling of consumption and politics. "These were the years of the highest voter turnout in our entire history. Americans of that era ... found it [politics] simultaneously serious and entertaining, both intellectually and emotionally satisfying."

On the other hand, pleasure struggles to justify itself in accounts of modern political communication; it is not accepted as "proper" political discourse (Street, 2012). Infotainment, showbiz, attractiveness, and likeability of politicians are at best beside the point of proper politics; at worst they are sickly confections to mislead, trivialize, and capitalize on our irrationality and weakness as cognitive misers (Pratkanis and Aronson, 1991). Analyses of campaigns and media coverage of elections typically distinguish between substantive content (policies, issues, record, etc.) and nonsubstantive issues (personality, image, horse race, etc.). Typically, we regard the former as a genuine contribution to the democratic information environment; the latter is almost inherently troubling. It is as though the very idea of the light side, of entertainment or pleasure, belittles politics.

This takes us to the point, highlighted by Quelch and Jocz, that contrasted the paucity of political efforts to encourage participation compared to the considerable resources devoted by consumer markets to make shopping a comfortable, convenient, and pleasurable experience. The contrast is exemplified by the language of campaigning.

In commerce, the complexities of purchase decision lead marketers to radically conflicted views of consumers, summarized in the common marketing metaphors of love and war (Quelch and Jocz, 2007: 31). "The customer is someone to be conquered" as marketers attempt to "capture market segments" with "rifle versus shotgun marketing." At the same time the customer is also someone who needs to be "romanced over a long time through multiple exchanges and not just a single transaction," and thus marketing is replete with relationship metaphors. Marketing promotion, from design to delivery, is full of the language of love: relationship marketing, customer care, flattery of customer good taste and sense, and, of course, the overt wooing of customers with displays of attractiveness, glamour, and sex appeal.

In politics, war metaphors predominate. Campaigns are strategized in the "war room"; "war books" determine the lines of defense and offense in strategies and tactics. The "ground battle" denotes the fight to turn out target voters in the decisive districts, while campaigns wage "air wars" to set the agenda on television news and to outwit opponents in the advertising battle. Military metaphors are standard in modern campaigning, while, from the late 1980s on, negative advertising and hard-hitting attacks on opponents became hallmarks of the "modern" or "Americanized" campaign. It is not much of an exaggeration to suggest that the language of hate, certainly more than the language of love, is a distinctive characteristic of political contrasted to commercial marketing. Again, this was especially noticeable in the United States, even before the Arizona shootings of January 2011 sparked a national debate about the state of public discourse (Mutz and Reeves, 2005; Jamieson and Cappella, 2008). For many years now U.S. campaigns have tended to be exceptionally negative by international comparison. Tom Rosshirt (2008: 34), formerly speech writer for President Clinton, claims,

For the last nine elections, the Republicans have tried to define the Democratic nominee as "not one of us." He can't be for us, he's for the blacks ... gays; ... he hates the flag; ... he's against the military; ... he mocks religion; ... he's an elitist who looks down on us. The goal in its crudest form, is to convince millions of Americans that Democrats hate them, which is virtually the same thing as convincing millions of Americans that they should hate Democrats. It's tribal politics.

The United States may be exceptional in its polarized negativity, but since the mid-1990s Europe too witnessed widespread concern at what became commonly accepted as "crisis of public communication," involving a three-way breakdown of trust among media, politicians, and citizens (Coleman and Blumler, 2009). As Coleman and Blumler's influential "crisis" thesis summarizes, citizen interest is sidelined in a media/political game that squeezes the public spaces for constructive dialogue about policy. The mediated public sphere becomes a less welcoming place for citizens, dominated by "insiders," the spin doctors, and an increasingly disdainful media, whose dissection of the motives of spin was seen as encouraging cynicism.

However, romance is not completely absent in politics, and it is most evident in the personal appeal of leaders and candidates. Chapter 3, on the rebranding of Blair, offers a clear example of the analysis of a leader's popularity in terms of a romance gone wrong with voters. Blair is a paradigmatic example of the phenomenon of personalization, which itself is a defining characteristic of "modern" campaigning throughout the democratic globe (Swanson and Mancini, 1996). In truth, personalization is a complex concept that, despite its ubiquitous use in accounts of campaigning, is curiously underexplored empirically. Langer (2011) distinguishes between three facets of personalization, which although overlapping in practice are conceptually distinct and raise significantly different normative issues: the redistribution of power (from cabinets to leaders), increased campaign and media attention to leaders at the expense of other party actors, and, most troubling, a heightened focus on private qualities of personal life. The latter is what Langer calls the "politicization of private persona," and it is here that both the potential and the anxieties about personalization reside. The distinction matters; attention to leaders and their capacity to govern (strength, competence, intelligence, education, and so on) fit fairly comfortably within the traditional domain of rational political discourse. These are clearly legitimate "rational" questions for citizens to ask of would-be leaders. Increasingly, however, politicians reveal aspects of their private lives that have no obvious connection to their governing capacity: the nature of their family relationships, the movies, music, and sports they like, their favorites on *X Factor*, and even if they prefer (as in the case of David Cameron) to wear boxers rather than briefs. It is this politicization of the private that most clearly distinguishes modern personalization from earlier forms of leader emphasis. It is, argues Langer, an attempt by politicians to show themselves as "authentic" human beings and not merely distant leaders. This is the fault line that divides opinion about personalization as a force for good or ill.

It can be seen as "profoundly depoliticizing," as Hay (2007: 119) argues: as parties squabble over the center ground, so policy choices are insulated from public scrutiny, while "at the same time, it also serves to politicize a series of more ephemeral and non-policy matters – as personality contests replace the clash of competing policy trajectories in the determination of electoral outcomes." Personalization replaces politics: it creates a pseudo intimacy with citizens that can divert attention from the harder substantive politics of policy and record. Furthermore, it may, in a world of Peter Pan politics, be almost inevitably destined to disappoint, as superheroes are found to have feet of clay; almost inevitably in the real-world muddle of political compromise they may come to be seen as guilty of hypocrisy. Moreover, as politicians pour more of their private lives into the public arena so they become more vulnerable to the voracious media appetite for sex and personal scandal (Thompson, 2000; Castells, 2009).

Conversely the democratic potential of personalization resides precisely in its challenge to the rigid privileging of the "rational" in political discourse: "There is still not enough recognition in political communication that the personal, as well as the aesthetic and the emotional, are legitimate dimensions of politics which can play a positive role" (Langer, 2011: 170). Thus, personalization may be a route to "bridge the representative gap and inspire a further democratization of democracy" (Corner and Pels, 2003: 13) by making politicians more approachable and understandable. Personalization of politics invites us to engage our emotional intelligence and evaluate politicians by the normal standards of popular culture. It links distant high politics to the everyday. As

Langer (2011: 172) says, "It may help citizens to feel that, even if not like them, leaders are at least living on the same planet and sharing the same discursive universe." It, at least, has the virtue of being concerned with citizens' enjoyment of politics. It is the most obvious soft sell in politics, and it stands out by its contrast to the overwhelmingly hard sell of most political promotion.

This debate echoes the emotion versus reason concerns raised about political branding. In practice, of course, branding and personalization are clearly linked as party leaders are selected and promoted precisely as "brand differentiators." Again the Blair example is paradigmatic: he was the embodiment of the new "in touch" Labour Party, a marker of change as much from "old" Labour as from the Conservatives. Following his lead, and copying many of his methods (Langer, 2011), David Cameron set out to "detoxify" the Conservative brand. In each case the personality of the leader was a deliberate and key means to achieving social, psychological, and cultural resonance with voters.

In the case of the brand, it was argued that emotional connection was a legitimate and necessary part of political promotion in order to mobilize and encourage participation. The democratic potential of personalization is essentially the same point; citizens need to feel that they are indeed occupying the same planet as would-be leaders. To use Philip Gould's phrase, politicians must seek "permission" to be heard in an age of declining deference. Thus, for personalization as for branding, the correct question is not *should* we be suspicious, but *when* should we be suspicious of political promotion located in personal (and brand differentiator) emotional and cultural connectivity. For example, the personal may enhance the credibility of political promises; it is a reasonable, emotionally intelligent judgment to assess the sincerity of these promises in relation to the life experiences of the politicians. To use the Cameron case, protection of the National Health Service (NHS) was a key policy in the Conservatives' 2010 election campaign, and Cameron's personal sincerity was crucial to the credibility of this claim because his party was not widely trusted on this issue. However, sincerity of motivation, stemming from Cameron's experience of NHS care for his disabled son, should not substitute for concrete analysis of his health reform proposals (Langer, 2011: 173). Thus, the literate political marketing question is not whether personalization strategies are being used, but how they are being used, how well connected to substantive issue positions and records, and whether we can detect an attempt to substitute personal sincerity for examination of the "hard" evidence of proposals and record.

THE LEGITIMACY OF PLEASURE IN POLITICS

The position we are now in, where pleasure must justify its place in proper politics, is, Schudson (2007) suggests, the legacy of a commendable, but ultimately joyless, modernization of politics over the turn of the nineteenth and twentieth centuries. The Progressives' reforms to eradicate corruption, patronage, and petty bribery also swept away mass enjoyment of politics. They caused, he suggests, the "purification of citizenship": a politics "cleansed of the souvenirs, the sensuous experience and the small everyday rewards that once enhanced political life. No more Election Day hooliganism ... no more festivity, no more emotionalism and soccer team style loyalties. The new voter should be motivated by ideas and ideals and information, not by social pressure or the social pleasure of a free drink and an extra dollar in the pocket" (Schudson, 2007: 245). Ultimately, he argues, removing the consumer-like pleasures from politics "is a task democracies undertake at their peril."

Schudson's point is made within the particular Puritan-influenced history of the United States. However, its conceptual thrust – the challenge to commonplace binary oppositions of citizen and consumer, substance and style, emotion and reason – has resonance way beyond the United States. It emerges whenever scholars find merit in the popular in political culture (e.g., Corner and Pels, 2003; Goodwin, Jasper, and Polletta, 2001; Langer, 2011; Richards, 2004; Scammell, 2003; Scammell and Langer, 2006; Street, 2012; Van Zoonen, 2004). The burgeoning literatures on, for example, social movements increasingly reject as a false dichotomy the opposition of emotion and reason. For Goodwin et al. (2001: 9), Max Weber set social science down a far too narrow path of associating emotion with irrationality, whereas, when we examine the world around us, we find that emotion accompanies "rational acts as fully as irrational ones, positive experiences as much as negative ones." In a similar vein, Pels (2003) uses the idea of emotional intelligence to justify "aesthetic politics." Contrasting the Romantic to the Enlightenment traditions of political thought, he argues that the former – politics as art, spectacle, style, and emotion – has become associated with radical right-wing projects, most obviously the fascism of Mussolini's Italy and Hitler's Germany. The Nazis are the terrifying epitome of aesthetic politics, and their legacy is so powerful that it continues to structure modern debates, rendering as suspicious any political manifestation of "style over substance." In fact, Pels says, aesthetic stylization is an inherent feature of mass politics, democratic as well as totalitarian; there is no necessary, "essential" connection between aesthetic politics and the irrationalism (or antirational) as embodied in totalitarianism. To champion the importance of style and aesthetics in democratic politics is "not to sell-out to irrationalism," rather it is to redefine "the domain of political rationality ... broadened in order to encompass the emotional political intelligence of ordinary citizens" (Pels, 2003: 57).

These critiques help unlock us from rigid dichotomies of thought. And this is a vital first step if we want to develop standards for evaluating political communication in terms of "fidelity to democratic ideals," as Street (2003: 97) puts it. Surely a good campaign will appeal to our minds and hearts, invite our senses, and stimulate our intellects. This is not to deny that there are important distinctions between emotion and reason, style and substance, and citizen and consumer. These distinctions are essential at an analytical level as we attempt to find ways to distinguish the democratically good from bad. However, it is to say that these distinctions are not binary oppositions; attention to style does not necessarily diminish substance. The lesson from marketing is to the contrary, that we examine how substance and style work together and how harmoniously they are linked.

SUMMARY AND CONCLUSION

This chapter started from two premises: that marketing of some sort is inscribed in the process of competitive representative democracy, and that political marketing as it currently exists is often problematic. It neither satisfies competitive elite theory that elections should return those most fit to rule, nor does it appear particularly effective at mobilization, in the light of continuing concerns at low levels of participation around the democratic globe. What value then does marketing have for democracy?

We sought answers by first looking at commercial marketing and its relation to democracy, drawing on Quelch and Jocz's examination of marketing set against Dahl's five conditions of ideal democracy: effective participation, inclusion of all adults, equal counting of votes and equality of opportunity to vote, enlightened understanding of citizens, and opportunity for citizen control of the agenda. Quelch and Jocz compared the U.S. commercial and political markets by these criteria and found that on virtually all counts commerce outperformed politics. In its essentials, then, marketing is democratic; but its capacity to contribute to socially desirably ends requires strengthening of "citizen sovereignty": fair competition, regulation of promotional claims, consumer protection, reliable information, monitoring of ethical standards, encouragement of consumer choice and activism, and mutual respect between buyers and sellers. This discussion led to two key points: the importance of the structure of the marketplace and the need to attend to the quality of the consumer experience in order to encourage participation.

The importance of structure echoes the increasingly urgent attention to democratic design in political theory and practice. It is becoming increasingly clear that electoral systems, regulation of the campaign, and the media environment are significantly correlated with citizen satisfaction with the way democracy works. There are huge constitutional issues here that remind us that political marketing is just a small part of the process, on the one hand, and on the other, that political marketing is not one undifferentiated model. How the marketing is conducted is the product of overall democratic design and cultural specificity.

The importance of the experiential dimension is marketing's most distinctive contribution and raises questions at the levels of both the theory and practice of political communication. At the level of theory, it challenges the normative grip of the informed citizen in accounts of proper democratic discourse. The necessity of informed, reasoned decisions renders suspicious anything that might seem to undermine rationality, and thus aesthetics and emotion are deemed inherently troubling. The marketing approach encourages us to consider that the personal, the aesthetic, and the emotional are all legitimate dimensions of political discourse, and are spurs to political participation. At the level of practice, we see political marketing discourse that is grounded in ideas of battle. It is as much about belittling opponents as inviting participation. Parties struggle to do what comes naturally to social movements (Goodwin et al., 2001), where art, music, consumption, and popular culture generally are entwined with activism. Passive party members, as long as they pay their checks, have benefits for leaders; after all, activism can be troublesome and tend to the extreme. However, the risk is a disconnect of politicians from popular culture. Attempts at pleasure and entertainment are injected top-down into the campaigning process and, unless in the hands of highly skilled political performers, come across as clumsy, gimmicky, and inauthentic.

It is a simple point, that political participation will be encouraged by attending to citizens' experience and pleasure. However, it is a fundamental one, not just for parties but for an active citizenry generally. To paraphrase Schudson, removing pleasure from politics is a task democracies undertake at their peril.

Conclusion

Hope Not Fear

This book ends as it began, with a spirit of optimism. This is not the Panglossian cheerfulness of some marketing gurus that all is for the best in the best of all possible worlds; that good ethical business will pick up the baton dropped by politicians to deliver a greener, more sustainable, more human-rights-conscious world. It is not either simply a personal preference for hope over fear, because it is hope that makes life worth living. Nor is it afraid of the skepticism of realism, since a constant and critical weighing of the good with bad is a necessary condition for genuine optimism. However, it is upbeat about our consumer democracy. Here's why.

STRONG CITIZEN COMMITMENT TO DEMOCRATIC VALUES

Public support for democratic values remain strong and, if anything, is rising, despite the huge and continuing concerns at crises of participation and democratic deficits around the globe. The anxiety indicators are well known: declining electoral turnout in many advanced industrial democracies, party memberships collapsing, and survey evidence of mounting public distrust in the formal institutions of politics. Political marketing and aggressive, sensation-seeking media are often cited as contributory factors to our modern dissatisfactions. Specifically, marketing is said to squeeze the scope of public debate, emphasize the negative, and foster naïve individualism over collective solutions (Stoker, 2006; Hay, 2007), while consumer culture generally is alleged to promote "infantile" instant gratification over the "adult" recognition of complexity in negotiation of the public good (Barber, 2007).

"Crisis" has become a more or less permanent condition of our times. We are always in one crisis or another. However, this is not to dismiss crisis claims; the theories valuably turn our attention to the evidence, and are especially useful if we unbundle the various meanings of "crisis" and consider it not as collapse but as "turning point." The crisis debates have produced some compelling evidence of changing patterns of citizenship and repertoires of engagement around the world: declines in deference to traditional authorities, the rise of "post-materialist" values (Inglehart, 2008), the expansion of lifestyle and citizen-consumer activism (Bennett, 1998). Dalton, Scarrow, and Cain (2004: 124) summarize, "Fewer people may be voting, but more are signing petitions, joining lobby groups, and engaging in unconventional forms of political action." Underlying these changing patterns of citizenship, cross-national surveys consistently show worldwide support for democratic principles. This support is especially marked in the established "trilateral" democracies of Western Europe, North America, and Japan. Dalton (2007), using data from the World Values Surveys (WVS), even while noting trends to increasing distrust of politicians and parties, found that citizens remained resolutely attached to democratic values. Furthermore, Norris's (2011) examination, also of WVS data, found that "enlightened democratic knowledge" is particularly associated with the longer-established democracies, with their free flows of information and relatively high educational attainment. Moreover, Norris's study of democratic deficits internationally cast doubt on the common wisdom that public support for the political system has eroded consistently in established democracies; rather, she says, support has varied over time in what she calls a "trendless fluctuation."

Beyond this there is also evidence of a high degree of public commitment to democratic egalitarianism even in the United States, the epicenter of consumer democracy. The United States is "hypercommercial" compared to other advanced industrial democracies (Canada, Western Europe, Japan, Australia, and New Zealand), according to an index created by Jeffrey Sachs (2011: 79–82) that measures public-private dimensions of social choice. Even in the United States Sachs can cite compelling and consistent survey evidence of welfare-democratic values among a large majority of the population: commitment to equality of opportunity, commitment to government responsibility to take care of those in need, provide health care, and provide schooling, and broad agreement that income distribution was unfair and that the rich should pay more taxes. Stepan and Linz's (2011) review article on inequality and the quality of democracy buttresses Sach's argument. It is clear, they say, that the United States is the "most unequal long-standing democracy" in the developed world but dispute that public opinion is the fundamental cause. Public opinion and the "American spirit" are much less convincing explanations for U.S. inequality than institutional barriers to fundamental reform.

In short, we can say that public democratic values and knowledge are strongest in the older-established affluent democracies of the world, precisely the cradles of consumer democracy. This is not to deny tensions between markets and democracy. However, it is to say that we can assert with some confidence that consumer democracy is not destructive of democratic commitment and aspiration.

MARKETING IS INHERENTLY RECIPROCAL

This does not mean equality of interest or an equal power balance between consumers and producers, citizens and political institutions. There are clear asymmetries of resources and information, although that balance is shifting in our connected society, in some markets dramatically through the Internet and social media. However, the underlying logic of marketing is reciprocity;

that the best way for producers to achieve their goals is by being attentive and responsive to consumer interests throughout the entire production-consumption cycle. Yet, for good reasons, a huge concern of modern professionalized campaigning is that there is "no place for amateurs" (Johnson, 2001), that the skills and resources required for success in modern mediated politics are beyond the reach of ordinary citizens. This point was discussed in Chapter 2 in the account of the political professionals. It arose again in the discussion of consumer democracy and citizen consumers (Chapter 6). Politics is now commonly seen as something "done by them to us." The professionalization process increases the yawning distance between citizens and governments, and fuels the dissatisfactions that are regaled in the many accounts of crisis of democracy. In this sense political marketing, even while it seeks connection through its focus groups and market research, widens the professional-amateur divide.

Moreover, consumer marketing is associated with broad societal processes that create difficulty for structures of representative democracy. The individual sense of consumer choice and expression in the marketplace contrasts with the highly centralized, slow, messy collective compromises offered by political choice. Democracy seems "designed in disappointment" compared to the near-instant satisfactions of the market (Stoker, 2006). Political practitioners often concede this point, agreeing that our affluent consumer culture complicates political leadership. Consumers feel empowered through increased choice, hugely improved sources of information, brand loyalty strategies, and ever-increasing opportunities to engage directly whether through feedback mechanisms, "prosumption" possibilities, and on- and offline consumer communities. By comparison, politics seems distant, complex, and barely relevant – the preserve of remote intellectual and wealthy elites.

Yet, paradoxically, as politics adopts the insights of marketing, so more gaps are prized open for amateurs. The "brand" is the epitome of this process. Brand images, as vessels of "popular meaning" (O'Guinn and Muniz, 2010), can add colossal value to company worth, but at the same time they are permanently on trial and never purely under the control of the producers. Brand images cannot be simply transferred from producer to consumer; and this is to say more than that audiences are active, are selective, and negotiate meaning. It is to say that brands are cocreations between producers and consumers. More than this, as O'Guinn and Muniz (2010: 142) argue, the brand arises out of multiple interactions not just between producers and individual consumers, but between collectives of consumers and institutions including "media, retailers, equity markets, government and NGOs.... These institutions bring the weight of economics, norms, practice, sanctions, regulations and even law to the ongoing creation of brands." Thus, they argue it makes better sense to describe brands, not just as cocreations, but as "social constructions." This interactive quality is why the brand was such a ripe target for the "no logo" activism of the 1990s and why the brand emerged as the crucible of citizen-consumer, consumer-democracy debates. At one and the same time, the brand is the symbol of the triumph of consumer capitalism (and our complicity) and it is also the means by which democratic principles and ethics are brought into the marketplace (and thus reflect our expectations of social justice).

The consumer activism of the 1990s lit a fuse. Popular and expensively built reputations were exposed by protest that laid bare a reckless capitalism, plundering popular culture, violating human rights, inflicting cruelty on animals, and polluting the environment (Klein, 1999). However, and not so ironically, the wider resonance of this activism stemmed precisely from the same consumer attitudes that fueled the "cool" branding strategies in the first place. Klein (2010) makes the point well when describing her ambivalence at the marketing of corporations such as Nike, Apple, and Starbucks.

All of their high-priced market research had found a longing in people for something more than shopping – for social change, for public space, for greater equality and diversity. Of course the brands tried to exploit that longing to sell lattes and laptops. Yet it seemed to me that we on the left owed the marketers a debt of gratitude for all this: our ideas weren't as passé as we had been told.

Now it is a commonplace of market research that "consumers are increasingly concerned about environmental, social and economic issues, and increasingly willing to act on those concerns" (World Business Council for Sustainable Development, 2008). Arguably the success of consumer activism is seen not just in changes of behavior in targeted companies, but more importantly and sustainably in broad consumer choice (Ward and de Vreese, 2011). Consumer activism, perhaps especially in Europe, has had a profound impact on entire markets. What once were tiny niche markets for the educated middle class – organic produce, fair trade coffee, chocolate, and bananas, sustainably harvested fish and timber, ethical investment – are now familiar offerings in the high streets and supermarkets. Companies are increasingly forced to consider their reputations, not just in terms of legal compliance and product reliability, but as socially responsible corporate citizens. "Ethical consumption is perhaps the biggest movement in branding today," reported market researchers GfK (2008). Its five-country study (France, Germany, Spain, UK, United States) found that consumers are increasingly dissatisfied with commercial ethics and "are increasingly taking matters into their own hands and choosing to buy brands which they believe to be ethical. Of the five thousand consumers surveyed, 39 percent say that buying ethical products 'makes them feel good.'" Practice, of course, is not so simple. Businesses promoting sustainable and ethical consumption note a continued gulf between consumer attitudes and behavior; we are far more likely to say we prefer ethical products than actually to shop ethically. However, there is no doubting the vigor of the trend toward responsible and ethical consumption; GfK found that even amid the deepest recession for decades, brands considered by consumers to be ethical were growing five times as fast as those considered nonethical.

What does this citizen-like consumption mean for mainstream electoral politics? Can we see some sort of parallel with the political marketing of the major candidates for government? As parties lose members and citizen attachment to parties weakens, so the relationship with voters is rendered looser, more like brand loyalty than an expression of socially determined identity

(Himmelweit, Humphreys, and Jaeger, 1985). As parties and candidates come to conceive, research, and sell themselves as brands, do they not also open up, as in consumer markets, new opportunities for "amateurs," for critical citizens to expose political communication to equivalent sorts of ethical considerations? We are now starting to see some intriguing evidence of amateur activism in political branding. The YouTube "bling bling" satire on President Nicolas Sarkozy is a case in point, as too were the "airbrushed for change" online spoofs of advertising for Cameron's Conservatives in the UK in 2010. There are even some fledgling "compare the political market" websites, such as "pocketpolitics" and "compare the political parties" in the UK. The creation of the Obama brand was an outstanding example of reciprocity, bottom-up as much as top-down, although ultimately its ramifications may be as much a cautionary as inspirational tale. The strategy ran the risk of the kind of "pain of premium" suffered by New Labour, as former supporters may eventually feel excluded and betrayed by failure to live up to the promise of the brand. Moreover, the Obama example, while it generated huge interest around the globe, is a difficult example to follow. This is partly because of the qualities of the candidate; few have Obama's charisma. However, it is also because there is a noticeable reluctance from campaigners elsewhere – and the UK is a good example – to let go of the central reins and "open source" their campaigns.

This raises the question of how reciprocity is imagined and conducted by the parties themselves. The point made in Chapter 1 was that modern politics, like many consumer markets, had undergone a relative power shift away from parties (producers) and that this induced a nudge toward a "market orientation"; in short, that parties seeking to increase vote share and/or win elections would modify their product in line with their understanding of the wants and needs of potential voters. This does not necessarily mean a simple "follow the polls" strategy, because established parties do not come with empty slates, polls are often ambiguous, and voters' preferences are mutable, frequently not coming fully formed but emerging out of public debate about alternative political actions. Political supply, in other words, does not emerge in some kind of automatic fashion from demand. However, a market orientation does indicate heightened attention toward reciprocity; to researching and understanding the concerns and wants of citizens. In practice reciprocity plays out in multiple and context-specific ways, depending, for example, on competitive structures and the incentives to bridge across wide sectors of society or bond with sectional interest, on the strength of core values and ideologies of candidate/parties, and indeed on practitioner attitudes toward democracy itself and citizen capacity for enlightened political knowledge and participation. Thus, it is no surprise that the inherent reciprocity of the brand raises both opportunities and threats for parties. Amateur activism can engender enthusiasm and interest and add greatly to brand attractiveness, as in the case of Obama; equally it cannot be controlled, and thus it threatens the top-down marketing model.

Labour's (late) advisor Philip Gould (2011: 536) makes the optimistic case that the inherent reciprocity of our consumer societies has decisively changed the balance of power in democratizing fashion. He describes a "Copernican revolution" in political communication, one that exactly parallels consumer markets:

The old model was clear: commercial and civic institutions held both power and knowledge while the public was trusting and effectively deferential. Institutional knowledge and information were at the centre of our universe; they were our sun. The model has changed completely. Now it is the public who are the sun and politicians and corporations the orbiting planets, seeking to gain attention and win trust. It means that ... the old models of politics are effectively obsolete and that companies are increasingly answerable not just to shareholders but to a world in which both citizens and consumers have a voice.

Polling and focus groups are no longer enough to achieve connection between parties and citizens, he says. People have come to expect participation, and they are demanding higher ethical standards of both politics and business. "This sounds idealistic, but it is not.... Without a core of integrity, values and ultimately fairness, it is hard to gain and sustain success in this new world"

(Gould, 2011: 537). The potential, he suggests, could be hugely democratizing: a world in which "democratized knowledge is moving us from an age of deference to an age of discovery" (p. 536). Underlying his argument is a fundamental and fascinating question about the old established parties themselves. What now is their purpose? We have up until now assumed that parties are essential for representative democracies typically listing a set of necessary functions: parties aggregate interests, organize compromise among competing interests and worldviews, mobilize voters, select candidates for leadership, and so on. The question now is what kind of relationship parties have with citizens, given that the era of mass-member parties, with a more or less continuous presence in local communities, is over.

Gould's optimism depends in part on the activities of politicians, and their willingness to do well out of doing good. This in turn will partly depend on citizen behavior, and in this politics can take this lesson from consumer democracy: a critical mass of critical citizen-consumers can bring about significant changes in marketing and markets and can affect broad swathes of everyday producer and consumer behavior. In short, politicians' willingness to engage in more open, responsive, and socially responsible marketing depends in part on citizens' political marketing literacy.

THE IMPORTANCE OF LITERACY

Roughly from the mid-1990s onward, and propelled by the growth of the Internet, literacy was at the heart of the new wave of consumer activism. Traditional consumer watchdog organizations combined with a proliferation of compare-the-market websites to examine product reliability and value for money and to expose "rip-off" practices. Simultaneously brand activism dissected corporate cultures, contrasting their self-promoted reputations to their practices. In the era of neoliberal globalization, activists championed consumer power against the might of corporations. Shopping became the new politics, buying or boycotting the new mode of voting in societies where the axis of power seemed to shift away from the political institutions of nation-states. Part of the attraction for these consumer activists was precisely self-education. Ten years after the publication of *No Logo*, Naomi Klein (2010) recalled,

Looking back, what I liked most was the unapologetic wonkery of it all. In the two years after *No Logo* came out, I went to dozens of teach-ins and conferences, some of them attended by thousands of people, that were exclusively devoted to popular education about the inner workings of global finance and trade. It was as if people understood, all at once, that gathering this knowledge was crucial to the survival not just of democracy but of the planet. Yes, this was complicated, but we embraced that complexity because we were finally looking at systems, not just symbols.

In politics, research over more than fifty years has consistently shown a close correlation among political participation, democratic aspiration, and further or higher levels of educational attainment (Campbell et al., 1960; Norris, 2011). As concerns have increased at low levels of participation, particularly among the young, a growing number of democracies worldwide now include civics and citizenship education as a compulsory part of the school curriculum; the International Association for the Evaluation of Educational Achievement listed twenty-one such countries in its recent thirty-eight-country survey (Schulz et al., 2010). Gerry Stoker's acclaimed *Why Politics Matters* (2006) champions a broader conception of democratic literacy. The problem now, he says, is that democratic processes of decision making are collective and centralized and hence seem increasingly alien in our Western highly individualized, self-expressive cultures. The reinvigoration of participation in formal politics, as opposed to angry protest, requires more spaces and opportunities for "amateur" involvement "because that is all most of us want to be when it comes to politics"; but it should be an educated amateurism, less surprised and therefore less disappointed at the messy compromises that collective decision making often produces (Stoker, 2006).

Thus literacy is commonly accepted as essential in both politics and consumption, even allowing for difference in perspective.

Commercial marketing tends to assume engaged, interested, and literate consumers; political scholarship focuses on the disengaged and worries about the lack of knowledge and interest among broad swathes of the population. Moreover, a persistent anxiety in politics, as exemplified by Stoker and Barber (2007), is that our comfortableness as consumers may undermine our capacity as citizens. However, even while acknowledging inherent tensions in the citizen-consumer couplet, this book tends to the optimistic view. Marketing exists in our daily lives, whether in consumption or politics. We can regulate it, but we cannot wish it away; instead, just as in consumer-citizen activism, we can promote a more democratically desirable political marketing. A necessary first step for this is the development of political marketing literacy to understand what campaigners are doing, how and why they do it, but not to assume that all marketing is a synonym for lying. In short it is about finding ways to distinguish the democratically good from the bad.

The idea of political marketing literacy cuts to the heart of concerns about disaffected citizens and particularly the problem of cynicism. Politicians as a class have never commanded a popular reputation for honesty. They have been the objects of derision for as long as people have written about politics: Cicero observed the calculated vacillators of ancient Rome, King Lear's "scurvy politician" was the exemplar of hypocrisy, while for American iconoclast H. L. Mencken (1924) "a good politician, under democracy, is quite as unthinkable as an honest burglar." There is some protection in cynicism; the bursting of overblown bubbles is healthy for democracy. However, trust, or rather the lack of it, has come to be seen as one the great crises of our modern politics. It is worrying if cynicism becomes the intellectual zeitgeist. If we assume that all politicians by virtue of their profession are inherently scoundrels, how do we make rational choices between them? Ultimately, and this is the great fear about our personalized politics, it may boil down to likeability and personal empathy. As British media critic John Lloyd (2007) argues, there is something dangerously anti-Enlightenment in the fashion to deride all elected officials as liars and all signs of "honest doubt, compromise and the weighing of conflicting views (the true stuff of public life) as so much pettifogging weakness." For Lloyd, this risks shifting decisions about trust from the head to the heart, from rational assessments of politicians' actions to intuition about their personal sincerity. Thus, we have arrived at the paradoxical situation where we, the public, may prefer the "sincere liar," the politician who ignores the facts or stacks the deck because she or he *feels* a course of action is right, to the "honest hypocrite," whose awareness of a clash between political action and principle is betrayed in equivocating language and demeanor (Runciman, 2006). The first type (one can immediately think of Clinton, Blair, George W. Bush) appears sincerely motivated by good intentions, while the latter (perhaps Al Gore or Gordon Brown) appears hypocritical, motivated by base political exigency. The danger, as Lloyd puts it, is that sentiment trumps reason.

Both the concept of emotional intelligence, which has long guided marketing research, and contemporary political psychology doubt that reason and sentiment can be so easily divided; on the contrary they tend to work together. More fundamentally some affective investment is necessary for political action; we need to care at some basic emotional level if we are to participate. However, even though we may agree that "reason" has been overprivileged within the Enlightenment tradition and common accounts of "proper" politics, this does not mean that we can be content with entirely irrational or, worse, antirational politics. There is a legitimate and necessary place for sentimental types of criteria, but if they are the only criteria, if they displace substantive criteria, we are in trouble. Skepticism says that we should compare the brand appeal to the substance and then make a verdict; cynicism says that since they all lie, we might as well go with something that seems at least likeable and entertaining, if we bother to participate at all.

This book seeks to advance literacy by contributing to debates about standards for the evaluation of political marketing. In particular, it proposed the brand differentiator model (connecting substantive reasoning and social, cultural, and psychological factors), and a set of democratic dimensions to assess campaigns. Brand differentiation was discussed in relation to George W. Bush and was put forward primarily as an analytical vehicle, intended to show how the political brand distinctiveness model might be applied to the understanding of the construction of political images. It did not claim to be a comprehensive account of Bush's campaign. However, this example does indicate the usefulness of the model in analyzing image construction; it demonstrates the balance and weight given to various elements and the ways in which the boundary conditions are, or are not, smoothly connected to the cultural and psychological elements of the brand differentiators. In the Bush case the model showed how heavily he relied on emotional associations; even his one substantive claim, as a strong commander in chief, was promoted primarily through cultural and psychological associations. It also showed that overall, his portrayal did indeed, and as expected, capitalize on the war on terror, but not, as anticipated, through fear of enemies, but through a sunny and optimistic patriotism.

The political brand differentiation model does not of itself lead to normative conclusions, but it does valuably draw our attention to this perpetually troubling couplet of reason-emotion. It invites us to ask not if we should but rather *when* we should be suspicious of political identities that are located wholly or mainly in the region of brand differentiators. The model gives us the basis for assessment, by drawing attention to the balance and interconnections between substantive performance and differentiators. However, it does not assume that substance-weighted brand identity is "good" normatively while brand differentiators are normatively suspicious. This is partly a matter of the quality of the information: what substantive information is being presented, and how do we evaluate its accuracy and relevance to citizen concerns? However, it is also because we know now from political psychology that information is not enough to generate participation. Politics needs to raise our hopes and enthusiasm, and indeed to trigger anxieties that cause us to convert thought to action. Because of this we might equally be critical of political promotion that makes no attempt at emotional connection, or, in other words, that pays no attention to differentiators. Mobilization is widely considered to be one of the functional benefits to democracy of campaigns, and thus campaigns that make little or no attempt to invite emotional engagement might be considered as deficient as campaigns that do not provide even basic information about record and policy.

How then do we judge a good campaign? Chapter 5 revealed a wide gulf between practitioner and academic perspectives, the former focused on effectiveness while the latter raises an increasingly broad range of concerns covering the micro level (individual citizen's political knowledge, sense of efficacy, and mobilization) and the macro level, and the capacity of elections to deliver system benefits by inter alia increasing the stock of public knowledge, promoting elite responsiveness to public concerns, and, through fair contest and representation of the spectrum of public opinion, providing legitimacy for the democratic system as a whole. Academic criticism of campaigns around the world, and especially in the United States, focuses precisely on this apparent practitioner/democratic theory disjuncture. The great anxiety is that the goal of effectiveness runs counter to the ideals of democracy. Trent and Friedenberg's (2004: 395) question encapsulates the fears: "is contemporary political campaigning failing the nation?"

However, it is not inevitable that practitioner goals clash with democratic ideals. In Chapter 5 we proposed, as a tool of evaluation, a model of the democratic dimensions of a good campaign. Following Farrell and Schmitt-Beck (2002), it separates out civic (micro) and system (macro) dimensions. Most of these are standard in academic accounts of campaigning and revolve around the two big issues of information (individual citizen learning and the stock of public knowledge) and mobilization. In addition, the model advanced two criteria that are far less common in the campaign literature. First is the inclusion of the encouragement of affective investment. This point draws directly from the discussion of political brands and political psychology. The second criterion involves a separation of the ideas of responsiveness and accountability. Responsiveness refers to the democratic necessity for leaders to respond to public concerns, and in that respect political marketing, at least in theory, could enhance responsiveness. Accountability is the idea of a kind of contract between the people and governments, in which rulers and would-be rulers are held to account for their actions. The significance of the accountability dimension is that it highlights the importance of "good deliberation" (Mansridge, 2003). If campaigns are to promote accountability there is a clear need for adequate and reliable information and sufficient opportunities for scrutiny by the public and, on their behalf, by the media. Thus accountability directs our attention, not just to the quality of parties/candidate communication, but to the media environment and citizen engagement within it.

The democratic dimensions campaign model is offered as a contribution to a positive debate; not just what is going wrong but what ideally would we like to see in parties' and candidates' communication. Criticism is an essential task of the academy, and it is certainly true that campaigns are rarely examples of high-minded debate. We may see political marketing, judged by these democratic dimensions, falling short of ideals almost everywhere we look. However, we can also find examples of partial success, of responsiveness, of emotional connection, of openness to scrutiny and concerted efforts at mobilization. It is not axiomatic that the imperative of winning is inherently at odds with ideals.

The debate about standards is doubtless influenced by the local and thus in part relative. However, there is also the possibility that academics and practitioners might come together to do something that we never seem to do now. As we look across our countries and increasingly seek comparison with others, it should be possible to start building a canon, a broadly accepted selection of international examples of winning (effective) campaigns that are also compliant with desirable democratic goals. We should not expect perfection, but neither is it too difficult to find examples that at least are aspiring in the right direction, running with rather than against the grain of citizenship. Obama's 2008 campaign, for example, seized the attention of a fascinated world as we witnessed the enthusiasm, the extraordinary emotional connection, and the against-the-tide success at mobilization. It seemed an outstanding example of responsiveness, even if issues of accountability were less clear-cut. The development of a canon is a small step, but it is important. It will encourage academic critics to match the ideals to the concrete and deal in specifics, of campaigns and campaign environments encompassing the media and their role as well as electoral systems and regulations. It is also suggestive of possibilities of judgment, including aesthetic evaluation, that can be distinguished from personal taste and ideological preference.

Just as importantly it can encourage political marketers' own best instincts, to do well out of doing good. It can facilitate the development of the too-often-neglected issue of ethics in campaigning (Johnson, 2012; Nelson, Dulio, and Medvic, 2002; Thurber et al., 2000), encouraging a dialogue about campaign standards and how these relate to broader political cultures and specific electoral and media regulatory environments. There has been little in this book about campaign ethics, rather more about regulation. This is not because there are no ethics in professionalized campaigning. The American Association of Political Consultants, for example, requires all its members to sign a code of ethics that requires inter alia a commitment to honesty in dealings with the media and attacks on opponents and prohibits appeals to voters that exploit sexism, racism, and religious intolerance. However, in general ethics are both understudied and underdeveloped in the campaigning world (*pace* Nelson et al., 2002 and James Thurber and colleagues' Improving Campaign Conduct project). Practitioners who ought to see themselves as the "centurions of democracy" (Arterton, cited in Scammell, 1997) tend rather to operate flexibly, guided by legal frameworks and personal taste, both theirs and those of the leaders, candidates, and parties that they serve. In practice ethical guidance is often reduced to the fear of public exposure: "how would it look if such and such an activity came to light?" Ironically, the process of professionalization demands attention to ethics; self-regulating codes are typical and essential accompaniments to claims of "professionalism" in other walks of life, most obviously medicine, law, and accounting but also increasingly the communicative "professions" of marketing and journalism. The possibilities of effective self-regulation of political communication are rather limited. In this it is akin to journalism and for some of the same reasons; for example, the democratic necessity of open entry, and the difficulty and undesirability of establishing licensing authority. However, as we saw in Chapter 2, practitioners typically are politically motivated people, commonly with partisan attachment. There is both a significant degree of good will, in the sense of democratic commitment, and a long-term practitioner self-interest in questions of regulation and ethics.

Above all, the quest for literacy and the development of standards of evaluation can provide some balance to the overwhelmingly critical tide against political marketing. This is not to abandon critique and critical reflection but rather to harness them to reimagine a campaigning that runs with, rather than against, the grain of citizenship. Without this we are in danger of a permanent sense of loss, a narrative of decline that may be profoundly disempowering, feeding a spiral of cynicism among practitioners, media, and citizens.

CONCLUSION: MARKETING AND DEMOCRATIC POTENTIAL

Political marketing, as a distinct branch of political communication scholarship, has flourished over the past fifteen or so years with its own international journal, annual conferences, and specialist groupings in various academic disciplinary associations. It has become a vibrant, sometimes anarchic, mix of analysis and advocacy, welcoming input from practitioners as well as academics from business, political, and communications fields. There is no single, settled, dominant theory of political marketing but rather a shared sense that marketing provides a valuable analytic framework to understand organizational behavior in markets, profit or nonprofit, where there is competition to influence "the behaviour of publics, with an offer whose perceived value is ...

superior" to that of rivals (Lendrevie, Levy, and Lindon, 2006: 2). This starting point is part of the analytical attraction of marketing because it begins with realistic and reasonable definition of what it is that parties and candidates are actually doing. It starts from a wholly different place from most mainstream political communication accounts of mediated democracy. Typically (see Chapter 1), political communication scholars view "marketing logic" as an exterior, commercial influence in politics; practitioners enlist marketing logic as a way to manage an increasingly powerful media and manufacture difference among rivals who are no longer clearly demarcated ideologically. As such "marketing logic" invades politics in potentially troubling ways, depoliticizing, image elevating, personalizing, and manipulating. By contrast, political marketing analysis sees marketing logic as inherent in the competitive structures of democracy; candidates/parties compete to influence publics with rival offers that are essentially promises, and as such are hugely reliant for credibility on reputation (image).

These divergent starting points lead to quite different sets of questions with respect to the democratic good. The big questions of mainstream political communication focus on power relations between media and politics, with a strong and common sense that the media/politics relationship has become dysfunctional, to the detriment of political discourse in the public sphere. What, in short, are the media doing to politics? Arguments about "media-malaise" and a "crisis of public communication" have driven the political communications agenda for some thirty years, amid concerns that citizens are sidelined or, worse, demotivated by a discourse of confrontation and complicity among politicians, spin doctors, journalists, and media organizations.

The political marketing analysis set out in this book changes track on these debates. It does not dispute that media are the hugely significant shaping environments for politics, nor that political marketing in practice is often worrisome. However, its key questions are less about media/politics, and more about politics/citizen relations within the overall structure of competition. It does not see "marketing logic" as some kind of single, exogenous, media-induced, commercially derived entity, but rather as endogenous, context-dependent, related to the structure of competition including the regulatory environment, electoral system, and political culture. The marketing logic of Denmark, for example, with its much-admired PR system, would be expected to be much different from the marketing logic of the United States, with its well-resourced two-party monopoly competing in a relatively deregulated campaign environment. The big question for political marketing scholarship now is how we make political marketing practice better, more democratic, where "democratic" is broadly seen as meeting the criteria set out by Dahl (see Chapter 6) for participation, inclusion, and citizen sovereignty. Part of the answer, as suggested in this book, lies in the critical engagement of marketing literate citizens; the inherent reciprocity of marketing enables such engagement. However, more fundamentally, we are directed to the particulars of the underlying competitive structures. If we are concerned at political marketing practice that ignores vast swathes of the population (the partisans, the nonvoters, the citizens of nonmarginal constituencies) and instead relentlessly targets small voter segments in battleground territory – as is the case in the United States, the UK, and Canada, for example – we need to examine the competitive structures that incentivize that particular marketing logic. To put this another way, as Quelch and Jocz do (Chapter 6), citizen sovereignty over marketing requires a fair marketplace, with sufficient choice, reliable information, opportunities for active engagement, and mutual respect between buyers and sellers. Thus, ironically, marketing, which is so often considered as the superficial in contrast to the substance of politics, takes us to the fundamentals of political reform. It demands that we ask whether the political and electoral system is fair, and is perceived as such by citizens, and whether it offers sufficient choice and possibilities of participation. In short, political marketing analysis leads us into the key political science debates of democratic design. In so doing, it avoids the pitfall highlighted by Norris (2000; cf. Coleman and Blumler, 2009) in her long-running argument with the media crisis theorists; by blaming the messenger they may divert attention from the more profound issues of political reform.

Political marketing analysis is concerned with how competition and choice are played out in real markets. Because of this it lends a new perspective on issues of image, personality, and emotion in politics. As we look at political marketing practitioners and try to understand their work (Chapter 2), what we see is a fascinating, perhaps sometimes disturbing, combination of high politics and "nonpolitics": "cynical idealists" in Joe Trippi's phrase, ideologically motivated people, often invested in long-term political projects, employing the language and methods of apparently nonpolitical commerce and popular culture. Political marketing analysis tells us that there is no contradiction there, it is a reflection of how choice works in real markets. Classic economics supposes that buyers and sellers, parties and voters are utility maximizers, who will rationally calculate how to extract optimum benefit from any transaction. Analysis of real markets takes us to the contemporary dominance of the brand, whose value is predicated on its social, psychological, and cultural value over and above its functional benefit. In other words, choice in real markets is played out precisely around the dialectic of rational utility and emotional intelligence. It is only ideal models of economic and political choice that make emotion and rationality seem so oppositional.

This focus on the operation of real markets raises the question of the experiential dimension in participation. We are not an assembly of disembodied brains, weighing the merits of alternative offers, when we engage in either commercial or political markets. Rather, we are social beings, attracted or repelled by the quality of the experience. It was argued (Chapter 6) that sociability and the pleasures of consumption and popular culture go hand in hand with grassroots political participation. The ideal of a "purified" citizenship, cleansed of the pleasures of the senses, is ultimately both unrealistic, as the vibrant social movements continue to demonstrate, and potentially damaging for democracy. Political marketing in practice does make some attempts to enlist popular culture; the political marketing critique is not that they do so, but that these efforts are too often injected top-down and look like inauthentic packaging of politicians parachuted in from a distant planet. The danger is of a vicious cycle; the less "amateurs" are involved, the more parties become remote from popular culture, the more likely that their attempts to connect at a human, sociable level are regarded as merely campaigning devices. Equally, a virtuous cycle is imaginable, albeit not so easy; "connection," the mantra now of many political marketing practitioners, involves attention to the quality of citizens' experience of politics. To the extent that it is genuine, it is more welcoming of amateurs, who automatically bring with them cultural resonance and social pleasures, which in turn encourages more participation.

The work of practitioners returns us to where we started in this book, and the common perception that they are now the cynical villains of modern politics; the calculating power brokers and self-interested manipulators. While this is a partial characterization, it does well to remind us that we should be skeptical of the claims of marketing. Martin Kornberger's *Brand Society* (2010: 272) is one of the most perceptive contributions to the social significance of brands. After nine chapters in which he examines how brands transform management, lifestyle, politics identity, and culture, he concludes with total ambivalence. He still does not know whether brands are "good guys," creators of social value, champions of social responsibility, or "villains" in which the rich and powerful destroy the authentic, natural good guys. What kind of movie would the brand be: perhaps "a thriller around a conspiracy theory," or a comedy "depicting brands as nothing but the next chapter in the farce we call civilization"? He has never found an answer that satisfied himself for more than five minutes. It is ultimately, he says, a conclusion in which nothing is concluded, but with the profound hope and real possibility that the next chapter will be "co-created, co-written and co-produced by you."

It is a neat summary of the inherent ambivalence of marketing. Raymond Chandler joked that chess was the greatest waste of human intelligence outside an advertising agency. It is worse than that. There is something disconcertingly immoral about all those colossal resources and creative energy being marshaled in the service of our manipulation, especially if, as all too often, it is heedless of the human and environmental costs. However, at the same time, we recognize the utilitarian value of marketing. Products and services, no matter how functionally valuable, are no use to us if we do not know they exist or how to get them. Moreover, consumer society has delivered a standard of living that few of us seem willing to forego, even if we consider ourselves intelligent, socially responsible shoppers. We enjoy good marketing, perhaps especially if we do not identify it as "marketing." We simply appreciate the buzz, the courteous service, the good taste, the pleasing design, the marvelous functionality, and increasingly we seem to expect as standard that companies behave as though they are partners in our communities, that they too should be good citizens. Corporate social responsibility is decreasingly to do with the philanthropic disposition of owners and more to do with permanent demands on the brand.

Skepticism, as suggested at the outset, is the correct attitude toward marketing. It is essential if the democratic potential of marketing is to be developed. Moreover, in its duality of light and dark, marketing is no different from markets themselves. There are clear and generally accepted correlations between capitalism and liberal democracy; the marriage between the two historically has delivered widespread prosperity, public services, and comparatively high degrees of individual freedom and civil rights. However, as pluralist democratic theorists, such as Dahl and Lindblom, have insisted over many years, markets and democracy may need each other but are in a permanent state of antagonistic symbiosis. Left to their own devices markets can eat themselves; they can destroy competition, concentrate power in huge corporations, and engender potentially damaging levels of social inequality. Lindblom (1977) warned, some forty years ago, that the inequalities produced by untrammeled corporate capitalism might ultimately threaten democracy itself. The warning has renewed force now in the wake of the financial crash and global recession. Capitalism and its relationship with democracy is on public trial once again, with a renewed emphasis on fundamental issues of equality and social justice. An explosion of economic and political research challenges the Reagan-Thatcherite neoliberal orthodoxy of globalization, highlighting a variety of alternative settlements among capitalism, state, and society (see, e.g., Sachs, 2011; Hertz, 2011). These challenges remind us also that collaboration and cooperation are as significant features of markets as competition. Markets rely on networks of trust between and among suppliers and consumers.

Thus, ambivalence about marketing is not an excuse to withdraw from judgment, but rather is an invitation to consider how citizen sovereignty can be achieved. There is plenty of good in marketing. At its best it takes us seriously as adult citizen-consumers, is deeply concerned with what we think and feel, invites our participation, encourages our enjoyment, and seeks mutually beneficial long-lasting relationships with stakeholders. In all these ways, at the levels of both democratic systems and competing parties, politics can learn from the practice of marketing. The argument is not so much that more marketing is needed, but *better* marketing. Politicians must sell themselves to us. The point is not to lament that they do so; it is to find ways of encouraging more inclusive marketing, more in tune with democratic ideals.

References

Abramowitz, A. "The 2008 Presidential Election: How Obama Won and What It Means." In *The Year of Obama*, edited by Larry Sabato, 91–114. New York: Longman Pearson, 2010.

Aikman, David. *A Man of Faith: The Spiritual Journey of George W. Bush*. Nashville, Tenn.: Thomas Nelson, 2004.

Ansolabehere, S., and S. Iyengar. *Going Negative*. New York: Free Press, 1997.

Baker, M. "One More Time – What Is Marketing?" In *The Marketing Book*, edited by M. Baker and S. Hart, 3–9. Oxford: Chartered Institute of Marketing/Butterworth-Heinemann, 2008.

Bannon, D. P. "Relationship Marketing and the Political Process." *Journal of Political Marketing* 4, no. 2 (2005): 85–102.

Barber, Benjamin. *Consumed: How Markets Corrupt Children, Infantilize Adults and Swallow Citizens Whole*. New York: Norton, 2007.

Strong Democracy. 20th anniversary ed. Berkeley: University of California Press, 2003a.

"Which Technology and Which Democracy?" In *Democracy and the New Media*, edited by Henry Jenkins and David Thorburn, 33–48. Cambridge, Mass.: MIT Press, 2003b.

Barberio, Richard, and Brian Lowe. "Branding: Presidential Politics and Crafted Political Communications." In *Annual Meeting of the American Political Science Association*, Washington, D.C., 2006.

Barker, Rodney. *Making Enemies*. Basingstoke: Palgrave Macmillan, 2006.

Bartels, Larry M. "The Impact of Electioneering in the United States." In *Electioneering: The Comparative Study of Continuity and Change*, edited by David Butler and Austin Ranney, 244–77. Oxford: Clarendon, 1992.

Bartels, Larry M., and John Zaller. "Presidential Vote Models: A Recount." *PS: Political Science & Politics* 34, no. 1 (2001): 9–20.

Bartle, J., and D. Griffiths. *Political Communications Transformed: From Morrison to Mandelson.* Basingstoke: Palgrave, 2001.

Belt, Todd, Marion Just, and Ann Crigler. "Accentuating the Positive in US Presidential Elections." In *Annual Meeting of the American Political Science Association*, Washington, D.C., 2005.

Bennett, Stephen. "Know-Nothings Revisited: The Meaning of Political Ignorance Today." *Social Science Quarterly* 69, no. 2 (1988): 476–90.

"'Know-Nothings' Revisited Again." *Political Behavior* 18 (1996): 219–33.

"Political Ignorance Revisited." Public Opinion Pros. 2005. http://www.publicopinionpros.com/features/2005/dec/bennett.asp.

Bennett, W. L. "Communicating Global Activism: Strengths and Vulnerabilities of Networked Politics." *Information, Communication and Society* 6, no. 2 (2003): 143–68.

"The Uncivic Culture: Communication, Identity and the Rise of Lifestyle Politics." *PS: Political Science & Politics* 31, no. 4 (1998): 740–61.

Bennett, W. L., and R. M. Entman, eds. *Mediated Politics: Communication in the Future of Democracy.* Cambridge: Cambridge University Press, 2001.

Bennett, W. Lance, and Taso Lagos. "Logo Logic: The Ups and Downs of Branded Political Communication." *Annals of the American Academy of Political and Social Science* 611 (2007): 193–206.

Bennett, W. Lance, and Jarol Manheim. "The Big Spin: Strategic Communication and the Transformation of Pluralist Democracy." In *Mediated Politics: Communication in the Future of Democracy*, edited by W. Lance Bennett and Robert Entman, 279–98. Cambridge: Cambridge University Press, 2001.

Bernays, Edward L. "The Future of Public Relations." In *Association for Education in Journalism and Mass Communication (AEJMC) Convention*, 1992.

Propaganda. New York: IG Publishing, 2005.

Bernstein, Richard J. *The Abuse of Evil: The Corruption of Politics and Religion since 9/11.* Cambridge: Polity, 2005.

Blumenthal, Sidney. *The Clinton Wars.* New York: Plume, 2004.

The Permanent Campaign. New York: Simon & Schuster, 1982.

Blumler, J. G. *The Crisis of Public Communication.* London: Routledge, 1995.

Blumler, J. G., and Dennis Kavanagh. "The Third Age of Political Communication." *Political Communication* 16, no. 3 (1999): 209–30.

Blumler, Jay G., Dennis Kavanagh, and Tom Nossiter. "'Modern Communications Versus Traditional Politics in Britain: Unstable Marriage of Convenience." In *Politics, Media and Modern Democracy*, edited by David Swanson and Paulo Mancini, 49–72. New York: Praeger, 1996.

Blythe, James. *Principles & Practice of Marketing*. London: Thomson, 2006.

Bowler, S., and D. Farrell. *Electoral Strategies and Political Marketing*. Basingstoke: Macmillan, 1992.

"The Internationalization of Campaign Consultancy." In *Campaign Warriors: Political Consultants in Elections*, edited by J. Thurber and C. Nelson, 153–74. Washington, D.C.: Brookings Institution, 2000.

Bowler, S., D. M. Farrell, and R. T. Pettitt. "Expert Opinion on Electoral Systems: So Which Electoral System Is the Best?" *Elections, Public Opinion and Parties* 15, no. 1 (2005): 3–19.

Brady, Henry, and John McNulty. "Turning Out to Vote: The Costs of Finding and Getting to the Polling Station." *American Political Science Review* 105, no. 1 (2011): 115–34.

Brewer, Sarah. "Women Political Consultants: Who Are They, Where Are They?" *Campaigns & Elections* 22 (2001): 8–9.

Bruter, M., and S. Harrison. "Tomorrow's Leaders? Understanding the Involvement of Young Party Members in Six European Democracies." *Comparative Political Studies* 42, no. 10 (2009): 1259–91.

Burkitt, Catherine. "Are You Less Emotionally Intelligent Than Blair? And If So Why Should You Care?" In *Annual Conference of the Political Studies Association*, Aberdeen, 2002.

Butler, David, and Dennis Kavanagh. *The British General Election of 2001*. Basingstoke: Palgrave, 2002.

Butler, D., and A. Ranney. *Electioneering: A Comparative Study of Continuity and Change*. Oxford: Clarendon, 1992.

Butler, P., and N. Collins. "A Conceptual Framework for Political Marketing." In *Handbook of Political Marketing*, edited by Bruce Newman, 55–72. London: Sage, 1999.

Campbell, Alastair. *The Blair Years: Extracts from the Alastair Campbell Diaries*. London: Hutchinson, Random House, 2007.

Campbell, Angus, Philip Converse, Warren Miller, and Donald E. Stokes. *The American Voter*. New York: Wiley, 1960.

Campus, Donatella. "Mediatization and Personalization of Politics in Italy and France: The Cases of Berlusconi and Sarkozy." *International Journal of Press/Politics* 15 (2010): 219–35.

Cappella, J., and K. H. Jamieson. *Spiral of Cynicism: The Press and the Public Good.* Oxford: Oxford University Press, 1997.

Carroll, Archie B., and K. Shabana. "The Business Case for Corporate Social Responsibility: A Review of Concepts, Research and Practice." *International Journal of Management Reviews* 12, no. 1 (2010): 85–105.

Carville, James. *We're Right, They're Wrong: A Handbook for Spirited Progressives.* New York: Random House, 1996.

Carville, James, and Paul Begala. *Take It Back: Our Party, Our Country, Our Future.* New York: Simon & Schuster, 2006.

Carville, James, and Stanley Greenberg. "The Ass-Whuppin' Cometh." *Carville-Greenberg Memo: The National Memo* (blog). November 6, 2012a. http://www.nationalmemo.com/carville-greenberg/the-ass-whuppin-cometh/.

⸻. *It's the Middle Class, Stupid.* New York: Blue Rider Press, 2012b.

Castells, Manuel. *Communication Power.* Oxford: Oxford University Press, 2009.

Center for Responsive Politics. "2012 Election Spending Will Reach $6 Billion, Center for Responsive Politics Predicts." *OpenSecretsblog.* 2012. http://www.opensecrets.org/news/2012/10/2012-election-spending-will-reach-6.html.

Cohen, Lizabeth. *A Consumers' Republic: The Politics of Mass Consumption in Postwar America.* New York: Knopf, 2003.

Coleman, Stephen. "Review of Lilleker & Lees-Marshment: Political Marketing: A Comparative Perspective." *Parliamentary Affairs* 60, no. 1 (2007): 180–86.

Coleman, S., and Jay G. Blumler. *The Internet and Democratic Citizenship.* Cambridge: Cambridge University Press, 2009.

Collins, N., and P. Butler. "Positioning Political Parties: A Market Analysis." *Harvard International Journal of Press/Politics* 1, no. 1 (1996): 63–77.

Corner, John. "Mediated Persona and Political Culture." In *Media and the Restyling of Politics,* edited by John Corner and Dick Pels, 67–84. London: Sage, 2003.

Corner, John, and Dick Pels, eds. *Media and the Restyling of Politics.* London: Sage, 2003.

Cowley, P., and D. Kavanagh. *The British General Election of 2010.* Basingstoke: Palgrave Macmillan, 2010.

Curran, J., and S. Iyengar. "Media System, Public Knowledge and Democracy: A Comparative Study." *European Journal of Communication* 24, no. 1 (2009): 5–26.

Dahl, Robert. *Dilemmas of Pluralist Democracy.* New Haven, Conn.: Yale University Press, 1982.

⸻. *On Democracy.* New Haven, Conn.: Yale University Press, 1998.

Preface to Democratic Theory. Chicago: University of Chicago Press, 1956.

A Preface to Economic Democracy. Berkeley: University of California Press, 1985.

Dalton, Russell J. "Citizenship Norms and the Expansion of Political Participation." *Political Studies* 56, no. 1 (2008): 76–98.

Democratic Challenges, Democratic Choices: The Erosion of Political Support in Advanced Industrial Democracies. Oxford: Oxford University Press, 2007.

Dalton, Russell J., Susan Scarrow, and Bruce Cain. "Advanced Democracies and the New Politics." *Journal of Democracy* 15, no. 1 (2004): 124–38.

Davies, Philip, and Bruce Newman, eds. *Winning Elections with Political Marketing.* London: Haworth Press, 2006.

de Vreese, C., and S. Lecheler. "News Framing Research: An Overview and New Developments." In *Sage Handbook of Political Communication,* edited by Holli A. Semetko and Margaret Scammell, 292–306. London: Sage, 2012.

Delli Carpini, Michael, and Scott Keeter. *What Americans Know about Politics and Why It Matters.* New Haven, Conn.: Yale University Press, 1996.

Diamond, Larry, and Richard Gunther, eds. *Political Parties and Democracy.* Baltimore: Johns Hopkins University Press, 2001.

Diamond, Larry, and Marc Plattner. "Introduction." In *The Global Resurgence of Democracy,* edited by Larry Diamond and Marc Plattner, ix–xxiv. Baltimore: Johns Hopkins University Press, 1993.

Dowd, Maureen. *Bushworld: Enter at Your Own Risk.* London: Penguin Viking, 2004.

Downs, A. *An Economic Theory of Democracy.* New York: Harper Row, 1957.

Duran, Nicole. "Presidential Surge Strategy." *Campaigns & Elections* 28, no. 257 (2007): 36–40.

Duverger, Maurice. *Political Parties: Their Organization and Activity in the Modern State.* 3rd ed. London: Methuen, 1964.

Edmonds, Tom. "The Ass-Whuppin' Cometh." *Campaigns & Elections,* no. 314 (December 2012): 41–43.

"Being a Republican in 2006." *Campaigns & Elections* 28, no. 2 (February 2007): 27–28.

Enright, M. "The Marketing Profession: Evolution and Future." *Journal of Public Affairs* 6 (2006): 102–10.

Entman, R. M. *Democracy without Citizens: Media and the Decay of American Politics.* Oxford: Oxford University Press, 1989.

Esser, Frank, and Barbara Pfetsch. *Comparing Political Communication: Theories, Cases, and Challenges.* Communication, Society, and Politics. Cambridge: Cambridge University Press, 2004.

Ewen, Stuart. *PR! A Social History of Spin.* New York: Basic Books, 1996.

Farrell, D. "Campaign Strategies and Tactics." In *Comparing Democracies,* edited by L. LeDuc, R. Niemi, and P. Norris. Thousand Oaks, Calif.: Sage, 1996.

Farrell, David M., and Rüdiger Schmitt-Beck, eds. *Do Political Campaigns Matter? Campaign Effects in Elections and Referendums.* Routledge/ECPR Studies in European Political Science 25. London: Routledge, 2002.

Faucheux, Ronald, ed. *Winning Elections: Political Campaign Management, Strategy and Tactics.* New York: M. Evans, 2003.

Femia, Joe. "Machiavelli." In *Political Thinkers: From Socrates to the Present,* edited by D. Boucher and P. Kelly, 139–57. Oxford: Oxford University Press, 2003.

Fenn, Peter. "Hard Knocks: Lessons from Losing." In *Winning Elections: Political Campaign Management, Strategy and Tactics,* edited by Ronald Faucheux, 79–83. New York: M. Evans, 2003.

Finlayson, Alan. *Making Sense of New Labour.* London: Lawrence & Wishart, 2003.

Fleischer, Ari. *Taking the Heat: The President, the Press, and My Years in the White House.* New York: HarperCollins, 2005.

Frank, Thomas. *What's the Matter with Kansas?* New York: Metropolitan Books, 2004.

Franklin, B. *Packaging Politics: Political Communications in Britain's Media Democracy.* London: Arnold, 1994.

Franzen, Giep, and Margot Bouwman. *The Mental World of Brands: Mind, Memory and Brand Success.* Henley-on-Thames: NTC Publications, 2001.

Friedman, Milton. "The Social Responsibility of Business Is to Increase Its Profits." *New York Times Magazine,* September 13, 1970.

Frum, D. *Right Man.* New York: Random House, 2003.

Fullerton, R. "How Modern Is Modern Marketing?" *Journal of Marketing Management* 52 (1988): 108–25.

Gallagher, Michael, and Paul Mitchell, eds. *The Politics of Electoral Systems.* Oxford: Oxford University Press, 2005.

Geer, John G. *In Defense of Negativity: Attack Ads in Presidential Campaigns.* Chicago: University of Chicago Press, 2006.

Gergen, David. *Eyewitness to Power: The Essence of Leadership Nixon to Clinton.* New York: Touchstone, 2000.

Gerstle, Gary. "The GOP Is in Trouble but the Left Has Its Work Cut Out." *Dissent.* 2012. http://www.dissentmagazine.org/online_articles/the-gop-is-in-trouble-but-the-left-has-its-work-cut-out.

GfK. "Consumers and Ethical Consumption." 2008.

Glickman, Lawrence B. *Buying Power: A History of Consumer Activism in America*. Chicago: University of Chicago Press, 2009.

Goffman, Erving. *Frame Analysis: An Essay on the Organization of Experience*. New York: Harper & Row, 1974.

Goodwin, J., J. Jasper, and F. Polletta, eds. *Passionate Politics: Emotions and Social Movements*. Chicago: University of Chicago Press, 2001.

Gould, Jon B. "It Only Feels Like Death: 'Rebranding' the Democrats for a Post-2002 World." *Journal of Political Marketing* 2, no. 2 (2003): 1–12.

Gould, Philip. "Coping with the Post Advertising Age." *Market Leader*, 2006, 57–59.

"Labour Party Strategy." In *Political Communication: The General Election of 2001*, edited by J. Bartle, S. Atkinson, and R. Mortimore, 57–68. London: Frank Cass, 2001.

The Unfinished Revolution: How Modernisation Saved the Labour Party. London: Time Warner Books, 1998.

The Unfinished Revolution: How New Labour Changed British Politics for Ever. London: Abacus, 2011.

"What 'Permanent Campaign'?" *BBC News*, 2002. http://news.bbc. co.uk/1/hi/uk_politics/2499061.stm.

Greenberg, Stanley B. *Dispatches from the War Room*. New York: St. Martin's Press, 2009.

Greenberg, Stanley, and James Carville. *Solving the Paradox of 2004; Why America Wanted Change but Voted for Continuity*. Washington, D.C.: Democracy Corps, 2004.

Greyes, N. "The Untapped Potential of Social Media: A Primer for Savvy Campaigners." *Campaigns & Elections* 300 (2011): 44–47.

Grönroos, C. *Service Management and Marketing: A Customer Relationship Management Approach*. Chichester: Wiley, 2000.

Gummesson, E. *Total Relationship Marketing*. Oxford: Butterworth-Heinemann, 2002.

Habermas, J. *The Structural Transformation of the Public Sphere*. Cambridge: Polity, 1989.

"Three Normative Models of Democracy." In *Democracy and Difference: Contesting the Boundaries of the Political*, edited by Seyla Benhabib. Princeton, N.J.: Princeton University Press, 1996.

Hague, Rod, and Martin Harrop. *Comparative Government and Politics*. 5th ed. Basingstoke: Palgrave, 2001.

Hallin, D. C., and P. Mancini. *Comparing Media Systems: Three Models of Media and Politics*. Communication, Society and Politics. Cambridge: Cambridge University Press, 2004.

Hamburger, M. "Lessons from the Field: A Journey into Political Consulting." In *Campaign Warriors: Political Consultants in Elections*, edited by J. Thurber and C. Nelson, 53–64. Washington, D.C.: Brookings Institution, 2000.

Hamelink, Cees. "The Professionalization of Political Communication: Democracy at Stake?" In *The Professionalization of Political Communication*, edited by R. Negrine, P. Mancini, C. Holtz-Bacha, and S. Papathanassopoulos, 179–87. Bristol: Intellect, 2007.

Harrison, M. "On Air." In *The British General Election of 2005*, edited by D. Kavanagh and David Butler, 94–118. Basingstoke: Palgrave Macmillan, 2005.

Harrop, M. "The Rise of Campaign Professionalism." In *Political Communications Transformed: From Morrison to Mandelson*, edited by J. Bartle and D. Griffiths, 53–70. Basingstoke: Palgrave, 2001.

Hart, Roderick. *Campaign Talk: Why Elections Are Good for Us.* Princeton, N.J.: Princeton University Press, 2000.

Hay, Colin. *Why We Hate Politics.* Cambridge: Polity, 2007.

Heath, R. *The Hidden Power of Advertising: How Low Involvement Processing Influences the Way We Choose Brands.* London: Admap, 2001.

Heilemann, John. "John Heilemann and Joe Trippi Discuss the Democratic Primary Race over Instant Messenger." *New York Magazine*, March 10, 2008.

Hellweg, Eric. "Inside PricewaterhouseCoopers' Annual CEO Survey." *HBR Blognetwork*, 2013. http://blogs.hbr.org/hbr/hbreditors/2013/01/inside_pricewaterhousecoopers.html?utm_medium=referral&utm_source=pulsenews.

Henneberg, S. "The Views of an Advocatus Dei: Political Marketing and Its Critics." *Journal of Public Affairs* 4, no. 4 (2004): 225–43.

Henneberg, S. C., and N. O'Shaughnessy. "Political Relationship Marketing: Some Micro/Macro Thoughts." *Journal of Marketing Management* 25, 1–2 (2009): 5–29.

Henneberg, Stephan, Margaret Scammell, and Nicholas O'Shaughnessy. "Political Marketing Management and Theories of Democracy." *Marketing Theory: Special Issue on Political Marketing* 9, no. 2 (2009): 165–88.

Herbst, Susan. *Reading Public Opinion: How Political Actors View the Democratic Process* Chicago: University of Chicago Press, 1998.

Hertz, Noreena. *Co-Op Capitalism: A New Economic Model from the Carnage of the Old.* Manchester: Co-operatives UK, 2011.

Hilton, Matthew. *Prosperity for All: Consumer Activism in an Era of Globalization.* Ithaca, N.Y.: Cornell University Press, 2009.

Hilton, M., and M. Daunton. "Material Politics: An Introduction." In *The Politics of Consumption: Material Culture and Citizenship in*

Europe and America, edited by M. Daunton and M. Hilton, 1–32. London: Berg, 2001.

Hilton, Steve, and Giles Gibbons. *Good Business: Your World Needs You.* New York: Texere, 2002.

Himmelweit, Hilde T., Patrick Humphreys, and Marianne Jaeger. *How Voters Decide: A Model of Vote Choice Based on a Special Longitudinal Study Extending over Fifteen Years and the British Election Surveys of 1970–1983.* Rev. and updated ed. Milton Keynes: Open University Press, 1985.

Holbrook, Thomas. *Do Campaigns Matter?* Thousand Oaks, Calif.: Sage, 1996.

Holtz-Bacha, C. "Political Advertising in Germany." In *The Sage Handbook of Political Advertising,* edited by Lynda Lee Kaid and Christina Holtz-Bacha, 163–80. Thousand Oaks, Calif.: Sage, 2006.

"Professionalization of Political Communication: The Case of the 1998 SPD Campaign." *Journal of Political Marketing* 1, no. 4 (2002): 23–38.

Holtz-Bacha, C., and Pippa Norris. "'To Entertain, Inform and Educate': Still the Role of Public Television." *Political Communication* 18, no. 1 (2001): 123–40.

Honan, Mat. "Your Unconscious Has Already Voted." *Wired,* September 2009, 108–9.

Inglehart, Ronald. "Changing Values among Western Publics from 1970 to 2006." *West European Politics* 31, no. 2 (2008): 130–46.

Ivins, Molly, and Lou Dubose. *Shrub: The Short but Happy Political Life of George W. Bush.* New York: Random House, 2000.

Iyengar, Shanto, and Donald R. Kinder. *News That Matters: Television and American Opinion.* American Politics and Political Economy. Chicago: University of Chicago Press, 1987.

Iyengar, S., and Adam Simon. "New Perspectives and Evidence on Political Communication and Campaign Effects." In *Annual Review of Psychology,* edited by J. T. Spence, 149–69. Palo Alto, Calif.: Annual Reviews Press, 2000.

Jamieson, K. H. *Everything You Think You Know about Politics ... And Why You Are Wrong.* New York: Basic Books, 2000.

Jamieson, K. H., and J. Cappella. *Echo Chamber: Rush Limbaugh and the Conservative Media Establishment.* Oxford: Oxford University Press, 2008.

Johansen, H. P. M. "Political Marketing: More Than Persuasive Techniques, an Organizational Perspective." *Journal of Political Marketing* 4, no. 4 (2005): 85–105.

Relational Political Marketing in Party-Centred Democracies: Because We Deserve It. Farnham: Ashgate, 2012.

Johnson, Dennis W. "The Business of Political Consulting." In *Campaign Warriors: Political Consultants in Elections*, edited by J. Thurber and C. Nelson, 37–52. Washington, D.C.: Brookings Institution, 2000.

No Place for Amateurs. London: Routledge, 2001.

"Perspectives on Political Consulting." *Journal of Political Marketing* 1, no. 1 (2002): 7–22.

Johnson, Jason. *Political Consultants and Campaigns: One Day to Sell.* Transforming American Politics. Boulder, Colo.: Westview, 2012.

Johnson-Cartee, K., and G. Copeland. *Inside Political Campaigns: Theory and Practice.* London: Praeger, 1997.

Strategic Political Communication. Lanham, Md.: Rowman & Littlefield, 2004.

Jowett, G., and V. O'Donnell. *Propaganda and Persuasion.* 4th ed. London: Sage, 2006.

Just, Marion, Ann Crigler, Dean Alger, Timothy Cook, and Montague Kern. *Crosstalk: Citizens, Candidates and the Media in a Presidential Campaign.* Chicago: University of Chicago Press, 1996.

Just, M., A. Crigler, and W. R. Neuman. "Cognitive and Affective Dimensions of Political Conceptualization." In *The Psychology of Political Communication*, edited by A. Crigler, 133–48. Ann Arbor: University of Michigan Press, 2001.

Kahneman, Daniel. *Thinking, Fast and Slow.* London: Allen Lane, 2011.

Kaid, L. L., ed. *The Handbook of Political Communication Research.* London: Lawrence Erlbaum, 2004.

"Political Advertising: A Summary of Research Findings." In *Handbook of Political Marketing*, edited by B. Newman, 423–38. London: Sage, 1999.

"Political Advertising in the United States." In *The Sage Handbook of Political Advertising*, edited by L. L Kaid and C. Holtz-Bacha, 37–64. Thousand Oaks, Calif.: Sage, 2006.

Kaid, L. L., and C. Holtz-Bacha, eds. *The Sage Handbook of Political Advertising.* Thousand Oaks, Calif.: Sage, 2006.

Kaid, L. L., and A. Johnston. *Videostyle in Presidential Campaigns: Style and Content of Televised Political Advertising.* London: Praeger, 2001.

Katz, Richard S., and Peter Mair. *How Parties Organize: Change and Adaptation in Party Organizations in Western Democracies.* London: Sage, 1994.

Kavanagh, Dennis, and David Butler. *The British General Election of 2005.* Basingstoke: Palgrave, 2005.

Keith, R. "The Marketing Revolution." *Journal of Marketing Management* 24 (1960): 35–38.

Kerbel, Matthew. *Netroots: Online Progressives and the Transformation of American Politics*. Boulder, Colo.: Paradigm, 2009.

Kinder, Donald R. "Communication and Politics in the Age of Information." In *Oxford Handbook of Political Psychology*, edited by D. Sears, L. Huddy, and R. Jervis, 357–93. Oxford: Oxford University Press, 2003.

Kirchheimer, O. "The Transformation of Western Party Systems." In *Political Parties and Political Development*, edited by J. La Palombara and M. Weiner, 177–200. Princeton, N.J.: Princeton University Press, 1966.

Klapper, Joseph T. "The Effects of Mass Communication." Thesis, Columbia University, 1960.

Klein, Joe. *Politics Lost*. New York: Doubleday, 2006.

Klein, Naomi. "How Corporate Branding Has Taken over America." *Guardian*, January 16, 2010.

— *No Logo: Taking Aim at the Brand Bullies*. 1st Picador USA ed. New York: Picador USA, 1999.

Kornberger, Martin. *Brand Society: How Brands Transform Management and Lifestyle*. Cambridge: Cambridge University Press, 2010.

Kotler, P. "Business Marketing for Political Candidates." *Campaigns & Elections* 2, no. 2 (1981): 24–33.

Kotler, P., and N. Kotler. "Political Marketing: Generating Effective Candidates, Campaigns and Causes." In *Handbook of Political Marketing*, edited by B. Newman, 3–18. London: Sage 1999.

Kotler, Philip, and Nancy Lee. *Corporate Social Responsibility: Doing the Most Good for Your Company and Your Cause*. Hoboken, N.J.: Wiley, 2004.

Landor PSB Associates. "Presidential Image Power." August 18, 2004.

Langer, A. I. *The Personalization of Politics in the UK: Mediated Leadership from Attlee to Cameron*. Manchester: Manchester University Press, 2011.

Langmaid, R., C. Trevail, and B. Hayman. "Reconnecting the Prime Minister." In *Annual Conference of the Market Research Society*, London, 2006.

Lasswell, Harold D. *Propaganda Technique in World War 1*. Cambridge, Mass.: MIT Press, 1927/1971.

Lau, Richard R., and David P. Redlawsk. *How Voters Decide: Information Processing during Election Campaigns*. Cambridge Studies in Public Opinion and Political Psychology. Cambridge: Cambridge University Press, 2006.

Lazarsfeld, Paul F., Bernard Berelson, and Hazel Gaudet. *The People's Choice: How the Voter Makes Up His Mind in a Presidential Campaign*. 2nd ed. New York: Columbia University Press, 1948.

Lees-Marshment, J. *Political Marketing & British Political Parties.* Manchester: Manchester University Press, 2001.

Lees-Marshment, Jennifer, Jesper Strömbäck, and Chris Rudd. *Global Political Marketing.* Abingdon: Routledge, 2010.

Lendrevie, J., J. Levy, and D. Lindon. *Mercator: Théorie Et Pratique Du Marketing.* 8th ed. Paris: Duno, 2006.

Lijphart, A. *Democracies: Patterns of Majoritarian & Consensus Government in Twenty-One Countries.* New Haven, Conn.: Yale University Press, 1999.

Lilleker, D., and Jennifer Lees-Marshment, eds. *Political Marketing: A Comparative Perspective.* Manchester: Manchester University Press, 2005.

Lindblom, Charles. *Politics and Markets: The World's Political-Economic System.* New York: Basic Books, 1977.

Livingstone, Sonia. "The Changing Nature and Uses of Media Literacy." MEDIA@LSE Electronic Working Papers, London School of Economics & Political Science, 2003. http://eprints.lse. ac.uk/13476/.

Lloyd, John. "The Weak in Politics." *Financial Times,* March 30, 2007.

Lock, A., and P. Harris. "Political Marketing – Vive La Difference." *European Journal of Marketing* 30 (1996): 21–31.

Lucid Systems. "Neuro-Realism." November 2009. http://www. lucidsystems.com/ethics/qneuro-realismq.html.

Luntz, Frank. *Candidates, Consultants and Campaigns: The Style and Substance of American Electioneering.* Cambridge: Blackwell, 1988.

Lynch, Timothy. "Academics vs. Bush." *Political Studies Review* 8, no. 2 (2010): 208–17.

Maarek, P. "Political Communication and the Unexpected Outcome of the 2002 French Presidential Elections." *Journal of Political Marketing* 2, no. 2 (2003): 13–24.

Madrigal, Alexis. "When the Nerds Go Marching In." *Atlantic,* November 16, 2012.

Mair, P., and I. van Biezen. "Party Membership in Twenty European Democracies, 1980–2000." *Party Politics* 7, no. 1 (2001): 5–21.

Malchow, Hal. "New Campaign Targeting Techniques." In *Winning Elections: Political Campaign Management, Strategy and Tactics,* edited by Ronald Faucheux, 229–36. New York: M. Evans, 2003.

Mandelson, P. *The Blair Revolution Revisited.* London: Politicos, 2002.

Manin, B. *Principles of Representative Government.* Cambridge: Cambridge University Press, 1997.

Manin, Bernard, Adam Przeworski, and Susan C. Stokes. "Introduction." In *Democracy, Accountability and Representation,* edited by Adam

Przeworski, Susan C. Stokes, and Bernard Manin, 1–26. Cambridge: Cambridge University Press, 1999.

Mansridge, J. "Rethinking Representation." *American Political Science Review* 97, no. 4 (2003): 515–28.

Marcus, G. "The Psychology of Emotion and Politics." In *Oxford Handbook of Political Psychology*, edited by D. Sears, L. Huddy, and R. Jervis, 182–221. Oxford: Oxford University Press, 2003.

Marcus, George, Russell Neuman, and Michael Mackuen. *Affective Intelligence and Political Judgement*. Chicago: University of Chicago Press, 2000.

Marcuse, H. *One Dimensional Man: Studies in the Ideology of Advanced Industrial Society*. London: Routledge & Kegan Paul, 1964.

Matalin, M., and J. Carville. *All's Fair: Love, War and Running for President*. New York: Random House, 1994.

Mattinson, Deborah. *Talking to a Brick Wall: How New Labour Stopped Listening to the Voter and Why We Need a New Politics*. London: Biteback, 2010.

Mayer, W. "In Defense of Negative Campaigns." *Political Science Quarterly* 111 (1996): 437–55.

Mayhew, Leon. *The New Public: Professional Communication and the Means of Social Influence*. New York: Cambridge University Press, 1997.

Mazzoleni, Gianpietro. "TV Political Advertising in Italy: When Politicians Are Afraid." In *The Sage Handbook of Political Advertising*, edited by Lynda Lee Kaid and Christina Holtz-Bacha, 241–58. Thousand Oaks, Calif.: Sage, 2006.

McAllister, Ian. "World Opinion: Accountability, Representation and Satisfaction with Democracy." *International Journal of Public Opinion Research* 17, no. 3 (2005): 371–79.

McCombs, M. *Setting the Agenda: The Mass Media and Public Opinion*. Cambridge, UK: Polity Press, 2004.

McCubbins, Mathew D. *Under the Watchful Eye: Managing Presidential Campaigns in the Television Era*. Washington, D.C.: CQ Press, 1992.

Mellone, A., and L. Di Gregorio. "The Childhood of an Approach: Political Marketing in Italy." *Journal of Political Marketing* 3, no. 3 (2004): 17–40.

Mencken, H. L. *Prejudices, Fourth Series*. 1st ed. New York: Knopf, 1924.

Meyer, Thomas. *Media Democracy: How the Media Colonize Politics*. Cambridge: Polity, 2002.

Micheletti, Michele, and Dietland Stolle. "Mobilizing Consumers to Take Responsibility for Global Justice." *Annals of the American Academy of Political and Social Science* 611 (2007): 157–75.

Miller, Sean. "Building on Sand." *Campaigns & Elections*, no. 306 (September/October 2011): 45–49.

Moore, James, and Wayne Slater. *The Architect: Karl Rove and the Master Plan for Absolute Power*. New York: Crown, 2006.

Morgan, R., and S. Hunt. " The Commitment-Trust Theory of Relationship Marketing." *Journal of Marketing* 58, no. 2 (1994): 20–38.

Morris, Dick. *Behind the Oval Office: Getting Reelected Against All Odds*. New York: Renaissance Books, 1998.

"Money Can't Buy Votes." *Campaigns & Elections* 28, no. 256 (2007): 62.

The New Prince: Machiavelli Updated for the Twenty-First Century. New York: Renaissance Books, 1999.

Mutz, D., and B. Reeves. "The New Videomalaise: Effects of Televised Incivility on Political Trust." *American Political Science Review* 99, no. 1 (2005): 1–15.

Napolitan, Joe. "Napolitan's Rules: 112 Lessons Learned from a Career in Politics." In *Winning Elections: Political Campaign Management, Strategy and Tactics*, edited by Ronald Faucheux, 26–58. New York: M. Evans, 2003.

Needham, Catherine. "Brand Leaders; Clinton, Blair and the Limitations of the Permanent Campaign." *Political Studies Review* 53, no. 2 (2005): 343–61.

Citizen Consumers: New Labour's Marketplace Democracy. London: Central Books, 2003.

Negrine, Ralph, Paolo Mancini, Christina Holtz-Bacha, and Stylianos Papathanassopoulos, eds. *The Professionalisation of Political Communication*, vol. 3: *Changing Media, Changing Europe*. Bristol: Intellect, 2007.

Nelson, Candice, David Dulio, and Stephen Medvic, eds. *Shades of Gray: Perspectives on Campaign Ethics*. Washington D.C.: Brookings Institution Press, 2002.

Nelson, J. S., and G. R. Boynton. *Video Rhetorics: Televised Advertising in American Politics*. Urbana: University of Illinois Press, 1997.

Newman, B., ed. *Handbook of Political Marketing*. London: Sage, 1999.

The Marketing of the President. Thousand Oaks, Calif.: Sage, 1994.

Nielsen, Rasmus Kleis. *Ground Wars: Personalized Communication in Political Campaigns*. Princeton, N.J.: Princeton University Press, 2012.

Norris, Pippa. "Comparative Political Communications: Common Frameworks or Babelian Confusion? Review Article." *Government and Opposition* 44, no. 3 (2009): 321–40.

Critical Citizens: Global Support for Democratic Governance. New York: Oxford University Press, 1999.

Democratic Deficit: Critical Citizens Revisited. Cambridge: Cambridge University Press, 2011.

"Do Campaign Communications Matter for Civic Engagement? American Elections from Eisenhower to George W. Bush." In *Do Political Campaigns Matter? Campaign Effects in Elections and Referendums,* edited by David M. Farrell and Rüdiger Schmitt-Beck, 127–44. London: Routledge, 2002.

Electoral Engineering: Voting Rules and Political Behavior Cambridge: Cambridge University Press, 2004.

Political Parties and Democracy in Theoretical and Practical Perspectives. Washington, D.C.: National Democratic Institute for International Affairs, 2005.

Virtuous Circle: Political Communications in Postindustrial Societies. Cambridge: Cambridge University Press, 2000.

Norris, P., J. Curtice, D. Sanders, M. Scammell, and H. Semetko. *On Message: Communicating the Campaign.* London: Sage, 1999.

Norris, Pippa, and Ronald Inglehart. *Cosmopolitan Communications: Cultural Diversity in a Globalized World.* Communication, Society and Politics. Cambridge: Cambridge University Press, 2009.

O'Cass, A. "Political Marketing and the Marketing Concept." *European Journal of Marketing* 30, no. 10/11 (1996): 37–53.

O'Connor, Brendan. "Beyond the Cartoon: George W. Bush and His Biographers." *Political Studies* 3, no. 2 (2005): 163–74.

Ogilvy, David. *Confessions of an Advertising Man.* New York: Atheneum, 1963.

O'Guinn, Thomas, and Albert Muniz. "Towards a Sociological Model of Brands." In *Brands and Brand Management: Contemporary Research Perspectives,* edited by Barbara Loken, Rohini Ahluwalia, and Michael J. Houston, 133–58. New York: Psychology Press, 2010.

Ormrod, Robert. "Political Market Orientation and Its Commercial Cousin: Close Family or Distant Relatives?" *Journal of Political Marketing* 6, no. 2/3 (2007): 69–90.

O'Shaughnessy, N. "The Marketing of Political Marketing." *European Journal of Marketing* 35, no. 9/10 (2001): 1047–57.

The Phenomenon of Political Marketing. Basingstoke: Macmillan, 1990.

Politics and Propaganda: Weapons of Mass Seduction. Ann Arbor: University of Michigan Press, 2004.

Panagopoulos, C., D. Dulio, and S. Brewer. "Lady Luck? Women Political Consultants in U.S. Congressional Campaigns." *Journal of Political Marketing* 10, no. 3 (2011): 251–74.

Panebianco, A. *Political Parties: Organisation and Power.* Cambridge: Cambridge University Press, 1988.

Papathanassopoulos, S., R. Negrine, P. Mancini, and C. Holtz-Bacha. "Political Communication in the Era of Professionalization." In *The Professionalisation of Political Communication,* edited by R. Negrine, Paolo Mancini, C. Holtz-Bacha, and S. Papathanassopoulos, 9–26. Bristol: Intellect, 2007.

Patterson, Tom. *The Vanishing Voter: Public Involvement in an Age of Uncertainty.* New York: Knopf, 2002.

Pattie, Charles, Patrick Seyd, and Paul Whiteley. *Citizenship in Britain: Values, Participation and Democracy.* Cambridge: Cambridge University Press, 2004.

Pels, D. "Aesthetic Representation and Political Style: Re-Balancing Identity and Difference in Media Democracy." In *Media and the Re-Styling of Politics,* edited by J. Corner and D. Pels, 41–66. London: Sage, 2003.

Pew Research Center for People & the Press. "Low Marks for the 2012 Election." 2012.

Pharr, S., and R. Putnam. *Disaffected Democracies.* Princeton, N.J.: Princeton University Press, 2000.

Phillips, K. *American Dynasty.* New York: Penguin Viking, 2004.

Plasser, Fritz. *Global Political Campaigning.* London: Praeger, 2002.

Plouffe, D. *The Audacity to Win: The Inside Story and Lessons of Barack Obama's Historic Victory.* New York: Viking, 2009.

Podhoretz, John. *Bush Country.* New York: St. Martin's Press, 2004.

Polsby, N., and A. Wildavsky. *Presidential Elections.* Chatham, N.J.: Chatham House, 1996.

Popkin, S. "Campaigns That Matter." In *Under the Watchful Eye: Managing Presidential Campaigns in the Television Era,* edited by Mathew D. McCubbins, 153–70. Washington, D.C.: CQ Press, 1992.

The Reasoning Voter: Communication and Persuasion in Presidential Campaigns. Chicago: University of Chicago Press, 1991.

Pratkanis, A., and E. Aronson. *Age of Propaganda: The Everyday Use and Abuse of Persuasion.* New York: Freeman, 1991.

Price, Lance. *Where Power Lies: Prime Ministers v the Media.* London: Simon & Schuster, 2010.

Promise Corporation. "There's More to Brands Than Coca Cola." 2006. http://www.promisecorp.com/index.htm.

Quelch, John, and Katherine E. Jocz. *Greater Good: How Good Marketing Makes for Better Democracy.* Boston: Harvard Business Press, 2007.

Rawnsley, A. "Tony Blair Wants a Good Kicking." *Observer,* February 20, 2005.

Reed, S. F. "Introduction to the Inaugural Issue." *Campaigns & Elections* 1, no. 1 (1980): 1.

Richards, B. "The Emotional Deficit in Political Communication." *Political Communication* 21 (2004): 339–52.

Rosshirt, T. "Winning the Message War." *Campaigns & Elections* 29, no. 269 (2008): 30–34.

Runciman, David. *The Politics of Good Intentions: History, Fear and Hypocrisy in the New World Order.* Princeton, N.J.: Princeton University Press, 2006.

Saatchi, Maurice. "The Strange Death of Modern Advertising." *Financial Times,* June 21, 2006.

Sabato, Larry. "The Election of Our Lifetime." In *The Year of Obama,* edited by Larry Sabato, 33–76. New York: Longman, 2010.

The Rise of Political Consultants. New York: Basic Books, 1981.

Sachs, Jeffrey. *The Price of Civilization: Economics and Ethics after the Fall.* London: Bodley Head, 2011.

Sandel, Michael J. *What Money Can't Buy: The Moral Limits of Markets.* New York: Farrar, Straus and Giroux, 2012.

Savigny, H., and M. Temple. "Political Marketing Models: The Curious Incident of the Dog That Doesn't Bark." *Political Studies* 58, no. 5 (2010): 1049–64.

Scammell, Margaret. "Citizen Consumers: Towards a New Marketing of Politics?" In *Media and the Re-Styling of Politics,* edited by J. Corner and D. Pels, 117–36. London: Sage, 2003.

Designer Politics: How Elections Are Won. Basingstoke: Macmillan, 1995.

"Media and Media Management." In *The Blair Effect,* edited by A. Seldon, 509–34. London: Little Brown, 2001.

"Political Brands and Consumer Citizens: The Re-Branding of Tony Blair." *Annals of the Academy of American Political and Social Science* 611 (2007): 176–93.

"Political Marketing: Lessons for Political Science." *Political Studies* 47, no. 4 (1999): 718–39.

The Wisdom of the War Room. Cambridge, Mass.: Joan Shorenstein Center on the Press, Politics and Public Policy, Harvard University, 1997.

Scammell, M., and M. Harrop. "The Press: Still for Labour Despite Blair." In *The British General Election of 2005,* edited by D. Kavanagh and D. Butler, 119–45. Basingstoke: Macmillan, 2005.

Scammell, Margaret, and A. I. Langer. "Political Advertising: Why Is It So Boring?" *Media, Culture and Society* 28, no. 5 (2006): 763–84.

Scammell, Margaret, and Holli Semetko. "Election News Coverage in the U.K." In *The Handbook of Election News Coverage around the World*, edited by Jesper Strömbäck and Lynda Lee Kaid, 73–89. New York: Routledge, 2008.

Schudson, Michael. "Citizens, Consumers, and the Good Society." *Annals of the American Academy of Political and Social Science* 611 (2007): 236–49.

——— "Click Here for Democracy: A History and Critique of an Information-Based Model of Citizenship." In *Democracy and the New Media*, edited by Henry Jenkins and David Thorburn, 49–60. Cambridge, Mass.: MIT Press, 2003.

——— *The Good Citizen: A History of American Civic Life*. Cambridge, Mass.: Harvard University Press, 1999.

Schulz, Wolfram, John Ainley, Julian Fraillon, David Kerr, and Bruno Losito. *Initial Findings from the IEA International Civic and Citizenship Education Study*. Amsterdam: International Association for the Evaluation of Educational Achievement, 2010.

Schumpeter, Joseph. *Capitalism, Socialism and Democracy*. London: Allen and Unwin, 1943.

Séguéla, Jacques. *Le Pouvoir Dans La Peau*. Paris: Pion, 2011.

Seldon, A. *Blair*. London: Simon & Schuster, 2004.

Semetko, Holli, J. G. Blumler, M. Gurevitch, and D. H. Weaver. *The Formation of Campaign Agendas: A Comparative Analysis of Party and Media Roles in Recent American and British Elections*. Hillsdale, N.J.: Lawrence Erlbaum, 1991.

Severinghaus, Erik. "3 Lessons for Marketers from the 2012 Elections." *Forbes*, November 19, 2012. http://www.forbes.com/sites/theyec/2012/11/19/3-lessons-for-marketers-from-the-2012-elections/.

Shapiro, Ian. "The State of Democratic Theory." In *Political Science: State of the Discipline*, edited by Ira Katznelson and Helen Milner, 235–65. New York: Norton, 2002.

Smith, Gareth. "Conceptualizing and Testing Brand Personality in British Politics." *Journal of Political Marketing* 8 (2009): 209–32.

Smith, Jennifer. "Campaigning and the Catch-All Party: The Process of Party Transformation in Britain." *Party Politics* 15, no. 5 (2009): 555–72.

Stepan, Alfred, and Juan Linz. "Comparative Perspectives on Inequality and the Quality of Democracy in the United States." *Perspectives on Politics* 9, no. 4 (2011): 841–56.

Stephanopoulos, G. *All Too Human: A Political Education*. London: Hutchison, 1999.

Stoker, Gerry. *Why Politics Matters: Making Democracy Work*. Basingstoke: Palgrave Macmillan, 2006.

Street, John. "The Celebrity Politician: Political Style and Popular Culture." In *Media and the Restyling of Politics*, edited by John Corner and D. Pels, 85–98. London: Sage, 2003.

Mass Media, Politics and Democracy. Basingstoke: Palgrave, 2001.
"Political Culture and Political Communication." In *Sage Handbook of Political Communication*, edited by Holli A. Semetko and Margaret Scammell. Thousand Oaks, Calif.: Sage, 2012.
"Politics Lost, Politics Transformed, Politics Colonised? Theories of the Impact of Mass Media." *Political Studies Review* 3, no. 1 (2005): 17–33.
Politics and Popular Culture. Cambridge: Polity, 1997.
Strömbäck, Jesper, and D. V. Dimitrova. "Political and Media Systems Matter: A Comparison of Election News Coverage in Sweden and the U.S." *Harvard International Journal of Press/Politics* 11, no. 4 (2006): 131–47.
Strömbäck, Jesper, and Lynda Lee Kaid. "A Framework for Comparing Election News Coverage around the World." In *The Handbook of Election News Coverage around the World*, edited by Jesper Strömbäck and Lynda Lee Kaid, 1–20. New York: Routledge, 2008.
eds. *The Handbook of Election News Coverage around the World*. New York: Routledge, 2008.
Stutts, Phillip. "The Right's Early Vote Dilemma." *Campaigns & Elections*, no. 314 (November/December 2012): 45–46.
Sussman, Gerald. *Global Electioneering: Campaign Consulting, Communications, and Corporate Financing*. Critical Media Studies. Lanham, Md.: Rowman & Littlefield, 2005.
Swanson, D., and P. Mancini, eds. *Politics, Media and Modern Democracy*. London: Praeger, 1996.
Sweitzer, Thomas. "War without Blood: Military Roots of Political Strategy." In *Winning Elections: Political Campaign Management, Strategy and Tactics*, edited by Ronald Faucheux, 97–100. New York: M. Evans, 2003.
Taylor, Philip M. *Munitions of the Mind: A History of Propaganda from the Ancient World to the Present Day*. 3rd ed. Manchester: Manchester University Press, 2003.
Thompson, John B. *Political Scandal: Power and Visibility in the Media Age*. Cambridge: Polity, 2000.
Thomson, Alice. "New Tories Who Dare Not Speak Their Name." *Daily Telegraph*, March 12, 2005.
Thurber, J., and C. Nelson, eds. *Campaign Warriors: Political Consultants in Elections*. Washington, D.C.: Brookings Institution, 2000.
Thurber, J., C. Nelson, and D. Dulio. "Portrait of Campaign Consultants." In *Campaign Warriors: Political Consultants in Elections*, edited by J. Thurber and C. Nelson, 10–36. Washington, D.C.: Brookings Institution, 2000.

Trayner, Graeme. "Open Source Thinking: From Passive Consumers to Active Creators." In *Annual Conference of the Market Research Society*, London, 2006.

"The Role of Political Consultants in Sharing Knowledge between US and UK Elections: The Practitioner Perspective." In *Annual Conference of the American Political Science Association*, Washington, D.C., 2005.

Trent, Judith S., and Robert V. Friedenberg. *Political Campaign Communication: Principles and Practices.* 5th ed. Communication, Media, and Politics. Lanham, Md.: Rowman & Littlefield, 2004.

Trippi, J. *The Revolution Will Not Be Televised.* New York: HarperCollins, 2004.

Trish, Barbara. "The Year of Big Data." *Campaigns & Elections*, no. 314 (November/December 2012): 10–13.

Troy, G. *See How They Ran: The Changing Role of the Presidential Candidate.* New York: Free Press, 1991.

Tynan, Daniel. "GOP Voter Vault Shipped Overseas." *PC World*, September 24, 2004.

Van Zoonen, E. "Imagining Fan Democracy." *European Journal of Communication* 19, no. 1 (2004): 39–52.

Vavreck, Lynn. *The Message Matters: The Economy and Presidential Campaigns.* Princeton, N.J.: Princeton University Press, 2009.

Viguerie, Richard A. *America's Right Turn: How Conservatives Used New and Alternative Media to Take Power.* Chicago: Bonus Books, 2004.

Waldman, Paul. *The Strategy Behind the Bush Lies and Why the Media Didn't Tell You.* Naperville, Ill.: Sourcebooks, 2004.

Walzer, Michael. *Just and Unjust Wars.* 2nd ed. New York: Basic Books, 1992.

Ward, J., and C. H. de Vreese. "Political Consumerism, Young Citizens and the Internet." *Media, Culture & Society* 33, no. 3 (2011): 399–413.

Warren, Mark. *Democracy and Trust.* New York: Cambridge University Press, 1999.

Weber, Max. "Politics as a Vocation." In *From Max Weber: Essays in Sociology*, edited by Han Heinrich Gerth and Charles Wright Mills, 77–128. New York: Oxford University Press, 1946.

Wernick, A. *Promotional Culture: Advertising, Ideology and Symbolic Expression.* London: Sage, 1991.

West, Darrell M. *Air Wars: Television Advertising in Election Campaigns, 1952–1992.* Washington, D.C.: CQ Press, 1993.

Westbrook, Robert B. *Democratic Hope: Pragmatism and the Politics of Truth.* Ithaca, N.Y.: Cornell University Press, 2005.

Westen, Drew. *The Political Brain: The Role of Emotion in Deciding the Fate of the Nation.* New York: Public Affairs, 2008.

White, J., and L. de Chernatony. *New Labour: A Study of the Creation, Development and Demise of a Political Brand.* London: City University Business School, Barbican Centre, 2001.

Whiteley, Paul, Patrick Seyd, and J. J. Richardson. *True Blues: The Politics of Conservative Party Membership.* Oxford: Clarendon, 1994.

Wilentz, Sean. "The Worst President in History?" *Rolling Stone,* April 21, 2006.

Willmott, Michael. *Citizen Brands: Putting Society at the Heart of Your Business.* Chichester: Wiley, 2001.

Woods, Richard. "Creating Emotional Maps for Brands." In *Annual Conference of the Market Research Society,* London, 2004.

Worcester, R., R. Mortimore, and P. Baines. *Explaining Labour's Landslip: The 2005 General Election.* London: Politico's, 2005.

World Business Council for Sustainable Development. "Sustainable Consumption: Facts and Trends." 2008.

Wreden, Nick. "George W. Bush, Branding Guru?" 2006. http://fusionbrand.blogs.com/fusionbrand/2006/02/george_w_bush_b.html.

Wring, D. *The Politics of Marketing the Labour Party.* Basingstoke: Palgrave, 2004.

Yannas, P. "Political Marketing and Democracy: A Plea for Cross-Fertilization." *Journal of Political Marketing* 7, nos. 3–4 (2008): 205–16.

———. "Political Marketing in Greece Is Ready for the Take-Off." *Journal of Political Marketing* 4, no. 1 (2005): 1–15.

Index